Educational Psychology and the Internet

The first comprehensive, research-based textbook on Internet-infused education, *Educational Psychology and the Internet* offers students an accessible guide to important issues in the field. Michael Glassman begins with an overview of the evolution of the Internet and its significance for education. He outlines the current state of research, clearly defining terms that students will need to discuss larger concepts, such as hypertext and cyberspace. The second part of the book explores the practical applications of this research, which range from the individual-oriented to the generalized, including massive open online courses (MOOCs), open educational resources, and augmented reality. Key issues that affect teachers and students today, such as net neutrality and Creative Commons and Open Source licenses, are explained in straightforward terms, and often-overlooked differences – for example, between course management systems and learning management systems, and between blogs, social networking sites, and short messaging systems – are highlighted.

Michael Glassman is an associate professor in the Department of Educational Studies at the Ohio State University. He has published widely on Internet-related issues in education.

Educational Psychology and the Internet

Michael Glassman
Ohio State University

CAMBRIDGE
UNIVERSITY PRESS

32 Avenue of the Americas, New York, NY 10013-2473, USA

Cambridge University Press is part of the University of Cambridge.

It furthers the University's mission by disseminating knowledge in the pursuit of education, learning, and research at the highest international levels of excellence.

www.cambridge.org
Information on this title: www.cambridge.org/9781107479302

First published 2016

Printed in the United States of America

A catalog record for this publication is available from the British Library.

Library of Congress Cataloging in Publication Data
Names: Glassman, Michael (Michael J.) author.
Title: Educational psychology and the internet / Michael Glassman.
Description: New York, NY : Cambridge University Press, 2016. | Includes bibliographical references and index.
Identifiers: LCCN 2015032422| ISBN 9781107095441 (Hardback) | ISBN 9781107479302 (Paperback)
Subjects: LCSH: Educational psychology. | Internet in education. | Computer-assisted instruction. | Educational technology. | BISAC: PSYCHOLOGY / Applied Psychology.
Classification: LCC LB1051 .G555 2016 | DDC 370.15–dc23 LC record available at http://lccn.loc.gov/2015032422

ISBN 978-1-107-09544-1 Hardback
ISBN 978-1-107-47930-2 Paperback

Cambridge University Press has no responsibility for the persistence or accuracy of URLs for external or third-party Internet websites referred to in this publication and does not guarantee that any content on such websites is, or will remain, accurate or appropriate.

Contents

Contents

Introduction

I had my most significant Internet-driven education experience long before I realized the role that the Internet could play in creating a new type of education. It was as a participant in one of the most successful initiatives into Internet-infused education long before most anybody put the two ideas – Internet and education – together, before almost anybody had even considered using Web-based/Internet tools in teaching and learning processes. My experience in educational psychology and the Internet started in the mid-1990s. A colleague, David Kritt, knowing I was feeling separated from discussions of ideas that were close to my heart in my new job, suggested I join a listserv run out of the University of California San Diego called XLCHC established by Michael Cole and the Laboratory of Human Cognition. The initial reason behind the listserv was to maintain a vibrant educational community during a period of dwindling resources, especially for the type of socio-cultural/sociohistorical research central to the work of many of the laboratory's members and affiliates. The list was completely accessible to anybody who wanted to join. I can remember sitting in the second bedroom in our townhouse in Clear Lake Texas (just down the road from NASA), firing up my modem, which I used for very little in those days, listening to the crackle and the long beep, and typing in the Universal Resource Locator that David had given me, following the directions for joining and waiting. Hours or perhaps days later (at this point I can't remember) messages from members of the community started showing up in my mailbox.

The first few messages were welcomes to the list, one from David, a couple from people I had met at conferences. And then I experienced something that could be described as nothing less than extraordinary: Ideas started falling out of the list and into my computer. People were offering me (and of course the list) a continuous stream of ideas, sometimes three lines long, sometimes three pages long – and inviting comments, additions, counterarguments. Discussions could go on for days. Posters would make recommendations for reading, new individuals would emerge and push the discussion in new directions. Some of the list members were writing from California, some from New York, some from Europe, some from Australia, some from Japan – I had no idea where a lot of people were writing from. Sometimes people would drop out of the discussion for a few days and then pick back up without missing a beat. Some people would drop out of discussions and then reemerge in other discussions. Sometimes discussions would disappear for weeks and then suddenly gain new life through an insight or a long-forgotten reference. People would take chances with their thinking I had never seen before. Graduate students might challenge the most preeminent scholars in the field. And those scholars would challenge them back.

The listserv did not always work to its ideal but it always worked, and continues to work to this day – the type of sustainability that is rare for Internet communities, or really any initiative that does not have constant infusions of money. No matter who came, who left, who upset who, the XLCHC listserv that later became the XMCA listserv continued to pour new ideas into my mailbox – and yet I very quickly began to take the experience for granted. I have continued to log into that list for almost two decades. For most of that time I saw it as a chance to engage in academic discussion simply by opening my e-mail (to which I also never gave much thought). I found over the past few years as I became more interested in the Internet as a phenomenon that would impact human cognition and education that I would keep returning to the listserv less for the exchange of ideas (though it was always interesting) than to see how it was continuing to evolve as an academic discussion forum, but still not understanding its significance. It was not until researching this book – in particular the chapter on massive open online courses-that I understood the implications of XLCHC/XMCA for Internet-infused education and the role that it played, and continues to play, in my own thinking about education – not for the specific ideas discussed (though that is important) but for the way list activity reflected visions of what educationally oriented Internet initiatives could accomplish.

The XLCHC/XMCA is one of the great natural experiments of the Internet, along with Douglas Engelbart's oNLineSystem, Stuart Brand and Larry Bright's Whole Earth 'Lectronic Link, early Multiuser Dungeon games like *MirrorWorld*, and Mark Weiser's ubiquitous computing situations at the Palo Alto Research Center starting with the communal coffee pot (all of which will be discussed in some depth in this book), offering an early window into the workings of the Internet and how it might change the way we understand human-to-human interactions/ transactions in the context of an internetworked world as we move deeper into the twenty-first century – experiments that were not meant to control, were not looking to achieve some predetermined product or reach a planned endpoint, but evolving in their own directions within the open feedback loops encountered in the new cyberspace created by internetworking technologies. The Internet is an immersive technology – it creates new ecological contexts in which users work and play and explore. We don't really create within these ecologies, we co-construct or coevolve with it. This can often be difficult to grasp, partially because of the Internet's symbiotic relationship with stand-alone computers (and computer-like instruments like smart phones). I have come to recognize the XLCHC/XMCA listserv as one of the best, if not the best, examples of education reimagined for the online universe. The most successful Internet initiatives have been those that consume their participants; but because the participants are operating within an immersive technology, it is often difficult for them to step outside and understand the implications across a broader range of activity. I would argue XLCHC/LXMCA was and is more representative of many of the ideas behind the original massive online open courses than any of the more targeted experiments that refer to themselves as MOOCs (I know this will cause some confusion, so I urge you to come back and read this again after reading Chapter 9 and see if you agree).

XLCHC/XMCA was part of my ongoing life activity – there are almost daily entries in my mailbox – setting the context for a series of conversations I had with three graduate students. The first set of conversations was in the early years of the millennium – just as the Internet was coming of age as a popular medium. Connectivity was becoming easier, more mobile, and more universal; the idea of somebody running out to fix a server in the dead of night was a distant memory. Search engines were making it easier to navigate and find information on the Web. Communication was no longer as dependent on e-mail with the emergence of what-you-see-is-what-you-get writing programs. I was doing an independent study with Min Ju Kang on attachment and cognition, but the conversations naturally drifted toward, first, the impact that

Internet might have on attachment, and then what seemed to us like important relationships between the Internet and cognition. I was especially interested in the ways that the Internet reflected John Dewey's ideas of knowing, a particular passion at the time. It seemed to me that the Internet provided the perfect context for implementing Dewey's ideas on knowledge, teaching, learning, and Pragmatism in general – related to other projects Min Ju and I were working on together.

The second set of conversations took place a few years later. I decided to try and implement some of the ideas Min Ju and I had been developing in a graduate class. The class, discussed in the last chapter of this book, was a disaster. But Mitchell Bartholomew, one of the students, approached me about extending rather than ending my little experiment. He was the first person I met with a smart phone, which he was continuously checking. I can still hear him saying, "This is it, this is how we communicate with each other now. We have to get it into the classroom." There was an urgency in Mitch that was almost antithetical to the glacial pace of my colleagues in trying to understand and integrate new technologies into education. He was living a good part of his life online, not because of any type of addiction but because this was where a good part of his life now was. He urged me to get on Facebook, he urged me to get on Twitter, he urged me to get off Facebook, he (recently) urged me to get on Snapchat – none of which I did successfully (e.g., I am still on Facebook but with eleven "friends" who are barely acquaintances and I never communicate with). It was Mitch who designed and redesigned the blog-centric courses we tried out on undergraduates (initially much to their dismay).

The third person set of conversations was with Yunhwan Kim – almost the opposite of Mitch. Yunhwan took a more global view, wanting to understand the psychological mechanisms behind individuals' use of the Internet (interestingly I can't even remember if he had a smart phone). It quickly became apparent that there were any number of individual differences in the way students engaged with the blogs in class. Some students loved the blogs, and some students hated them. Some students would write long, expressive posts while other students would write short, targeted posts with relevant links to other sites, and still other students wrote as little as possible. Some students seemed highly motivated to engage in online dialogue, and some students seemed annoyed or even angered that it was part of the class. Yunhwan was using sociocognitive theory, in particular Bandura's self-efficacy construct, in his dissertation research and was looking to apply it to Internet-related behavior. The idea of individual differences among users and the role of different types of experience when considering integrating the Internet into the classroom became a pressing issue in our shared research.

The Eric Raymond article "The Cathedral and the Bazaar" (1999) and the idea of Open Source project development served as a backdrop to all of these discussions. The ideas describing the creation of the Linux development community along with further readings on Richard Stallman and the Free Software Foundation and the Apache Foundation merged with the work of Douglas Engelbart and the Augmentation Research Center to provide an underlying structure for our thinking about how we thought the Internet might change education in dramatic ways. At the same time I began reading sporadically existing research on Internet-infused education. The major difficulty is that much of the literature, even within the field of education, was very different from each other – creating a lot of confusion, at least for me.

What I didn't know about internet-infused education

One of the things I have realized in researching this book is that my haphazard entry into explorations of Internet-infused education is not unique. Theory and research on Internet-related education to this point has been something of a maze where different individuals and groups enter from various (intellectual) points, all looking to make it to a central understanding of what the Internet means in education and how best to integrate it into teaching and learning practices. We scurry through the maze using our initial conceptions and belief systems about the Internet and education as our compass, sometimes passing close to each other, overhearing interesting phrases like Web 2.0, hypertext, or affordances seeping through the walls that separate us. We take these phrases and quickly appropriate them to our own journeys, often not thinking what they mean in the larger context of the maze itself. It is ironic that the most powerful tool created to distribute information has suffered from communities studying the Internet being too distributed, or more particularly foregoing the other attribute of the Internet that makes distribution viable – as a tool for interconnection. Different groups develop their own meanings and trajectories of thinking about what the Internet means for the role(s) it will play in education. Different branches of Internet-infused education following their own routes through the maze developing expressions and definitions that are unique to their goals. On some levels this may be necessary, but the danger also exists of explorations into Internet and education not only losing some of their richest early conceptualizations to expediency but of the entire program breaking into a "tower of babble." We become so tied to our race to reach the center we forget that what is important is the journey and not the destination (which probably doesn't exist in any case).

I have been as susceptible to this "race through the maze" as anybody. It is not just that I didn't take the time to understand XLCHC/XMCA as an innovation in online education even as I was exploring the philosophies and practices of Internet education; I took phrases and ideas and quickly applied them or discarded them, not so much misusing them as losing their larger meanings and the ways in which they framed my research/discussion. Two examples are the phrases Web 2.0 – which I adopted – and cyberspace – which I discarded.

The phrases Web 1.0 and Web 2.0 were coined by Tim O'Reilly, (2005) an Internet innovator/entrepreneur (perhaps what William Gibson might refer to as a cyberspace cowboy), mostly as a means to differentiate the ways commercial organizations use the Internet (partially an attempt to maintain business-based interest in the Internet after some early, spectacular failures). In general O'Reilly opposes the more interactive Web 2.0 where users are invited into the website as participants to Web 1.0 more static websites – places users (are expected to) visit, take information offered, and either buy whatever wares the site is offering or depart toward other destinations. Web 2.0 has been used to describe pretty much any type of Internet technology where the user is – or can be – an engaged member in online activities that help in some small way to define the site (e.g., in business rating systems, reviews, or community projects, in education-readable/writable applications such as blogs, wikis, or discussion boards). I have come to think for various reasons that Web 2.0 is not a very valuable descriptor for Internet-infused education. First, it makes it seem like the development of the Internet and the Web has in some way been linear – where engagement has somehow followed information distribution. One of the most important things in understanding the Internet, especially the ways in which it might qualitatively transform education and unfortunately one of the most difficult to grasp hold of, is that online activity (can) foster nonlinear and nonhierarchical relationships between sources of information and the humans behind them (something not so central to commerce). The thinking that led to the invention of the Web was at least as much a precursor of the Internet as the Internet was a precursor of the world wide web (a discussion that can be found in Chapter 1). But, more important, simple participation is not the key difference in current Internet-infused educational initiatives: Almost all enterprises have at least some Web 2.0 components, including those that are primarily based in distributive frames. A more valuable differentiation for Internet-infused education might be taken from the work of information theorist/historian Iikka Tuomi (2002), one that has been central to the history of the Internet and plays an important role in debates about how we might use the technology in education – whether the Internet is used as a tool to augment the human intellect and develop community (collaboration and/or cooperation) or whether it is used as a tool to distribute information to a wider audience, to scale up educational practices and reach new populations in new ways.

On the other hand, before researching this book I avoided using the term cyberspace – mostly because hackers avoided it. After understanding the origins of the word in cybernetics, I realize the importance it has had in the development of our conceptualizations of Internet activities and the ways it pushes us to think in new ways about critical issues in developing educational programs: Do we try and anticipate the reaction of students, scaffolding their understanding and/or self-regulation through automated interventions based in closed feedback loops, or do we design educational programs so that students become explorers in an expanding information universe that we cannot and should not predict? In any number of instances I have had to go back and rethink my own beliefs about how to approach Internet-infused education. This book and my thinking continue to be a work in progress – its evolution partially mirroring Ted Nelson's original descriptions of hypertext (yet another among many of the concepts I have had to go back and reconsider, including multiple times while writing this book). At another point in time I might have suggested writing this book was an exercise in humility, so often did I have to go back and rethink and reorganize my suppositions. Perhaps the greatest lesson I have learned in writing this book is the need to revise our value systems about knowledge – what it means to others and what it means to our own sense of self – that knowing is always an active enterprise and knowledge a work in progress. This is not a new idea: John Dewey and Arthur Bentley stressed this in their book *Knowing and the Known* (1949). But the Internet creates a greater possibility for and a sense of urgency in recognizing that ideas, concepts, products, and projects are constantly open for revision or annotation, and the greatest dangers lie in forgetting this.

The structure of the book

This book is an attempt at a bird's eye view of the maze described earlier, a moment in time that looks to capture various maze runners in process – with the realization that even as I write these words the race continues. The book is divided into two parts: very generally the first part is devoted to the way students (and teachers and administrators) might learn through Internet-infused education, and the second part is devoted to modes of teaching using Internet-infused technologies. A good deal of crossover is found between the two parts, especially with the early chapters informing the later chapters.

The first chapter of the book outlines the development of thinking about internetworking leading to the creation of the Internet and the invention of the world wide web and the following applications – especially the what-you-see-is-what-you-get writing applications – that have popularized Internet activity. This is a topic too little discussed, especially recognition that the Internet and its precursors were about education issues and new trajectories of human thinking long before they were about commerce. The second chapter discusses how the Internet (might) change our views of intelligence, focusing on Vannevar Bush's web of trails, T. H. Nelson's hypertext, and the new attention being paid to collective intelligences, including collaborative intelligence, swarm intelligence, and collective agency. The third chapter looks at the way past and current research in educational psychology that developed separately from Internet activity has been applied in attempting to understand and implement Internet-infused teaching/learning processes. One of the bigger questions educational psychology and education in general are facing is how much should we take from earlier research and how much do we need to understand Internet activity in its own right – requiring new theoretical constructs for a new era of human thinking. This will be one of the most interesting but perhaps difficult issues to negotiate as we move deeper into the information age. (Many people are deeply invested in existing cognitive and educational theories – and if you give them up, to whom or to what are you giving them up? At what point are we throwing the baby out with the bathwater?) The fourth chapter is on agency and motivation in Internet-infused education. The Internet demands far more agency on the part of users than almost any other tool – a realization especially salient in educational contexts, where students are often treated as passive recipients of knowledge. How do we change the students' attitudes toward their own roles in traditional education contexts? Do we have to? The fifth chapter looks at the history and research of online social engagement. One of the most discussed aspects of online education is the abilities to establish new types of teaching/leaning communities through networked communications. There is also a growing line of argument that it is very difficult to establish well-functioning online learning communities without some level of social engagement of participants. Yet community is an elusive goal for most online learning initiatives. Online ecologies have very different constraints on social behavior than place-based contexts – how do we navigate these differences as we look to establish what Alfred Rovai (2002) refers to as classroom community?

The second half of the book is focused on Internet-infused teaching – whom we approach, the types of tools that are available to us – what they mean and what they don't mean. There is a lot of confusion about tools like Open Educational Resources, Internet-based learning applications like Course Management Systems, and Internet applications used for teaching/learning, such as blogs and wikis. The sixth chapter takes a philosophical look at the ways instructors go about integrating Internet technologies into their educational practices. One of the (currently) less talked about but important considerations in Internet-infused education is the development relationship between the traditional, place-based classroom (or indeed almost any learning context) and what Manuel Castells (2011) refers to as the new spaces of flows of information created by the Internet. The enclosed classroom has historically been used to define student thinking and help set it on specific trajectories that are meaningful to their bounded social group, but also to try and make certain that students understand their immediate social context and their place within it. The Internet by its nature invites students to explore possibilities of thinking and problem solving far outside traditional boundaries, and often not understood by the place-based contexts in which they must live their lives. Both place and space are important in educational practices going forward, and it is crucial to understand the developing relationship between the two. The seventh chapter looks at the Open Educational Resource movement, its history, its possibilities, and its trajectories for education. Chapter 8 looks at the different types of technologies used in the development of hybrid or blended classrooms. The ninth chapter goes into one of the most discussed yet least understood phenomena of integrating Internet capabilities into education practices, expansive, online education, which includes early innovative initiatives like PLATO IV, the originally named massive online open courses (MOOCs), the scalable online education initiatives that are called MOOCs because of a silly *New York Times* headline, and the possibilities of using the extended reach of the Internet for new forms of participatory education. The last chapter is an outline of a new (or not so new) approach to Internet-infused education; Open Source Educative Processes that looks to integrate some of the basic ideas of the Free Libre Open Source Software movement into everyday teaching/learning practices.

The fast and the slow of the information age

It is true that the Internet is moving quickly. I think back two decades sitting in the house of my son's childhood friend when the father received a phone call. He jumped from his chair, threw on an overcoat, and picked up his briefcase saying there was an emergency with his server. He had a small company with a friend connecting three hundred people to the Internet. I had no idea what he was talking about (I often wonder if he became rich or was completely destroyed by the oncoming freight trains of the Internet revolution). Today I am able to connect to the Internet faster using relatively low-speed broadband than I could have ever imagined plugging in my modem, listening to the funny noises, and waiting for my e-mails to load so it could deliver the next messages from XLCHC.

However, writing this book I also came to realize we are moving slowly, and perhaps sometimes backwards, in how we apply these new technologies to education. Again and again I am told (often lectured) that ideas like hybrid classrooms and scalable education are moving so quickly. Yet we seem to be stuck in our mazes, believing we are advancing simply because we are moving. We are still trying to understand the early successes of the Augmentation Research Center, the Palo Alto Research Center, the Whole Earth 'Lectronic Link, and I add to that XLCHC/XMCA. Some of the most important research endeavors discussed in this book are important because they are failures, because they remind us it is a long journey through the maze, no matter where we are going. The greatest enemy in integrating the Internet into education – perhaps into anything – is hubris. It is perhaps time to admit that the new technologies of the information age are not by themselves going to provide answers to questions about teaching and learning that we have been struggling with for decades, sometimes for centuries. Whispers from the past (and present) – from Vannevar Bush, from Douglas Engelbar, from J. C. R. Licklider, from Stuart Brand, from Michael Cole – should constantly remind us that at the end of the Internet-immersed day it is about human-to-human relationships.[1]

References

Castells, M. (2011). *The Rise of the Network Society: The Information Age: Economy, Society, and Culture* (Vol. 1). New York: John Wiley & Sons.

Dewey, J., & Bentley, A. F. (1949). *Knowing and the Known* (No. 111). Boston: Beacon Press.

O'Reilly, T. (2009). What Is Web 2.0. O'Reilly Media.

Raymond, E. (1999). The Cathedral and the Bazaar. *Knowledge, Technology & Policy*, 12(3), 23–49.

Rovai, A. P. (2002). Building Sense of Community at a Distance. *International Review of Research in Open and Distributed Learning*, 3(1).

Tuomi, I. (2002). *Networks of Innovation*. Oxford: Oxford University Press.

---

[1] This is actually a reconfiguration of a sentence Michael Cole wrote to me in an e-mail discussion about the Internet.

1 The internet: it was always about education

The use of the Internet and its applications as tools in formal, directed education is relatively new and, it can be argued, still in its infancy. This is especially true for uses that go beyond simple communication of content and grading/credentialing tools and attempts to explore the social and intellectual ramifications of the new types of relationships with knowledge and information and with other humans that the Internet (potentially) engenders. The fact that Internet-infused education is following so closely on the heels of (often failed; Cuban and Cuban 2009) attempts to introduce stored-program computer applications into the education infrastructure makes integration of the new technology even more complex and emotion laden. This is complicated by emerging multiple frameworks for understanding the role and the meaning of the Internet in education in particular and human life in general. Is the Internet meant to make educational experiences simpler or more difficult? Is the Internet meant to deliver information to the student or provide means for a student to move out into the world to find new information sources? Or is the Internet primarily for not only building new types of knowledge but also new types of knowledge building? Does the Internet separate us so that we are working individually devoid of traditional human relationships, or does it bring us together into virtual learning communities that stimulate new types of productive relationships? Is the Internet a tutor or a junior partner, or is it actually an extension of ourselves out into the world, creating unanticipated feedback loops? All of these, sometimes contradictory, questions are central as we look for effective strategies in Internet-infused education – strategies that fit institutionally determined educational goals or perhaps (creatively) destroy them. To understand why these questions are so important and often so implacable, it helps to put them in the context of the complex motivations and thinking that led to the creation of the modern Internet: from its first science fiction–like rumblings in the middle of the twentieth century to what seems like the minute-to-minute development of new Web applications as we move toward the middle of the twenty-first century and the information age.

The Internet today is pervasive in everyday life – at least among some populations: Internet access gives new and multiple meanings to the phrase *digital divide*. It is easy to forget that the Internet as we know and use it today developed a relatively short time ago and was based primarily on the ideas and vision of a single individual. This last statement will no doubt be extremely controversial, and from a purely technical perspective the Internet had many extraordinary innovators nurturing its inception and early first steps, some of whom will be mentioned in this book: J. C. R. Licklider, Douglas Engelbart, Vincent Cerf, and Tim Berners-Lee, to name just a few. It is also true that the backbone of what would eventually become the Internet was dependent on organizations such as the NSF and the (Defense) Advanced Research Project Agency (DARPA). But the Internet and its most influential applications such as the Web and hypertext mark-up language, and especially its relationship to human thinking, can also be traced back to the vision of a single individual – the proverbial spark that lit the flame. The term *visionary* is overused, especially when it comes to technology, but if that title can be used for any person it can be used for the engineer Vannevar Bush. Bush wrote a short article in a popular journal that must have seemed like fanciful musings to many at the time. The article "As We May Think" (1945a) outlined in its own way the scope and the breadth of the Internet, the Web, search engines, and hypertext in a short ten pages at a time when most people didn't even know what a computer was. One of the most important and possibly unappreciated aspects of Bush's vision is that it was basically a treatise on education and innovation as they might develop in the near future.

From the memex to the oNLineSystem

Two visions of computers in education – interaction and transactions

It is important to differentiate between the technological advances offered by the Internet and the stored-program computer, especially in

discussions about computers and education. Yet the two are often conflated, perhaps because they both use the same or similar hardware and
graphical interface. There are some important similarities. The Internet
and the stored-program computer can be tied back to individuals
working and experimenting with human relationships to information
before and during World War II, the life-and-death urgency of the war
spurring the thinking of Bush and Alan Turing into new realms of
possibility. The stored-program computer is often traced back to Turing,
a mathematician in England who worked on processing information
to break preexisting codes. Turing started developing his ideas for an
information-processing machine (the Turing machine) a few years before
the war. He combined these initial ideas with his experiences as a
cryptologist developing (with apologies to John von Neumann)[1] the
design for the first stored-program computer – where the programs used
to process data are stored inside the memory of the machine making it a
stand-alone entity, an on-call computational tool that could be used to
accomplish complex calculation tasks quickly and efficiently when
needed. Any number of histories are available about Turing and the
Turing machine, and they are often mentioned even in Introduction to
Psychology texts, so there is little need to go deep into the story and the
impact of Turing and the stored-program computer on our understanding of human thinking.

Vannevar Bush was an engineer and inventor who oversaw the office
of scientific research and development for the U.S. military during World
War II. While Turing's task was primarily in understanding and breaking
codes through mathematical wizardry, Bush's office was in a race to
develop new inventions nobody had considered or even thought of even
a few years before, to turn the tide of the war. The stakes of the
innovation race were high, in part determining the fate of human
civilization. In his role overseeing research and development for the
war effort, Bush experienced first-hand the ways new ideas emerged,
developed, came to fruition, or were discarded in highly compressed

---

[1] The first stored-program computer was actually developed in the United States, and various
researchers worked on the design, including Presper Eckert and John William Mauchley. John
von Neumann wrote the paper describing the architecture, so he received much of the credit
(which is why everybody rushed to publish the first paper). However, it was Turing who took
the more psychological, information-processing approach, attempting to re-create the mind in
the machine.

periods of time – one of the great natural experiments in human invention in history. Bush came to recognize that the sharing of information in the service of productive problem solving and invention was taking on a new and important character during a period when the world was quickly shrinking while possible information sources were expanding. In the most successful instances information was shared quickly, ideas were promoted based on intuitive links, and individuals shared ideas in nonhierarchical, rapid-fire fashion. There was no ownership of innovation – the focus was on the invention itself and not the role any single scientist/engineer played in its development.

At approximately the same time Turing was outlining an intellectual trajectory for development of the stored-program computer, Bush published what many consider an outline for the modern Internet in "As We May Think." The article was a merging of technical and humanistic visions of how human relationships to information might change over the coming decades. It was highly futuristic and would remain so for years to come. In many ways it laid the groundwork for the combination of engineering and poetry that is the Internet. Like the Turing machine it was based on a prewar idea that was expanded in new directions through Bush's experiences during the war – a stark reminder of the impact of human events on technological development.

Central to Bush's thinking and the article was an information search tool he referred to as the *Memex machine*. Bush saw the Memex as an augmentation or extension of the human mind, envisioning an interconnected system of microfiche[2] readers linking together books, documents, and other types of open communications that scientists, engineers, and really any potential inventor could reach out for at any time while sitting comfortably at their desk. Bush saw the Memex machine as part of a natural progression of the coming information revolution changing both human memory and abilities to incorporate new, unanticipated information pools into problem solving/research. But even this stunning, early concept of the Internet was not the most important part of the short article. Bush combined his idea of a Memex machine (which predated the war) with his observations of fast-moving

---

[2] Microfiche is a system for storing and transferring information. Texts are reduced in size and placed on film. Individuals access the information by putting the film into a specially constructed machine that reexpands the text on a lighted screen.

scientific innovations through streams of quick, intuitive leaps and communications where there was no obvious direct, linear relationship between initial research idea and ultimate discovery. Bush suggested the Memex could be used to create fluid, asynchronous interrelationships (individual users could access the Memex when they wanted or needed to) where scientists could simultaneously be consumers and producers of relevant data and theory by easily retrieving the work of others and adding their own thinking processes into reframing and/or reworking the information before sending it back into the shared universe.

Bush believed that human thinking is at its most productive when it can reach out to use webs of connections that mirror the natural activities of the brain. The search for new information should be open to any direction, any trajectory of thought, jumping from idea to idea through a series of intuitive leaps – creating what Bush referred to as a "web of trails." The Memex machine's primary purpose was to act as an augmentation of these connecting capabilities, allowing the web of trails to move out into a larger information universe of shared human thinking, informing and being informed by the intuitive links and unique thinking trails of other minds. Turing was looking to develop a machine that could re-create the processes of the controlled human mind, where stored thinking processes could act almost as a junior partner in directed problem solving. (What is cryptology if not advanced problem solving with a definite end point/ solution?) Bush was looking to develop a machine that could extend the natural proclivities and inclinations of the human mind as an adventurer – making connections between ideas and information sources leading to unique, innovative discoveries that may serve as immediate solutions but more importantly as jumping-off points to new possibilities. The changing documents (at the time microfiche) could be exchanged quickly between system users, open to commentary and annotation so that engaged nodes (scientists) could build on each other's thinking without thought to individual ownership or control – an idea that would eventually lead to the concept of hypertext (Nelson 1974).

Bush was suggesting dramatic changes to human relationships in problem-solving/discovery-oriented contexts – processes he had witnessed in real time and believed to be the future of creative human endeavours. Bush's vision of a collaborative human learning in which there is no individual mind (or ego) was deeply influenced, however, by the life-and-death struggles that served as the background to his experiences during World War II. He hypothesized that the Memex machine (or something very much like it) would naturally emerge based on human adaptation to an evolving information ecology and would push humankind toward hypertext-based learning[3] and innovation. It was a (prescient) bet Bush was placing on the role of technology in continuing development of human thinking.

The transactional field

In discussing how we conceptualize and understand the actions and behaviors in which we engage and observe, John Dewey (Dewey and Bentley 1949) differentiates between interactional-based fields of analysis and transactional-based fields of analysis. In interactional analysis we focus on the immediate relationships between two objects or subject and object. Causality is recognized as being linear and for the most part encapsulated by boundaries of the immediate relationship. The causal relationship is often relatively easy to observe, but even easier to misinter-pret. For instance, in an educational context students' performance is often judged in terms of their relationships with their teachers (e.g., teacher evaluation measurements). If the student learns, it is because of the rela-tionship with the teacher or with the teaching approach. A more transac-tional model of analysis takes into account various causal elements in constant motion, some directly observable and some part of a larger field of action (distanced by time and space). Any number of interlinking relationships can exist in this field of activity, leading to a particular circumstance/state of a subject or object, many of which are not apparent from direct observation of or experience in an immediate relationship.

A child may have trouble learning in a particular situation, but the causes may go far beyond the direct relationship with the teacher or even the immediate components of the classroom – there are the child's rela-tionships with the family, the child's previous relationships with other teachers, the rewards the child has received for different types of actions in and out of the classroom, the teacher's relationship with other students, and the teacher's own history as a student. All of these come together in a dynamic field that is constantly shifting based on strengths and

---

[3] The term hypertext came a few decades after Bush, but there is probably no better word to describe Bush's thinking.

weaknesses of different relationships at any particular point in time. Dewey (Dewey and Bentley 1949) suggested that although other areas of study such as physics and biology had developed analyses based on these types of transactional fields, the study of human behavior/education was lagging behind – primarily because they lacked the same types of tool sets for studying dynamic fields of action. One of the first attempts to explore the possibilities of transactional systems was the field of cybernetics – an important influence on the development and understanding of the Internet. But even here the modes of analysis were much more successful in the material and biological sciences than the human sciences.

The Memex machine and internetworking technologies could theoretically provide access to these types of transactional fields in ways that no human tool had before. Distributed perspectives are displayed and archived so any user can examine direct and indirect relationships leading to the current status of the object/subject. It is important to differentiate between the relationship between the user and the immediate feedback loops of tools such as the stored-program computer, which is often portrayed as interactional (Human Computer Interaction is an important descriptor), and the user(s) and more open ecologies that can (possibly) be offered through the Internet (an in-depth discussion of this idea is given in Chapter 6). As will become apparent through the course of this book, the differences between human-computer interactions and human-computer transactions are important for how Internet-infused educational initiatives are conceptualized, developed, and implemented. At times the book will use the phrase *human-Internet transactions* in place of traditional *human-computer interactions*.

ARPANET and the human network

ARPANET was the first incarnation of the system of networked computers and servers that would eventually become the Internet. It was funded by the Department of Defense's Advanced Research Project Agency. The agency supported cutting-edge technology development, with its ethos falling very much into the "let researchers be researchers" model laid out by Vannevar Bush in his report to the president, *Science: The Endless Frontier* (1945b). On the frontier of new technologies in the 1960s were researchers looking to push the recent invention of the computer in different directions and explore the possible purposes of the new machines. The most important element for the development of the Internet was that these computers were rare and expensive. A very big problem for the research community for many years was too many computer researchers and not enough computers (which were prohibitively expensive and cumbersome). The scientists in the Behavioral Sciences Command and Control Unit at ARPA led by J. C. R. Licklider along with his second in command Robert Taylor (who would later go on to be founding director of the Palo Alto Research Center) created a system of off-site time sharing (of computers) where different users at different locations could go online at different times, sometimes leaving an intellectual footprint, a work product for those who followed – the beginnings of asynchronous communication/learning. The original network, which came to be known as ARPANET, had four major computer centers – three in California (UCLA, Stanford, and Santa Barbara) and one in Utah.

One of the enduring questions, one even might say mysteries, of the beginnings of the Internet is why the Department of Defense was willing to fund and even expand the Behavioral Science Unit and their research using ARPANET over some years and with little oversight (the Augmentation Research Center [ARC], which was one of the research groups, did some particularly un–Department of Defense things; Bardini 2000). Various theories exist, which are not mutually exclusive. One possibility is that it was partially in homage to Bush whose political star was in decline but was still recognized for his fundamental contributions to the war effort. A second theory is that the early sustainability of ARPANET was deeply indebted to the vision and energy of Licklider and his successor, Taylor, as they used the research forum to push the envelope of the new concept of (hu)man-computer symbiosis (Licklider, 1960) into the realm of computer communication (Licklider and Taylor 1968). A third theory is that many of the scientists working for the Department of Defense during the Second World War were part of the original cohort using ideas culled from their experiences to develop the field of cybernetics. Much of the work being done at, and even the name of, the Behavioral Sciences Command and Control unit incorporated many of their ideas. One of the most common theories is that the Department of Defense was looking for ways to concretize Paul Baran's (1962) ideas on the survivability of a distributed communication system (especially important as we were entering the tension-filled years of the nuclear age).

The early development of ARPANET was not monolithic: Just as the network itself was distributed, the early researchers of ARPANET and its intellectual tributaries sometimes had very different visions of where the new tool of connected computer centers would take human activity and experience. Tuomi (2002) suggests the development of four *technological frames*: the augmentation frame (a continuation of Bush's vision as described in his seminal article, based on researchers' abilities to log on, find the left-behind thinking of others, and incorporate it into their own thinking), the online communities frame (partially based on what would become hypertext and the ways in which time sharing allowed individual researchers to create shared communities that transcended the usual boundaries of time and space); the communication frame (concerned primarily with Baran's ideas of distributed communications and influenced by the most popular early application of ARPANET – electronic mail); and the electronic services frame (concerned mostly with how electronic networking might change practices in delivery of services). For this book (and perhaps the Internet as it evolved over time) it makes sense to combine the augmentation and the online community technological frame (they shared many of the same early researchers) and to combine the communication and service frame. Most Internet-infused education models, it can be argued, still reflect either a combined augmentation/community frame or a combined distributed communications/electronic service frame. An enormous difference exists between considering education in one of these two technological frames.

Stahl and colleagues, (2006) discuss the importance of differentiating between e-learning and computer-supported collaborative learning – suggesting the former is primarily concerned with dissemination of digitized content (i.e., in the communication/services technological frame) whereas the latter focuses on more complex collaborative learning activities (i.e., falling primarily within the online community frame, but also in many cases the augmentation frame). This differentiation is helpful and important, but it is also dependent on how broadly one is willing to define computer-supported collaborative learning. It may be more descriptive and encompassing (and, admittedly, clumsier) to focus on the differences between educational initiatives within the differentiation communication/service frame(s) and those within the augmentation/community frame(s).

Augmentation and community

One of the pioneers in using ARPANET to explore the nexus of augmentation of the human mind and the development of distributed, goal-oriented online communities (what would soon be referred to as virtual communities) was Douglas Engelbart. Engelbart had read Bush's article soon after it was published, and it convinced him to pursue a career in engineering and eventually develop the type of (machine-) augmented thinking and collaborative development of dynamic information sources championed by Bush. Funded by the Advanced Research Project Agency (the Department of Defense had not yet officially attached their name) Engelbart formed and led the ARC at the Stanford Research Institute (Bardini 2000), one of the four original computer hubs in ARPANET. Engelbart began to experiment with some of Bush's ideas, using the nascent computer network to explore what he was beginning to see as a new stage of human thinking (Tuomi 2002), opening the human mind to new possibilities for using symbols to create asynchronous collaborative communities. He combined Bush's ideas on augmentation with Licklider's concept of (hu)man-computer symbiosis; computers were not meant to replace human thinking but to complement it, offering just-in-time support to creative problem solving and intellectual exploration. The work was radical and confusing to those outside of ARC (and to a certain extent even those within ARC): It was both a natural extension of Bush's initial thesis and really the first attempts to integrate computer capabilities directly into goal-driven activities so that it qualitatively changed not only the nature of computer-enhanced activity but also the types of thinking used in accomplishing collective goals.

Engelbart was especially taken with the idea that the computer was not a companion or a junior partner but an extension of the mind. His research projects focused on erasing boundaries or dividing lines between the computer and the human, creating a continuum from the individual mind, to computers as tools that could support and extend thinking by reaching out into the larger universe, to a problem-solving space shared with other minds, and back again. This idea of augmentation or extension manifested itself in two ways at ARC. First and most material in the short run was the center's focus on computer-based innovations that worked to expand the augmentation/community frame so that it became more obvious and accessible for the user.

ARC invented the computer mouse, the first hyperlinks, and the concept of "windows" along with many other critical components of human-computer/Internet relationships – which Engelbart presented at a single conference in what has been termed "the mother of all demos" (1968). These inventions are so natural to current everyday activities with computers that it is easy to forget just how far-reaching the ideas behind them were. The mouse acts as a natural extension of the human mind into the computer, merging processes of thinking and navigating the computer, breaking down the traditional hard dividing line between the human mind and the Qwerty keyboard (which has almost no intuitive properties)[4] – the beginnings of what would become the concept of ubiquitous computing. The early version of hyperlinks was the first foray into the idea of fast-moving texts both affecting and controlled by a combination of augmented individual thinking and collaborative engagement accessed through the (mouse into the) mind. The early windows, forerunner of the windows users are familiar with through their personal computer operating systems, could concretely allow users to switch between texts or other types of media with a click of the mouse button.

But perhaps even more important over the long term than these consequential inventions (at least for education) was an abstract realization. In Bush's Memex machine, documents (eventually every document in the world) are transferred to microfiche and interconnected so they can be reached through augmented cognitive connections. But what if everything we did, we thought, we acted on could potentially be documented immediately and easily accessed by off-site users? Essentially we could take what is in our minds – minds that never slept – and extend it out into a public work space where it could meet and work together with other interested users. In many ways it is part of the same thinking that led to the invention of the mouse – developing continuous activity from individual thinking to human-computer interaction to human-Internet transactions. All traditional boundaries to collaborative thinking, planning, and creating could be broken down. It was an idea that came to dominate Engelbart's world and partially led to the demise of ARC, perhaps too far ahead of its time (ARC had various other problems that had nothing to do with augmentation).

---

[4] Engelbart also attempted to develop a new, much more intuitive method of human-computer interaction that bypassed the Qwerty keyboard.

The oNLineSystem

Engelbart developed the oNLineSystem (NLS), which merged Bush's concept of continuous, dynamic knowledge building (what T. H. Nelson would come to call hypermedia), the complementary support of (hu) man-computer symbiosis, and the new possibilities offered by an inter-connected network of users sharing time in a problem-solving space that could offer new and often unanticipated feedback loops. Engelbart's commitment to a knowledge-building system presages the development of Internet-infused education. The original purpose of ARPANET and the one that received the most administrative support was time sharing and storage of and access to information – a storage device similar in concept to the stored-program computer (Abbate 2000). The most popular application of ARPANET was one of the earliest tools for distributed communication, the electronic messaging application, which was efficient, fast, and convenient but really not that qualitatively different from other communication systems.

Engelbart tried to use the interconnected nodes of ARPANET as a way of extending thinking into open, shared spaces, where information is dynamic in nature, changing continuously through the collaborative input of users, providing a constant flow of information feedback loops. He saw the participants in the shared community as "knowledge workers" where individuals were not simply distributed nodes in a system sharing information but actually working to build new knowledge together in their shared electronic space. At the center of the NLS was an online journal where users could post information, comment, offer suggestions, and/or change posted information at any time while maintaining an archive of all communications (so that any user could trace back the reasons behind any changes made). All this could be accomplished by users working at different time points from different places.

The online journal is perhaps the (originating) exemplar of collaboration through online hypermedia that has become a central component for many models of Internet-infused education. In some ways the NLS may have been ahead of even current models of augmentative/community-based education with its attempts to integrate off-line work into online activity. But a major difficulty with it and with Engelbart's model of augmentation was its complexity – a primary reason that the NLS for all its creativity and possibilities did not expand much beyond the "knowledge workers" at ARC. Engelbart believed that a direct flow of activity from the user should go through the computer and into the shared space, but he also believed these relationships, as well as the rules and processes behind them, should not be easy ones for the user. Users should have to struggle to develop mastery of the collaborative system, taking time and effort to recognize new possibilities available through the system – a process he referred to as bootstrapping. (This idea of planned complexity was not unique to Engelbart, as will become apparent in later discussions of the development of Multiuser Dungeons – the earliest incarnations of online gaming – and the Whole Earth 'Lectronic Link – one of the first and perhaps most important applications of computer conferencing.)

Engelbart's ideas on bootstrapping focused on using the computer for processes of discovery and development rather than simple information gathering or even everyday community building. Users should be put in a position of always wanting to look for the next idea, to take chances in making the intuitive leaps that Bush believed so important to creative processes. Users should never really be comfortable in what they are doing at the moment, feeling as if they have reached some end point or plateau in their search. Each discovery should open up new problems and avenues of thought leading to a virtuous cycle of frustration, search, discovery, and innovation. The NLS was at its core a demanding knowledge-building tool. The idea of making computers user friendly came a bit later during the development of the personal computer (Glassman 2012). There is some irony when considering many current uses of the mouse and windows. They were tools originally designed for a dynamic hypermedia environment, part of making collaborative processes more complex by integrating the human mind into a larger, dynamic network of activity. These inventions were appropriated during the personal computer revolution to make computer activity more user friendly, taking responsibility away from the user and perhaps giving more control to the designer. Robert Taylor, who worked with Engelbart, was an original member of the "mother of all demos" presentation team and took several top researchers from ARC when he started the Palo Alto Research Center; the integration of the tools into a user-friendly approach may have been partially a backlash against Engelbart and his vision. The inventions emanating from ARC mirrored human thinking, but they were also meant to challenge human thinking.

The personal computer revolution emphasized the former but really had no way of addressing the latter. Engelbart's fear of making the entry into the bootstrapping process too easy for too many may have been prescient, as modern social networking sites (e.g., Facebook) have overtaken the idea of online knowledge-building communities.

The NLS and then ARC and then ARPANET faded out of existence. Yet the argument can be made that when people refer to the Internet within an augmentative/community technological frame (especially in educational contexts) they are actually talking about activities originating through Engelbart's NLS – promoting the types of human-Internet transactions in collaborative learning spaces where hypermedia allows for (hu)man-computer symbiosis as originally envisioned by Licklider, dynamic project development, and archived communications.

Bush from another angle: hypertext and hypermedia

Perhaps the most important concept for the Internet (certainly the most used) initially had relatively little to do with ARPANET, the Internet, or internetworking between computers. T. H. Nelson, a philosopher, sociologist, and all-around technologist, influenced by the work of Bush and to a lesser extent Engelbart, developed the concept of hypertext and hypermedia (hypertext is a branch of hypermedia but also preceded it in Nelson's (1974) thinking); Hypertext is an attempt to re-create Bush's idea of constant annotation and reworking of ideas by individuals as they move through the information universe, not only using the information they find in a "web of trails" in their processes of discovery and problem solving, but also leaving behind their own intellectual footprint. Nelson's vision of hypertext includes the concept of "transclusion," which involves the nonsequential reuse, intercomparison, and reorganization of shared information as part of collaborative project activity that really never stops in the creation of shared databases. Hypertext is dynamic and adapting to the immediate circumstances of the user. There is no individual ownership of ideas; they belong to whoever uses them. There is no such thing as expertise because information is malleable and adaptable to circumstances; it can be improved relative to immediate needs anytime, anywhere.

Nelson originally attempted to implement or concretize the concept of hypertext through a computer program he named Xanadu. He was never successful, but the concepts emerging out of his failures had an important influence on the development of applications that democratized and popularized the Internet. Nelson was also committed to the idea of education through hypermedia, intimately involved in PLATO IV, one of the earliest platforms for asynchronous and synchronous online education, and a forerunner of what are currently referred to as massive open online courses (much of this will be discussed in depth later in the book).

The development of the internet and the web

It is difficult to say if the Internet was just an expansion of ARPANET or a full-on technological speciation. The major linkages between ARPANET and the Internet, and the bridging NSFNet, were the Transmission Control Protocol/Internet Protocol (TCP/IP) developed by Vinton Cerf and Robert Kahn that was used through all three systems and the development of a concrete backbone of interconnected servers (the system of regional computers that tied all the networked computers together into a single system). ARPANET was slowly folded in to NSFNet (they existed simultaneously for a short while), which looked to connect computers at different university centers in the United States, originally to allow National Science Foundation (NSF) researchers to stay in touch with each other and the foundation. The emphasis was very much on simple, distributed, but also restricted, communicative channels. Much of the hard technology developed for ARPANET was transferred to NSFNet. Leonard Kleinrock presented a report to Congress based on his experiences with ARPANET and NSFNet, "Toward a National Research Network" (1988), which led to initial funding for expanding the backbone.[5] Kleinrock had not been working within the Bush/Engelbart technological frame of using computers to augment human thinking and develop online, collaborative working communities (Toumi 2002). He was more concerned with distributed, high-speed communication, similar to the work of Paul Baran. It was determined, after a great deal of debate and political maneuvering (Abbate 2000), that the new internetwork (connecting of different computer networks) would be developed using the NSFNet's backbone and Cerf and Kahn's TCP/IP as its protocol suite.

---

[5] Referred to as the "Gore Bill" because of the strong influence of Al Gore in developing and promoting the bill.

Two interesting issues in the demise of ARPANET and the creation of NSFNet as a bridging network would eventually lead to the development of the Internet – but the involvement of both is mere conjecture. The first was that ARPANET was based primarily in California, often with researchers who had little if any connection to traditional academic communities at the time. This may have given those working with ARPANET something of a "Wild West" mentality, willing to push the envelope on what this new internetworking technology could and should be used for – nothing less than changing the way we understand human thinking. The NSFNet was primarily based on the East Coast and then extended into the Midwest. Researchers using the internetworking capabilities provided through the backbone may have been more conservative and circumspect in their approach to the new technology. The second idea is that because the bill for continuing with and expanding NSFNet was based on Kleinrock's committee presentation and because he was also committed to an Internet framework that promoted a distributed, communicative community of researchers sharing work they did offline (rather than a collaborative, goal-driven collaborative community creating new work online), less attention was paid to ideas of augmentation, changing ways of thinking, and building online, collaborative communities championed by Engelbart – and the augmentation/community technological frame so important to educational initiatives such as computer-supported collaborative learning.

The NLS, which may have been the most revolutionary part of ARPANET, would receive little if any initial attention from traditional academia and education during the early development of the Internet. Perhaps the most important result of this historical trajectory of the Internet from an education perspective is that the majority of early programs were implemented within a communication/service frame. The Internet was a way of staying in touch with students in different locations, of sending and receiving critical information. Teachers could use e-mail to stay in touch with students or post their syllabus on dedicated websites. The Internet was less often thought of as a tool for nonhierarchical, nonlinear collaboration. Many of the early tools for using the Internet for educational purposes, particularly course management systems such as Blackboard (or even the Open Source Moodle), were geared toward and used primarily for these communication/service purposes.

Saving the internet: the web, mosaic, and google

Early internetworking researchers and developers who worked on ARPANET and NSFNet led development teams that set about creating a structure for the Internet (based on the NSFNet backbone), attempting to internationalize its reach. Other internetworking approaches were developing outside of the United States, separate from the early ARPA-NET researchers, sometimes with broader possibilities for distribution and sharing of information (Abbate 2000). The current Internet is the result of decisions made for a variety of reasons, some involving polit-ics, some involving ego, some involving blind faith in a certain trajec-tory for the new tool. The shared focus was on development of a backbone that could act as a nonhierarchical system of nodes that were interdependent but not reliant on each other. No one server, more importantly no one institution controlling a server, could dominate the flow of information. This remains one of the most important attri-butes of the Internet. Information packets could be rerouted easily and quickly if a server was shut down for any reason. All information might not be created equal, but once it entered the system it would be treated as equal. This system of interconnected network servers would be governed by an independent body – the Internet Corporation for Assigned Names and Numbers (ICANN).

The initial Internet backbone also created a system of nodes as indi-vidual resource sites holding static information in the form of files that could be accessed only if you knew where the information was and the transmission control protocol needed to retrieve it. It was in many ways a re-creation of traditional academic discourse where information sharing was limited to small, bounded communities of researchers highly protective of their own sources. The major difference was the infor-mation on the Internet could be archived and transferred quickly, but only with the help of those who "owned" the data. It was during this time that the Internet took the descriptor "the information superhighway." Its primary purpose was similar to a national highway system –intercon-nected routes between predefined information hubs. The routes were transit channels that served the needs of the hubs. The Internet at this point was little known among the larger population and was frustrating to use, even for those who had access to one of the connected computer centers and experience in using the system.

Even though the NLS was not part of the initial transition from ARPANET to the Internet (it was by design difficult to use and when combined with the new technology of the Internet might have been overwhelming), it was in the intellectual DNA of the evolving technology. Tim Berners-Lee was a programmer with CERN (the Conseil Européen pour la Recherche Nucléaire or European Center [or Council] for Nuclear Research) first as a contractor and then as a fellow. Berners-Lee had read Bush's article and studied the ways Engelbart and Nelson extended the initial skeleton of the Memex concept (Berners-Lee and Fischetti 2000). In 1980 during his first stint as a contractor for CERN, Berners-Lee suggested and developed ENQUIRE, a prototype for a hypertext system for researchers to quickly share information that in many ways resembled the Memex machine. He returned to CERN in 1984 as a fellow just as it was beginning to use the TCP/IP technology, developed by Cerf and his group, to interconnect the information across its (massive) internal computer structure. In 1989 CERN opened up its first external Internet connections. Even working just within the CERN intranet Berners-Lee became frustrated with the limitations of needing to know about information pages to retrieve them – not really that different from browsing through the stacks in a library. The early Internet had extraordinary potential with little payoff – which became even more frustrating when CERN's intranet became part of the global Internet.

Working with Robert Calilou, Berners-Lee combined his ideas on hypertext with the TCP/IP technology to develop a system that linked together all the information controlled by servers through HTTP – hypertext transfer protocol – which is not just an identification protocol (like TCP) but a request for response protocol. Users are able to sit at their desk and (at the time theoretically) reach out and find information archived on any interconnected computer by submitting a request for a specific information page – by clicking on an underlined name or an icon – turning the Internet into a giant Memex machine – which Berners-Lee called the World Wide Web (in partial homage to Bush and his idea of human thinking as a "web of trails"). HTTP took the power of information transfer out of the hands of the "owners" and put it into the hands of potential information consumers.

The casual Internet user becomes an active agent in his or her own information search by typing a universal resource locator (URL) into a Web browser. Web browsers began to become more user friendly, developing graphical interfaces that made it easier to access links – using a mouse almost like a finger to point at a potential new idea (or link; bringing it closer to Engelbart's original reason for inventing the tool). Perhaps the most important (though not the first) of these early web browsers was Mosaic. Mosaic, integrating technology from previous browsers, developed a user screen (graphical interface) that was inviting and simple to read and became the model for all browsers that followed. It is hard to know whether the reason that Mosaic made the Internet more popular was ease of use or because the design encouraged a web of trails approach to the Internet – or a combination of both.

One issue with the Internet's early move back in the direction of hypertext through HTTP and browsers was that the agency of the user was limited to prior knowledge obtained outside of Internet activity. At this point the Internet was almost antithetical to Nelson's idea of hypertext as a shared community database that any person who could read would be able to access at any time. A user needed to know not only that the web page existed but the full URL for retrieval into the browser (CERN, for instance, kept a directory of web pages that users could refer to). Early Internet search activities were still based in information retrieval, interactive rather than transactive, and capabilities for online knowledge development or shared discovery were very limited (application of Unix-to-Unix copy [file-sharing] programs and Multiuser Dungeons did allow for transactive/knowledge development activity for a very small population). What allowed the Internet to realize its potential in augmentative/community technological frame envisioned by Bush and Engelbart among a broader population was the invention of the search engine. The search engine is a web page but one based on multidirectional relationships with the user and other Web pages across the Internet. It is capable of searching Web pages for specific words and phrases entered by the user and pointing the Web browser to likely candidates. A searcher could type in different combinations of key words in an effort to find new information – they could go through the retrieved hyperlinks quickly by pointing to and clicking on the URLs – and if not satisfied with the information could return to the search engine page and refine the search. (The "back" command, often taken for granted, was one of the most important innovations of the early Internet.)

Google developed a search engine using online algorithms that could work in dialectical relationship with users' thinking, creating the type of bootstrapping continuum Engelbart had been attempting to work toward years before (leading to a question of whether search engines would have ever been as successful without the mouse, let alone windows and hyperlinks). Users could theoretically become better at searching through the process of searching – or in Engelbart's terms engage in an ongoing process of online bootstrapping. It was thus the combination of the World Wide Web, the development of browsers, and the development of advanced search engines that set the Internet back on an augmentation/community technological frame trajectory. The user was able to put his or her thinking about a topic or subject or idea online and access information placed online by other contributors to the shared database. Previous knowledge (or at least lack of confidence in Internet-developed knowledge) may actually be a hindrance (as discussed in later chapters).

The influence of Bush, Engelbart, and Nelson on Berners-Lee's thinking suggests that he was seeing the global Internet very much within the augmentation/community frame. Berners-Lee is clear in his own writings and research (Berners-Lee and Fischetti 2000; Berners-Lee et al., 2001) that the initial Web was a first step toward an encompassing, collaborative knowledge-building NLS – initially restricted by technological capabilities. Hypertext is unique not just because the user can move quickly and easily between information pages accessing knowledge as needed, but because the text itself is dynamic. Berners-Lee envisioned communities of knowledge workers engaging in Nelson's transclusion practices in ongoing knowledge development across the Internet – leading to a dynamic, unified hypertext library. The Web opened up the Internet for a new generation of applications that created possibilities for the development of collaborative knowledge-building communities based on the concepts of nonsequential intuitive links, online bootstrapping, and hypertext-based learning communities.

The popularization of the readable/writable web

Perhaps the most important applications in popularizing the web (to date) are those that integrate rich text editing/"What You See Is What You Get" writing programs allowing individuals to create or add text to Internet sites as easily as typing with a word processing program. Applications employing these technologies offer users the abilities to easily create their own online documents with dedicated user resource locators and/or add text to existing documents. Engelbart might not have readily approved of "What You See Is What You Get" technology where users can see how the text will appear in the document as they are typing (and in shared documents the text actually changes as they are typing). He might wonder whether the ease of use in some ways trivializes the possibilities of internetworked communications – promoting simple, empty communications over focused knowledge building. At the same time the continued development of readable/writable technologies democratizes the Internet, making it less exclusive to small, often insular groups heavily invested in computer technology and more open to new populations (early bulletin board systems and blogging were basically the province of computer/ technology nerds). The new technologies also open educational coursework to ideas on learning first proposed by Bush and Engelbart to the common educational experience. Although these new applications make casual use of the web as a communication/services device easier, they can create opportunities for intensive hypertext experiences that challenge both teacher and student – one of Nelson's primary goals. Moving students (and teachers) from their easier Internet experiences (e.g., casual communications on social network sites) to complex and challenging shared educational experiences in hypertext environments is one of the greatest challenges facing Internet-infused education. This tension emerges in design of Internet-infused educational ecologies. Do inviting graphical interfaces, for instance, make in-depth teaching/learning processes less or more difficult?

Evolution of the internet and evolution of internet-infused education

It is almost impossible to be precise with terms associated with the Internet. People, for instance, will often say that there is a difference between the Internet and the Web, but there is a complex relationship between the two terms. The development of the Internet has been like the crafting of a matryoshka doll where new technologies are nested within existing technologies and ideas. The Internet both as concept and concrete infrastructure serves as the outer layer. The Web is an Internet application, a subcategory (as all applications are) that currently dominates use of the Internet in everyday activities – but it could not exist outside the structure of the Internet. Very few people actually envision a concrete series of servers interconnected by cables and falling under the aegis of ICANN when they think of the Internet – they instead associate the Internet with whatever Web browser they see on their screen when they turn on their computers or mobile devices. In the same way, "What You See Is What You Get" writing applications such as wikis and blogs are not the Web, they are a subcategory of the Web (and the Internet) that produce Web pages with editable text. When people use the term *Web* they generally don't think of the hypertext transfer protocols they must locate and request – they basically think of clicking on a requested hyperlink in a Web browser or posting on their social network site or commenting on a blog. One of the most famous cartoons of the Internet is a man sitting by his computer telling his wife: "I can't go to sleep, somebody is wrong on the Internet." Somebody is wrong on the Internet, but that is because they are wrong on the Web, and that is probably because they are wrong on some targeted application such as a blog or wiki. The terms *Internet* and *Web* will be used mostly interchangeably in this book, as will *Web* and subcategories of applications. When it is important to be precise there will be an attempt to make the language very precise – otherwise the Internet will be treated as the gorgeous, intricate matryoshka doll it is.

The evolution of Internet-infused education has been as complex and nonlinear as the Internet itself. One can make a very strong argument that the earliest vision and use of an internetworked world – from Bush to Licklider to Engelbart, from the Memex machine to ARPANET – was as an information ecology for a new type of human learning and creativity – a different type of education where learners had to adapt to the breaking down of physical and social boundaries while access to information was increasing exponentially, where the increasing complexity of human problems and the higher stakes for quickly finding solutions would require ever higher levels of exploration and collaboration. These early researchers saw the human mind as the next great frontier. Bush and those who followed recognized that productive thinking would be based on open exploration of a continuously evolving information universe (massive open online courses rather than being some great new realization were one of the original philosophical drivers of the concept of the Internet).

ARC led by Engelbart in many ways was attempting to apply Bush's vision to the emerging technologies – and develop technologies that were adaptive to Bush's vision, that is, to create a model for human teaching and learning (knowledge building) where, to quote Licklider, "there will be plenty of opportunity for everyone (who can afford a console) to find his calling, for the whole world of information, with all its fields and disciplines, will be open to him – with programs ready to guide him or to help him explore" (Licklider and Taylor 1968, p. 40). Learning in this new environment would be a "right," and the internet-worked world would serve as a great equalizer in education, a "boon to humankind" beyond measure as Licklider saw it.

The Bush/Engelbart/Licklider vision of the internetworked world as a great new educational force that would open all of humankind to a new information universe retreated into the background as the concrete structure of the Internet materialized. The focus was on the outer layer – the intricate, nested layer of education needed to wait – but in the waiting many of the most salient ideas of augmentation and collaboration began to fade. Various historical reasons are probably responsible for this. The tipping point may have been the development of advanced search engines prior to the readable/writable web. The Internet became more about information retrieval than the search for solutions. The dream of a shared problem-solving universe promoting new types of collaboration survived, but mostly in particular niches, in the virtual communities that emerged out of the bulletin board systems made possible by file-sharing programs, or in the Open Source knowledge-building communities such as Linux and Apache (Glassman 2013).

When educators first started applying new Internet technologies it was primarily in a communication/service model (e.g., the pervasive course management systems such as Blackboard and WebCT). The Internet's most dominant use in education was as a basic communicative tool for dispersed populations. Information developed outside of the context of the Internet is posted on a server. The Internet is used as a high-speed communication device to deliver critical information to a (sometimes) highly distributed audience. Students develop content outside of the Internet (write papers) and then send it back to the instructor. It is actually not that different from a glorified version of the electronic messaging that was so popular in the early days of ARPANET. The actual Internet activities have very little to do with attempting to extend the minds of the users by creating a shared space for knowledge building. There is nothing necessarily wrong about this communicative/service framework, but it does not lead to any type of qualitative change in the way we educate. Some might argue it has almost no impact on traditional models of teaching and learning.

The idea of interworked knowledge-building communities began to reemerge with increases in capabilities for connectivity (e.g., broadband technology) and the availability of rich text editing/"What You See Is What You Get" programs. Recognizing the power of these new capabilities, educational researchers restarted Engelbart's program (most of the time without realizing that was what they were doing) at ARC of trying to understand how to build high-functioning knowledge-building communities through the new connectivity – attempting to navigate the high levels of both possibilities and difficulties. There were three lines of research, all descending in one way or another from Bush and ARC but based on different near histories of the Internet. There is research focused directly on knowledge-building communities descending from the work of Bill English, Engelbart's primary collaborator, brought to the Palo Alto Research Center by Taylor, who looked to extend his ideas through the development of the intranet technologies. Bereiter and Scardamalia's *Knowledge Forum,* which started with intranet technologies, is a primary example of this trajectory, along with other researchers focusing on computer-supported collaborative learning. There is a second line in which researchers attempt to re-create the types of sociability leading to community similar to those developed on the bulletin board systems that emerged in the 1970s and 1980s – one of the earliest forms of ongoing, transactive social relationships on the Internet, what Rheingold (1993) referred to as virtual communities. These lines of research include the Community of Inquiry and Classroom Community as well as research programs on developing social space. A third, less developed line of research is based on the Open Source communities exemplified by online development programs such as Linux and Apache (Raymond 1999). This trajectory focuses more on the development of the type of online community infrastructure leading to sustainable, goal-oriented communities.

These three trajectories share various assumptions – the differences are primarily in focus. They are all, however, qualitatively distinct from educational initiatives based in the Internet as a communication/service technology, and they all focus on the Internet as a new, open cyberspace for understanding and extending the human condition. The chapters that follow focus for the most part on the augmentation/technological frame as context for educational psychology and the Internet.

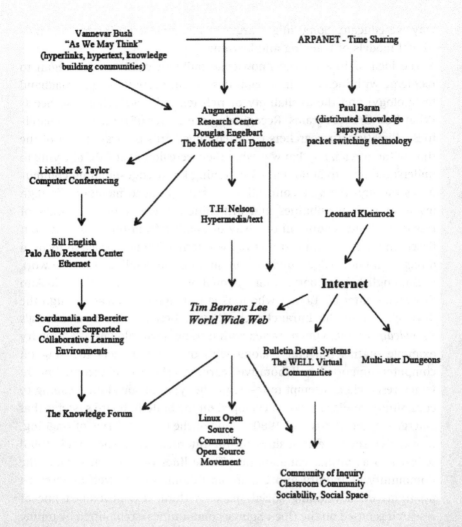

References

Abbate, J. (2000). *Inventing the Internet*. Cambridge, MA: MIT Press.

Baran, P. (1962) *On Distributed Communications Networks*. Santa Monica, CA: RAND Corporation. http://www.rand.org/pubs/papers/P2626.

Bardini, T. (2000). *Bootstrapping: Douglas Engelbart, Coevolution, and the Origins of Personal Computing*. Stanford, CA: Stanford University Press.

Berners-Lee, T., and Fischetti, M. (2000). *Weaving the Web: The Original Design and Ultimate Destiny of the World Wide Web by Its Inventor*. New York: HarperCollins.

Berners-Lee, T., Hendler, J., and Lassila, O. (2001). The Semantic Web. *Scientific American*, 284(5), 28–37.

Bush, V. (1945a). As We May Think. *Atlantic Monthly*, 176(1), 101–108.

(1945b). *Science, the Endless Frontier: A Report to the President*. OCLC 1594001. Washington, DC: U.S. Government Printing Office.

Cuban, L., and Cuban, L. (2009). *Oversold and Underused: Computers in the Classroom*. Cambridge, MA: Harvard University Press.

Dewey, J., and Bentley, A. F. (1949). *Knowing and the Known* (Vol. 111). Boston: Beacon Press.

Glassman, M. (2012). An Era of Webs: Technique, Technology and the New Cognitive (R)Evolution. *New Ideas in Psychology*, 30, 308–318.

Glassman, M. (2013). Open Source Theory. 01. *Theory & Psychology*, 23(5), 675–692.

Kleinrock, L. (1988). *Toward a National Research Network*. National Academies.

Licklider, J. C. R. (1960). Man-Computer Symbiosis. *IRE Transactions on Human Factors in Electronics*, (1), 4–11.

Licklider, J. C., and Taylor, R. W. (1968). The Computer as a Communication Device. *Science and Technology*, 76(2), 1–3.

Nelson, T. H. (1974). *Dream Machine*. Chicago: Hugo's Book Service.

Raymond, E. (1999). The Cathedral and the Bazaar. *Knowledge, Technology & Policy*, 12(3), 23–49.

Rheingold, H. (1993). *The Virtual Community: Homesteading on the Electronic Frontier*. Cambridge, MA: MIT Press.

Stahl, G., Koschmann, T., and Suthers, D. (2006). Computer-Supported Collaborative Learning: An Historical Perspective. In R. Keith Sawyer (ed.). *Cambridge Handbook of the Learning Sciences*. Cambridge: Cambridge University Press. 409–426.

"The Mother of All Demos." (1968). https://www.youtube.com/watch?v=yJDv-zdhzMY.

Tuomi, I. (2002). *Networks of Innovation*. Oxford: Oxford University Press.

2 Visions of intelligence in an interconnected world

The Internet, at least when being used within an augmentation/community technological frame, is about human thinking – what it means, how we use it in our lives, the ways in which active, engaged thinking can confound expectations and wreak havoc on belief systems. The Internet is an inherently social tool (there need to be at least two interconnected nodes involved in any activity), creating possibilities for human connectivity that have never existed before – a connectivity that has little need of historical or physical contiguity, transcending traditional boundaries of time and place. But opportunities for social connectivity, even fulfilled opportunities, do not necessarily lead to productive engagement, let alone what Dewey (1916) referred to as vital learning activities. Potential participants in a community enterprise have to be able and willing to reach out into the unknown in a search not just for contact with other minds/nodes but for solutions to the problems that plague them – to put exploration in the quest for discovery ahead of practices and belief systems that have evolved over decades, even millennia, as part of place-based cultures. Users as potential learners need to open themselves up to new, unexpected trajectories of thought and action, and their place-based communities have to not only allow them this freedom but support them in it. Connectivity needs to be tempered with intelligence to be meaningful to the human condition, with a developing dialectical relationship between the two. The augmentation/community trajectory of the Internet from the beginning (i.e., the work of Bush, Engelbart, and Nelson) has been about this relationship.

One of the greatest challenges facing educators in using the Internet as an educational tool is reconfiguring our understanding of human intelligence to take advantage of new possibilities for learning. As ideas of education and human intelligence have merged over the last century, we have examined and assessed them primarily at the individual level. The Internet pushes ideas such as distributed intelligence and collective intelligence to the forefront, suggesting the new technology is more than a potential source of knowledge, but a generator and sustaining force in human thinking.

This chapter outlines three distinct types of collective intelligence that can be loosely paralleled to the three lines descending from the augmentation/community technological frame outlined at the end of Chapter 1: (1) *Collaborative/hypertext intelligence* – based on ideas explored by Engelbart's Augmentation Research Center and Licklider and Taylor's (1968) discussion of the (computer-enriched) conference as a new type of collaborative process. The asynchronous availability of critical knowledge, archived and retrievable at any time, along with the ability of individual members of a learning community to annotate and redefine its meaning using hypertext tools (usually embedded in intranet or Internet technology) supports the creation of qualitatively enhanced and potentially highly distributed collaborative learning communities capable of creating intricate webs of exploration and understanding. (2) *Swarm intelligence* where individuals coalesce around compelling issues, attempting to solve immediate problems by quickly building a consensus of action, often making decisions based on the consensus of what has been referred to as "smart mobs" (Rheingold 2007). This idea can be tied back to the some of the transient (and sometimes not so transient) communities that emerged through early bulletin board systems and UseNet where individuals could come together to discuss specific topics and/or problems for a day or a month or a year in an intellectual free-for-all environment. (3) *Open Source/ collective agency intelligence*, the creation and maintenance of ongoing, usually targeted problem-solving communities capable of developing their own lasting contributory and decision-making protocols. This type of collective intelligence can be traced back to early models for virtual community such as the Whole Earth 'Letronic Link (WELL) discussion forum as well as some of the early Open Source communities such as Linux and Apache, which organically developed infrastructures capable of supporting sustainable, focused project communities. These different forms of intelligence are not linear (although Open Source/collective agency can be more complex because it needs to maintain connected relationships between participants over time, it does not necessarily follow swarm intelligence), and they are not mutually exclusive (all three can be part of combined intelligent action).

Internet-derived collective intelligence is dependent to a degree on individual choice and decision making, probably far more than earlier conceptions of collective intelligence where collaboration is partially dependent on social groups with (sometimes long) standing shared social and cultural histories (e.g., Putnam's description of social capital; 2000). With Internet-derived collaborative intelligence, potential participants have to be ready, able, and willing to join and become productive members of online collectives – to engage individuals with whom they may have no prior or even potential future relationships, in complex, demanding activities. The social group does not enmesh the individual in its thinking processes – the individual chooses to become a member of a learning community, developing membership on the fly.

The internet was always about intelligence (at least partly)

Bush named his seminal article "As We May Think" (1945a) because he recognized the changing nature of productive human thinking as we moved deeper into the information age – especially as related to scientific discovery. His basic idea was that coming innovations would dramatically augment the mind's associative powers to build new trails of thinking that go far beyond what Andy Clark (2004) calls our "sack of skin." Our thinking would become intermingled with the thinking of other extended minds with dynamic information serving as the combustible substance pulling individuals looking for solutions to important problems together into communities of invention and driving them forward. It is important to remember how radical these ideas were in 1945 for a man trained in physics and engineering. Bush was proposing a new system of intelligence and learning far different from the static system in which he himself was educated and where he prospered.

At the same time Bush was developing his advanced design of the Memex machine he was helping change approaches to research and innovation in the United States as a whole with his report to the president *Science: The Endless Frontier* (Bush 1945b). He suggested in the report that science should be a self-governing initiative where scientists feel comfortable following their own associative trails, turning in new directions, not answerable to market demands or predetermined end points: True innovation is at least partially the result serendipity between explorations of interesting ideas and human needs. To try and control and/or commercialize research is to hinder or even destroy science. Bush wrote *The Endless Frontier* the same year he published "As We May Think," and it is important to see the relationship between the two in the development of the Internet, both historically and present day.

Bush's idea of innovation through a combination of open research and serendipity certainly played out in the evolution of the Internet. ARPA-NET was first created as a tool for sharing limited resources, but even from the beginning many users did not see or use the new network in that way. Engelbart almost immediately recognized ARPANET connections as tools for new types of knowledge building – developing the oNLineSystem to take advantage of new possibilities. Other researchers initially used the Internet for new forms of communication – adapting their behavior most quickly and easily to electronic messaging systems (Abbate 2000), the first and still most popular inter- and intranetworking application. Electronic mail was only a first and easily accessible step in showing how human behavior and thinking could be changed by the internetworking of remote sites. E-mail is generally quick interactions, probably closer in type to conversation than written communication. The difficulty with conversation is that as soon as a person has finished saying something it is lost – at least the exact wording. Both speaker and listener must work hard to remember what was said, and as the child's game of telephone shows there is always degradation of original information, even over a few seconds. E-mail augments both communication and memory in transparent ways by preserving conversation in retrievable form – once written and posted an e-mail becomes what Hakkarainen (2009) refers to as a knowledge-laden artefact – an artifact that can be retrieved at any time, and pretty much anywhere (as long as you had an Internet connection), by either speaker or listener. It is no surprise then that communicative/service community would become the early dominant technological frame of the Internet in education.

The internet and distributed intelligence

Both the communicative/service and the augmentation/community technological frame lay claim in different ways to the distributive potentials of internetworked communications. The concept of distributed knowledge/intelligence, however, is probably most central to those working within a communication/service technological frame. Internet-working communications have moved far past the simple electronic messaging of ARPANET in their complexity and abilities to engage in one-to-many and many-to-one communications (e.g., lecture capture, pod casts, interactive web pages). One of the key benefits and driving forces of the evolution of the Internet is that it could serve as a highly distributed, fast-moving communication network where dispersed communities could share and preserve knowledge.

The idea of internetworked systems as tools for distributed information/intelligence is usually traced back to the work of Paul Baran. Baran in a report to the RAND Corporation (1962) suggested that the Department of Defense develop distributed communication networks to enhance surviv-ability in the case of enemy attack. This report was submitted at the height of the Cold War so it received a great deal of attention from the depart-ment, which was funding (and would soon formally subsume) the Advanced Research Projects Agency. A mythology has grown up around the Internet that it was originally developed by the Department of Defense so that government command and control systems could withstand a nuclear attack. Most histories of the Internet dispute this. Baran's work was influential, but the early years of the Internet mostly followed Bush's dictum – research is conducted for the sake of research – that through serendipity matched up with human (including defense) needs or wants.

The importance of distributed information system lies in the idea that (especially critical) knowledge has a much greater chance of being sustained in its original form if it is widely distributed in easily assem-bled pieces or packages among the many rather than consolidated in the (important) few. Since social groups are dependent on key information/knowledge systems for survival, it is to their benefit to find ways to distribute information among interconnected but independent nodes. Even if some nodes are destroyed, there is (or should be) enough infor-mation that survives to reassemble a reasonable facsimile of the whole. A second attribute of a distributed system is that once information is dispersed into small packages, knowledge has less of a chance of being corrupted when retrieved and/or transferred to different sources. (This type of distributed information system was realized in packet-switching technology developed independently by Baran in the United States and

Donald Davies in the United Kingdom: Pieces of information are distributed throughout the different networks and then reassembled at a requested destination – the Internet Protocol address.) A third important attribute of a distributed system is that it is more difficult for a single destination to amass and hoard information as a means of control over the rest of the network. The nodes carrying information are interdependent and equally important to the network, so it is more difficult for one node in the system to become dominant.

The idea of a distributed system has become almost the ethical core of the Internet. It was a critical influence on the development of its backbone/infrastructure, has been important in the decentralized development of applications, was vital to the Open Source (programming) communities and independent virtual communities that have surfaced over the last few decades, and, it could be argued, is even a key component of the role-playing games that have become in some quarters a large part of the Internet experience (e.g., Multi-User Dungeon systems were developed based on principles of distributed knowledge). It is also the reason why so many Internet advocates fight so hard for net neutrality (the idea that no one node should become dominant through controlling flow of information on the Internet).

The combination of apparent, easy-to-use applications such as electronic mail and its communication-based descendants along with its obvious and immediate (and, it can be argued, often overstated) benefits led a number of fields to try and adapt their activities to the distributive possibilities of the new technology – education being one of those fields.

One-to-many and many-to-one communicative communities: e-learning

Much of e-learning is variation on a communicative theme based at least partially on ideas of distributed information. These educational approaches are basically electronic messaging writ large. In a one-to-many format the one who holds information/knowledge can re-create it in accessible form, archive it, and disseminate it at will to distributed locations simultaneously (any amount of locations anywhere). The information is preserved in its original form so it encounters less of a chance of corruption or misinterpretation. The many can access the distributed information at a time and place of their choosing. It is also possible for the many to communicate back to the one (or intellectual hub) at a time and place of their choosing using e-mail or some other direct (e.g., Dropbox) or indirect (e.g., message board) communication application. As these approaches evolve, interventions are geared toward making communications more continuous, more efficient, and more user-friendly. Little use is made, however, of more augmentation/community-oriented activities such as intuitive search, hypertext, or anything resembling Engelbart's oNLineSystem. Intelligent activity is conducted offline and then communicated online (e.g., delivery of a paper, taking a quiz). This is not to say e-learning within a communicative framework has no or little worth. But this type of distributed communication approach does not use Internet-based technologies to qualitatively change or enhance human thinking. It can, when done well, increase sustainability of current relationships with information, but it does not do anything to change that relationship. Reaching back to Baran, e-learning approaches are often more about sustaining a system of knowledge than building new knowledge.

Collective intelligence: many acting as one

It is important if not critical to recognize that Vannevar Bush was fascinated by the human mind and the interrelationship between thinking and the tools that enable and enhance it. Bush wasn't a psychologist, he didn't think – or at least it wasn't important to him – that tools could change the functioning of the mind or the structure of the brain; he was an engineer and was looking to develop a device or application that worked in sync with the unique qualities of human thinking (Nyce and Kahn 1989) in ways that might augment experimentation and discovery. Some have described Bush as an associationist (Houston and Harmon 2007) because he believed thinking was at its apex (most creative) when motivated individuals landed on an idea and quickly made associative links to other ideas. The Memex machine was envisioned as an augmentation of this uniquely human ability to search for new possibilities beyond their initial thought horizons – turning knowledge development through association of ideas into an extended, collective enterprise. For Bush these associations are not predetermined, held in some storage unit, with the user working to correctly solve a puzzle. The associations that users make are instead highly personalized, very much dependent on immediate needs within the current situation and the thinking of the user in the context of that situation. Bush was, whether he realized it or not, working within a Pragmatist or contextualist framework. Jenkins (1974) describes the difference between associationism and contextualism:

> Associationism asserts that there is one correct and final analysis of any psychological event. ... The contextualist takes the much less comfortable position that a *complete* or *final* analysis is a myth, that analyses mean something only in terms of their utilities for some purposes. (p. 787)

The idea that Bush was a contextualist (again, Bush was an engineer and never defined himself in philosophical terms – the closest he came was considering himself a connectionist) is important for understanding his idea of search as a personal journey. Bush did not see search as looking through an index for something that already existed (e.g., it was not like looking something up in a dictionary or encyclopedia), but as the search for an idea that is as yet unknown. This was at the time, and for many years that followed, a radical idea in the new information world Bush had helped to create and was looking to impact (Nyce and Kahn 1989). Even though many in the information field embraced the Memex machine as outlined in "As We May Think," as T. H. Nelson (1973) pointed out, for the next quarter century Bush's ideas ran "counter to virtually all work being pursued in the name of information retrieval. Such systems are principally concerned either with indexing conventional documents by content, or with somehow representing that content in a way that can be mechanically searched and deciphered" (p. 442). The reasons for the discrepancy between Bush's vision and the development of (computer-based) information retrieval systems were partially technological – few if any tools could mimic the workings of the human mind as collective action in the ways that Bush proposed prior to the invention of the web. But a large part of the reason for the discrepancy may have also been sociological/psychological. Bush was proposing a search-based intelligence fundamentally different from the ways we measured (and continue to measure) intelligence in educational contexts and society in general.

Bush's ideas on search (or, as he called it, selection) were a major break in the ways intelligence is measured in traditional educational settings.

Intelligence tests as developed in the United States have been based on individual abilities to recall static, noncontextualized information in a limited amount of time for almost a century (Gould 1996). Arguments made against these types of intelligence measurements are often concerned primarily with lack of access to or agreement on this type of predetermined information. Many traditional classrooms center their assessments on individual abilities to retrieve relevant information (the right answer) within specific time frames. Bush thought about intelligence in terms of scientific discovery and invention. Again, this wasn't based on any overt psychological argument on Bush's part. This was how he saw invention progressing during one of the major periods of scientific innovation in history (World War II). The Memex machine provides an open space for establishing dynamic, collective thinking, and memory so individuals could reach out – rather than reach within – as they considered pressing problems. It changes the model of scientist from brilliant expert to daring explorer.

There is a second aspect to these early musings on information age intelligence. Bush recognized that the web of trails that individuals develop are for the most part transitory – but to different degrees: "trails that are not frequently followed are prone to fade" (Bush 1945a, p. 106). The human mind needs to be able to recognize those trails of ideas that have meaning – differentiated from those that lead down dark alleyways – and push their thinking in the service of new solutions and discoveries in those directions. Those trails that offer few possibilities for moving an idea forward should be abandoned quickly. The ability to differentiate between valuable information selection in the discovery process and information of less worth, or disadvantageous by offering misdirection, is critical. Attempts to claim ownership over trails of thinking is highly detrimental to innovation because individuals might hold on to those trajectories long after they have faded from their initial potential value.

Hypertext and the failure of Xanadu

Bush's ideas were initially limited because they were based on the individual having specific tool sets not yet invented – not just a computer but analog search tools that served as extensions of human thinking patterns. (Bush knew little about the emerging digital technology of stored-program computers and was not really that interested in it; Nyce and Kahn 1989.) The importance of tool development for this new type of thinking is exemplified by the story of T. H. Nelson and his attempt to bring Bush's and Engelbart's ideas to fruition through the development of a massive computer program (Nelson's proposed methods for achieving a hypertext ecology evolved/changed over the years).

Nelson suggested the terms *hypermedia* and *hypertext* in 1965 as a way of describing Bush's and Engelbart's ideas on open access to ideas and the collaborative development of those ideas. Nelson was originally a filmmaker and took his design of a hypertext information universe (something he later called a docuverse; 1992) from the way quickly moving film shots linked together to build an effect. Hypermedia is an umbrella term that denotes the role of user agency in branching of "presentational systems of all kinds" (Nelson 1974, p. 44). Branching is a media presentation that changes what it does based on what the user/audience does, and while suggesting that film, text, audio presentations, and slide presentation fall under this umbrella, he offers only a short description of hyperfilm, followed by a long and intricate discussion of hypertext. Nelson offers only one example of hyperfilm, a Czechoslovakian film project in which the audience could determine the ending based on their presuppositions about where the story should go; however, he never actually saw the film and later described the process of audience determination as something of a fraud. The concept of hypermedia is mostly undefined outside of hypertext, and although it is not necessarily wrong to use the two interchangeably, it can be misleading. Nelson is also clear that hypermedia and hypertext should not be confused with directed computer-assisted learning systems. In hypermedia the original media/text developer is not attempting to control or manipulate the response of the user/audience and does not anticipate how the original presentation will change in response to the user.

The idea that media (including text) is responsive to the user and not manipulated by the initial developer is critical to the definition of hypertext and can lead to misinterpretations when not taken into account. Hypertext is often presented, for instance, as nonsequential writing, which is technically true, but it is important to understand why it has a nonsequential structure. Bush suggests reaching out into an information universe to explore new possibilities for ideas based on intuitive leaps rather than a stepwise process. The individual needs to be able to follow this idea through finding information that meets their specific (creative) needs of the moment – the information is responsive to the individual's natural course of thinking (rather than attempting to control or limit that thinking). The responsive text is nonsequential because it is responding to potentially multidirectional intuitive leaps of the individual. The trajectory of thinking is controlled by the user and not the system designer.

A very simple, nontechnological example of hypertext is the portrait of the scholar researching a difficult question often portrayed in film, paintings, and literature. The scholar is sitting at a table with books strewn all around concentrating on a single text. All of a sudden the scholar stops in a moment of realization and starts searching for another book. The scholar reads that book for a few minutes and then tosses it aside for another book. At some point the scholar looks up in a moment of insight. The search between texts is being driven by a series of intuitive leaps. What Nelson (and Bush) are arguing is that the new information age will allow all users to have all of these books at their fingertips (literally) at any given moment. Nonsequential text outside of the context of responsive information sources is simply random facts. One of the difficulties with the research on hypertext and cognitive load is that nonsequential text and links are treated separately from the intellectual needs and desires of the users. Hypertext, at least theoretically, brings the nonsequential texts and thinking of the user into balance as part of a process so they are constantly playing off of each other – the action of the scholar moving quickly from book to book is not a dramatic moment but the way that humans engage in research on a regular basis. It is important to recognize that all links are not hyperlinks (a concept that merges together Nelson's and Engelbart's lines of research). A hyperlink is not simply a secondary information source, it is both a footprint and an invitation – a footprint that allows the reader to follow back the history of the text, and an invitation to take the role of that scholar, to select a new book in search of a moment of insight.

Nelson's original conception of hypertext has two (or possibly three) components: nonsequential writing where individuals could move back and forth easily between documents, the ability to annotate/comment on these documents so that users could take them in different directions, and an interconnected document system where these documents could be linked by the same or similar phrases. If an individual is reading a document and suddenly has an idea based on a particular phrase, they could use that phrase to search/select similar pieces of information in the larger catalogue (very similar to modern search engines). Perhaps more important, and more difficult, the individual could then annotate the found information to lead other interested searchers in the direction of the evolving trail of ideas as it crosses the shared community database. For instance, somebody working on the idea could recall the document and, noticing ways it was added to or changed, could use a phrase from the new text to retrieve other work by the most recent author.

Nelson suggested different levels of hypertext that interestingly enough predict the evolution of the web: *discrete, basic, or chunk style hypertext* that "consist of separate pieces of text connected by links" (1974, p. 19). Ordinary prose appears on the computer screen, but some type of embedded prompt takes the reader on command to a new related document/piece of information (understand that Nelson was writing this in 1974). He describes discrete hypertext systems as footnotes, upon footnotes, upon footnotes – except it is the user and not the author who decides which trail of footnotes to follow. There is *collateral hypertext* where users could have parallel texts and annotations available – predicting multiple windows. There is *stretchtext hypertext* where text can change continuously – predicting the readable/writable web and especially wiki applications. And there is *grand hypertext*, shared databases that could be accessed and annotated at will – predicting the evolving interconnected web or perhaps the coming semantic web. One of the difficulties in discussion of online tutoring/scaffolding systems using "hypertext" is that although they use linked chunks of texts they also involve designed anticipation of user response patterns. This puts the linked texts in many of these tutoring programs close to but outside Nelson's original conception (which can be an important boundary). Rather than developing a completely new term it might be more worthwhile to take some philosophical license and split discrete hypertext from basic/chunk hypertext, with chunk hypertext being chosen text that at least to some degree anticipates user response.

Nelson called his potential hypertext program Xanadu (after the summer capital of Kublai Khan), which would become perhaps the most long-running and interesting failure in the history of the information age (Wolf 1995). Despite having a well-developed vision, some of the strongest and most enlightened members of the early programming community as colleagues, and some influential and deep-pocketed backers, Nelson was never able to make Xanadu a reality. There was no way he could turn a computer program into a next-generation Memex machine: Hypertext is concerned with human-to-human relationships, not human-machine intelligence.

The vision of a new type of information age intelligence suggested by Bush and outlined by Nelson lay dormant for the next few decades, making few if any inroads in education. Of course, the major reason was there was no web technology to support the concepts. Many of the original ideas have reemerged in the twenty-first century in annotated fashion (as perhaps Bush would have predicted) through conceptions such as computer-supported collaborative learning, development of socially viable online learning communities, and Open Source communities (all of which will be discussed later in this chapter). In some ways the issues faced by Bush and Nelson have been flipped on their head by the evolution of Internet applications. Engelbart, Licklider, Nelson, and their contemporaries recognized new ways of understanding intelligence but lacked the tools to realize them in any concrete sense. Today educators and psychologists have the tools to pursue ideas such as intuitive search, hypertext, and distributed, asynchronous collaboration past their initial stages but lack well-developed theories of Internet intelligence to truly understand emerging human-human relationships in a transactional information ecology.

Collaborative/hypertext (knowledge building) intelligence

It is possible to make the argument that Bush (and by extension Engelbart and Nelson) dabbled in ideas of human intelligence – but they were more concerned with the ways in which the information revolution and the tools it might (and did) create could extend the natural inclinations of human thinking. A key and perhaps primary topic of those exploring the concept of intra- and internetworking of information was the development of knowledge-building communities engaged in hypertext-driven collaboration. It is a quirk of history that there is not really a direct line between Bush, Engelbart, and Licklider and the development of the Internet (as an entity). Perhaps the most important thinker emerging from the Augmentation Research Center was working just down the road (both physically and figuratively) from the early meetings of the group setting up the structure and governance foundations of an emerging internet-working initiative (at the time the Internet based on TCP/IP was one of multiple possibilities for a dominant network; Abatte 2000).

At first it seems incongruous that Bill English and other members of the Augmentation Research Center were working with ideas very similar to the Internet group but had very little to do with their project. Part of the reason is that English and others had moved with Robert Taylor to the Palo Alto Research Center, which engaged in proprietary research (they were funded by the Xerox Corporation). But there was a much deeper philosophical reason, one representative of the split between the augmentation/community and the communication/service technological frames. English was determined to preserve the oNLineSystem but became convinced that time sharing computers was not the right tech-nology for collaborative work (it would take the development of Internet applications years later to bring the concepts behind the oNLineSystem back to the Internet). English looked to implement the oNLineSystem – and the core principle of extending the individual mind into a shared hypertext environment along with Licklider and Taylor's ideas of how the computer could be used as a multidirectional, multisite conferencing tool – by interconnecting a (small) group of computers in a closed network so that users could easily engage at a high level of online discourse. The system was meant to foreground collaboration – with the dream of an interconnected information universe being secondary. Members of the interconnected community could immediately see what other members of their community were working on, offer commentary visible to all members of the network, and suggest new trajectories for ideas. The PARC OnLineSystem (POLOS) was one of the earliest attempts at establishing an intranet and a forerunner to Ethernet technology.

Scardamalia and Bereiter (1994) built their ideas of intelligence in the information age (although they refer to the "knowledge age" in their writings, actually closer to the original intentions of Bush and Engelbart) based mostly on twin pillars of the psychological theory of connectionism and the idea of a computer-connected community of knowledge builders as realized in classroom communities – what they came to refer to as Computer Supporter Intentional Learning Environments. When Bereiter discusses connectionism he is referring to the "new connectionism" (Bereiter 1991), which moves past traditional associationism in much the same ways that Bush's conception of search/selection does, building on the work of modern connectionists such as McClelland et al. (1986). In this new connectionism critical rule systems are not those that naturally lead to specific knowledge (e.g., logical positivism) but are part of dynamic, ongoing knowledge-building processes. This (pragmatic) associationism serves as theoretical/philosophical foundation for developing communities of knowledge workers through intranetworking activities. The ability to find new connections becomes a collaborative, community enterprise as opposed to an individual phenomenon.

The basic building blocks for collaborative, hypertext intelligence in the combined activity of intranetwork participants using software is not that different from the original oNLineSystem. The major difference is that while Bush and Engelbart were engineers who recognized and/or developed information tools that adults could and should struggle with in explorations of ways of knowing, Bereiter and Scardamalia are more educational psychologists who recognize possibilities for intelligence and then go looking for information based tools to enhance it. Bereiter and Scardamalia actually use the concept of discrete hypertext (they have referred to this as emergent hypertext; Bereiter 2002a) according to its original meaning as suggested by Bush and proposed by Nelson – dynamic, continually changing texts shared by goal-oriented project groups – except in this case the groups are groups of students. Knowledge is created publicly through nonsequential writing that is offered back and forth between students, open to continuous annotation, with all contributions archived so any member of the group could reexamine the trajectory of ideas. In a sense Bereiter and Scardamilia are looking to re-create Xanadu using English's ideas on the applicability of intranet technology. The students are encouraged to reach out into a dynamic knowledge ecology and "search" for new knowledge – not in terms of finding the right answers but finding the next level of understanding.

Bereiter's (2002b) concept of relational understanding helps put the concept of discrete hypertext in an educational/psychological context that is more easily applied to teaching/learning processes. Understanding something is not simply understanding the static characteristics of an object of knowledge. It is instead having a dynamic relationship with processes of knowing that can, at least potentially, support intelligent, forward-looking actions. The most intelligent actions a person can take with an object involve developing further understanding, extending thinking about the object out in new, innovative directions. Bereiter offers some interesting examples: for instance, students searching for an answer as to why HIV can be spread through hypodermic needles but not mosquitos (which can spread malaria). It is the understanding of how HIV can and cannot be spread that pushes students to look toward more complex understandings of the phenomenon, searching out experts that can flesh out and extend their understanding in ways they had not considered. The advance of collective knowledge is based in collaborative exploration and recognition that text is dynamic and potentially linked to other texts across an information universe rather than any didactic instruction. The students do not just learn new facts about HIV; their relational understanding places them in the process of a web of trails leading to more intricate and complex ways of knowing moving beyond their initial, individual thought horizons.

Bereiter and Scardmalia are careful to say that their concept of knowledge building works in sync with computer-supported learning and hypertext but is not dependent on it. This actually reflects the engineering perspective of Bush and Engelbart. Hypermedia (and the Internet by extension) are not powerful tools in human thinking because they in some way re-create the human mind – no tool can do that (Nelson 1974). They are powerful because they support the most productive, innovative inclinations of human thinking – inclinations that are sometimes forgotten in the rush toward certain knowledge and promises of control. The thinking that inspired the Memex machine predated even the earliest thought of an Internet. Scardamalia and Bereiter are looking to use computer technology to re-create the types of collaborative intelligence that Bush experienced overseeing scientists and engineers during World War II, that Engelbart desired, and that Nelson and English looked to bring to fruition in different ways – and do it in the everyday classroom. Their next generation of software intervention, the *Knowledge Forum*, brings Internet technology back into the equation, but the emphasis is still on the collaborative community.

Virtual communities, swarm intelligence, and smartmobs

Virtual communities are among the first recognizable phenomena of the Internet and are much better known than the oNLineSystem-based knowledge-building, collaborative communities of Engelbart and

English. Virtual communities are where users tap into the distributed reach and open communication of the Internet to create communities focused on specific topics and/or projects. Whereas hypertext/collaborative intelligence focuses on ongoing exploration and redefinition of knowledge by a (relatively) small, well-defined group of participants committed to a cooperative, knowledge building environment – whether it be a project meeting or classroom assignment – virtual community/ swarm intelligence is centered on the abilities of new, online communities to quickly emerge based on immediate needs and interests of potential participants. Individuals enter and leave those communities based on the degree to which those needs are being met on an individual level and/or to which their desire for human connections are being met at a group level. The assumption is that these emergent communities can create positive solutions or intellectual or behavioral trajectories through the momentum of collective actions – often based on the concept of swarm intelligence.

Swarm intelligence has its roots in sociobiology and in particular the collective behavior of ant colonies (Gordon 2010). Ant colonies are able to create more efficient routes for transferring food when working together as a large collective as opposed to working individually. Natural functions exist that allow groups to prosper from a hive, flock, or swarm mentality. One of the important implications of swarm intelligence for education is the concept of emergence – where there is an interaction between rules at a local level, making their systems of activity smarter at the community level, more adaptive to immediate ecological circumstances/needs (Johnson 2001). The higher-level intelligence emerges through individual agents working toward shared goals by following local rules systems, with members of the community taking different roles and different action trajectories to meet the immediate needs of the hive, swarm, or from a human perspective community. Agents discovering the most efficient, well-defined activity trajectories establish paths that other members of the swarm will naturally follow based on recognition of the efficacy of the proposed trajectory. In ant colony behavior, ants leave behind an excretion while searching for food that other ants naturally follow, building up a critical mass in the use of the new path (Huang and Liu 2009).

For humans recognition and choice of the most intelligent path forward is not biologically driven (at least not directly), but mostly a matter of collective wisdom or what has been referred to as the wisdom of crowds (Bonabeau et al. 1999). These types of emergent activity/learning environments are often not possible in directed education scenarios. Knowledge-seeking activities in place-based educational contexts are often restricted not just by physical contiguity, but by strict historical and cultural information/knowledge trajectories – focused on transmission of what has been referred to as crystallized intelligence (Cattell 1963). It is rare for individuals in these environments to break free of socially imposed constraints on their thinking. When members of a potential community are drawn together to work on interesting/important problems that in some way challenge these constraints they are able to recognize interesting action trajectories with each other that they may not be aware of when working on their own. Place-based emergent communities are possible, but they often come together in nontraditional situations that the larger social organization has not planned for and are usually spontaneous, difficult to predict, and short lived. The general psychology behind swarm intelligence is that disparate potential members of a group are naturally drawn to a developing collective wisdom. This can be conceptualized as a dialectical relationship between problem-solving activity of the participants and the (very generalized) evolving rules systems of the activity group (Huang and Lui 2009).

Online self-organizing virtual communities began developing early in the history of the Internet, suggesting that the connective structure of the Internet could serve as a new type of emergent learning ecology under the right user-oriented circumstances. Users were able to use (or manipulate) widely distributed, early computer operating systems such as Unix that included programs for sharing computer files between different computers called a Unix-to-Unix copy program (UUCP, a variation on the sharing of resources model that for some reason has never really become a popular use of Internet or for that matter intranet technology; Abbate 2000).

UUCP programs were used to develop electronic bulletin board systems where users could reach out to each other in cyberspace, posting continuous message threads on pretty much any subject. One of the most well known of the UUCP forums was UseNet. UseNet was similar to bulletin board/computer conference systems (such as the Whole Earth 'Lectronic Link) in their use of message threads to establish ongoing, online dialogues, but there was no dedicated administrator. Any user could participate in any discussion from almost any server. A user with a modem could search the UseNet discussion universe and find other users with similar interests and spontaneously develop a community around almost any subject (e.g., cooking). No predetermined geographical, or time, or social boundaries were set for these communities – you had an interest, you joined, and you made a contribution that was disseminated and "remembered" by the discussion system. Each forum was in a constant state of evolution through new contributions but maintained an archive of all communications where users could track the changes over time.

The bulletin board/computer conference systems and UseNet may have been clumsy, but they were one of the first real demonstrations of the power of hypertext in building information-based communities. The most famous of the electronic bulletin board systems was the Whole Earth 'Lectronic Link system, or the WELL. It was based on his activity as a member of the WELL online community, or as a "WELL Being," that Howard Rheingold (1993) first put forth the idea of virtual communities. And it can be argued that much of our understanding about the development and maintenance of online communities (e.g., the importance of social presence, the development of online relationships within a new type of social space) comes from the documented early experiences of WELL Beings (e.g., Hafner 1997; Matei 2005; Rheingold 1993).

A "WELL Being" like Rheingold could go home, start their modem, and through the Internet participate in a community with people anywhere in the world with shared interests and/or goals. Understanding and harnessing the power of these virtual communities could mean opening a new chapter in human goal-driven activities and the ways that hypertext enhance abilities to innovate through collaboration. The experience that Rheingold was having on the WELL and its meaning in society became a topic of a (WELL-based) conference, which is where the concept of virtual communities seems to have emerged. From an educational perspective it is important not to take the wrong lessons from these early virtual communities by focusing too much on the tools without understanding how they worked in tandem and extended the human mind in practice. It was not the discussion system used by the WELL or emergent UseNet communities per se that were important (the WELL system was complex and difficult to use), but the ways in which communications through them were used to develop very early emergent communities based on a combination of interest and social engagement. It is also important to recognize the differences between these early online groups. The WELL, which depended heavily on administrators and moderators, was able to develop a community structure that has lasted three decades. The more anarchic UseNet (no formal administrators) created more of a "Wild West" atmosphere where groups were more transient and volatile.

Rheingold extended his ideas on virtual communities to include the concept of smart mobs (2007) – based on the abilities of newly developing Internet applications to quickly bring together distributed individuals into emergent, goal-oriented groups and the ways this process could promote swarm intelligence focused on immediate contexts. Smart mobs are less concerned with information search (which has been meliorated by search engines) and more with immediate, adaptive goals of distributed individuals coming together to meet those shared goals. These smart mobs are self-organizing (using some of the precepts of complexity theory) and based in the types of interconnectivity where individuals can be drawn into a central activity, idea, or purpose, work together toward meeting a goal, and then disperse (e.g., flash mobs). Smart mobs can become transient vehicles for quick problem solving (or at least addressing problems) and for the development and recognition of collective wisdom (Surowiecki 2004), but they are difficult to control and sustain. It is difficult (if not impossible) to predict who in the group will emerge as trailblazers – able to lay down virtual markers that other members of the emerging group/mob follow.

Smart mob trajectories can be dependent on preexisting bureaucracies, organizations, and/or belief systems. Humans sometimes tend to follow those paths they already know, accept, and/or feel comfortable with (Kreiss et al. 2011). They can also be dangerous in that they have neither the centripetal force of social/cultural rule systems (crystallized intelligence) to delineate acceptable activity nor the organic rules systems and basic trust of ongoing virtual communities. Swarm intelligence among humans can lead to regressive group actions like lynch mobs or riots (Rheingold 2007) just as easily as it can lead to new problem-solving capabilities. Smart mobs are also often based for a particular problem or issue. It is the immediate problem that draws potential members of the community together, and once the problem is resolved, even with an emergent new intelligence, there is nothing to hold the group together to create new trajectories for collective action, to take the next intuitive leap that moves the group beyond the particular problem to create something new. For example, political protests based primarily on swarm intelligence can have an extraordinary immediate impact but then die out quickly without establishing new possibilities for governance (Clemens 2013).

A few examples can be given of tapping into smart mobs and swarm intelligence phenomena to promote learning processes. Sugata Mitra's *Hole in the Wall* experiment (2005) suggests the power and the difficulties of promoting smart mobs (although Mitra does not use this phrase in his work) as a teaching method, especially for difficult-to-reach populations. Mitra put Internet-connected computers in kiosks in children's play areas of a slum neighborhood in an Indian city. The children were able to teach themselves how to use different Internet functions by self-organizing into groups that developed an emergent intelligence about computers and Internet use far beyond anything they could have accomplished on their own. Semet and colleagues (2003) have attempted to develop a more controlled approach to swarm intelligence in formal education settings by creating virtual pheromones that reflect successes and failures of students as they navigate a graph for problem solving. Huang and Liu (2009) offer a more sophisticated, process-oriented approach to swarm intelligence in educational settings. Their research suggests that creating technology-infused environments that promote swarm intelligence factors (defined as *self-organization, multiagency,* and *cohesiveness*) made it more likely for students to appropriate larger system processes, which in turn led to more effective learning. But again this is dependent on having a well-functioning in-place system, students who are already motivated at least to some degree to learn from that system, and the natural centrifugal force of the preexisting educational structures.

The online, interest-driven communities that emerged out of early bulletin board systems such as the WELL and even UseNet and the ideas behind swarm intelligence have parallels with some of the more social/community-oriented approaches to Internet-infused education. One of the goals in approaches such as the Community of Inquiry (Garrison and Arbaugh 2007), classroom community (Rovai 2002), and explorations into social space (Kreijns et al. 2004) is to create the same types of emergent, problem-centered online communities. To create learning environments where the student wants to log on and share who they are with the community, to learn and connect – which is not that different from Rheingold's descriptions of the early bulletin board/computer conferencing systems. The approaches are often looking for the swarm intelligence factors of self-organization, multiagency, and cohesiveness. They look to develop (transient) classroom communities out of students' interactions. Much of the research focusing on virtual community/swarm intelligence looks to develop strategies that promote the types of activities leading to collective learning environments and problem solving.

A swarm intelligence approach also poses difficulties that to this point have not been adequately discussed. Emergent communities based on social interactions of disparate users/nodes can be highly volatile. They can be dominated by students with strong, online social presence and/or abilities to manipulate overt and covert social rule systems to their advantage. What happens if a dominant presence offers the burgeoning community virtual phronemes that take the group in unanticipated or even destructive trajectories? Approaches such as Community of Inquiry attempt to ameliorate these dangers with added variables such as teacher presence and cognitive presence. But as the history of online communities suggests, well-functioning, trusting virtual communities may take far longer than a sixteen-week semester to develop, and quickly forming, smart mob communities such as those on UseNet, or from a more modern perspective Reddit, can be difficult to control and predict.

Collective agency/open source intelligence through sustainable community collaboration

Collective agency intelligence (this signifier is a work in progress) is the most recent of the online intelligences to emerge, based in part on the free software movement of the 1980s and 1990s and the desire of many programmers/hackers to use online tools to cooperatively develop open software (Glassman 2013). Collective agency intelligence is central to the creation and sustainability of problem-solving communities where participants have (or develop) vested interests in the viability of long-term, goal-oriented activity through the Internet. It is in many ways a combination of collaborative/hypertext intelligence and virtual communities with high levels of social capital such as the WELL and collective efficacy (Bandura, 2001). Collective agency intelligence involves establishing protocols and governance systems that differentiate quality of users (e.g., trusted or transient) and value of information/knowledge added (e.g., recommend, comment systems). Social capital is highly dependent on interrelationships between context, evolving agent rule systems, and community development over time (i.e., sustainability). Collective efficacy – whether the group members perceive the group can actually be successful in achieving its goals – influences how well community participants use their available resources (e.g., information sources), the amount of effort and time they put into achieving short- and long-term goals, and their abilities to remain members of the community in the face of obstacles (including early project failures and trolling).

Both the willingness to organize into an ongoing, goal-directed community and the establishment and evolution of rule systems through collective activity is more of a conscious choice of the participants connected to shared goals than in more swarm intelligence–oriented communities – both in decisions to remain part of the community and in determining the community's efficacy for solving problems. Members of communities with collective agency intelligence make a choice to join and participate in the target community over time with focus on progress toward goals rather than tangential relationship issues. It can also be argued that because community activity is overtly forward looking (usually based on shared motivations to accomplish a task) there is less of a chance of communities based in collective agency intelligence falling into behaviors because they are familiar, based on social/emotional/cognitive predispositions. Once established, the community is capable of moving toward nonhierarchical, nonlinear decision-making models where individual participants merge their own needs with those of the community at large. The greater the investment of time and resources the participant puts into the shared goals of the community, the more responsibility that individual is given in system governance. The caveat is that other (especially core) members of the community must see these investments as valuable. Collective agency intelligence is more difficult to achieve (online or off) and more dependent on specific circumstances for establishing the collective.

Online development of communities based in collective agency intelligence emerged about a decade after the first bulletin board/computer conferencing systems and UseNet online discussion forums. The most influential of these material goal-focused groups (at that point mostly free software/programming) was the one that created the Linux operating system (Raymond 1999). A young programmer named Linus Torvalds used a UseNet discussion group on a GNU (Richard Stallman's

General Public Licensing)[1] operating system thread to post a message that he was developing a new free operating system and that anybody in the community who wanted a copy to test should e-mail him. Torvalds would then send the program through a UUCP along with a request for comments. There was immediate interest from the programming community (especially hackers without institutional affiliation) because all well-functioning operating systems had recently turned proprietary, closing off the ability to use, share, and adapt the code. After sending out an early version of Linux, Torvalds was inundated with comments and patches, many of which he incorporated into his evolving program. When the program changed significantly enough he would again post its availability, changing its tail to reflect the changes (e.g., adding a ".01" to the signifier) and go through the same collective revisions process again.

The history of Linux is fascinating in itself, but most important for education is that it was a watershed moment in the development of online goal-driven communities using the Internet to develop hypertext-based communications for advancing specific goals over time – a goal of educational processes to this day (which can even be found in the proposed *Common Core* teaching approach if not the actual standards). Not only were a distributed group of programmers with no previous relationship(s) or even knowledge of each other able to work collaboratively on a program far superior than any of them could have created individually, but in the process Torvalds and his most ardent and committed respondents were able to craft a unique governance structure that ensured the problems and issues of the program would take precedence over the needs of any individual participant (including Torvalds). The Linux program would continue to evolve no matter who left or joined the community. The Linux operating system continues to this day, becoming so popular with desktops, servers and especially "smart" devices that there is a good chance that almost any person reading this book had some contact with the OS in the very recent past.

---

[1] Richard Stallman's General Public License – an important forerunner of the Creative Commons that will be discussed later in the book – was developed through the Free Software Foundation and was the first attempt to develop an organized system for sharing computer programs, partially to allay fears of programmers of free software that their work wasn't be misused and/or be taken advantage of. The GNU operating system, including its source code, was sent to any person who requested it with an open invitation to try it and improve it.

Verdegem and Fuchs (2013) suggest a critical attribute of intelligence in virtual communities that is particularly important for online goal-driven communities – sustainability, "the long term form and effects of a social system" (p. 7). Learning communities need to remain viable long enough to create opportunities for participants to develop infrastructure that engenders trust in expressing and developing shared ideas (social capital) and community governance (e.g., development of trusted user systems). A critical component in the development of sustainable, virtual communities with collective agency for most self-organizing communities such as Linux is not just motivation but urgency of the participants to engage in long-term problem solving around a topic (the members of the Linux community had both political and practical reasons for working together on an open operating system). One of the biggest questions in the development of Internet-infused education is how educators can tap into this collective agency/Open Source intelligence that pushes the learning community to the next level in situations where students tend not to have high levels of motivation and/or a sense of urgency. This may take high levels of creativity and flexibility in educational design (something traditional educational institutions are not known for).

Open source intelligence

Open Source Intelligence (Glassman and Kang 2012) is one but certainly not the only way of conceptualizing collective agency intelligence. Much as Bereiter and Scardamalia developed their concept of knowledge building as an extension of new connectionism, Open Source Intelligence is an attempt at an information age extension of Cattell's (1963) conceptions of fluid and crystallized intelligence. Open Source Intelligence is based on two components of the augmentation/community technological frame: (1) Bush's concept of search/selection as leading to a web of trails and the ancillary capabilities of being able to organize and differentiate new information in a hypertext-based environment and (2) the willingness and the motivation of users to annotate and/or re-create the texts discovered online and then being open to other members of one's virtual community doing the same – recognizing all source material as a dynamic, ongoing community project that is considered by all and owned by none. These are skills that are relatively new to the ways in which we traditionally conceptualize intelligence, as well as to formal educational environments.

We can identify interrelated individual and collective components that are part of Open Source Intelligence. Individual components include the willingness to extend the mind in search and selection of new knowledge in the service of discovery and innovation, the ability to organize the fruits of these searches into coherent narratives for problem solving in ways that can be easily understood and annotated by other members of a shared information universe, and the abilities to differentiate worthwhile information from information that adds little or no value to the common project – to separate signal from noise. There are parallel community components to these augmentative skills. Search takes the individual user beyond not only what is known, but who might know it. Internet-working suggests a knowledge frontier where individuals are looking not only for new ideas but for communities where these ideas might be both nurtured and redefined (in many cases a single process). Organization helps the individual integrate new ideas and themes into an ongoing community – but also gives members of a new community opportunities to recognize the value of newly offered information and knowledge and to edit or annotate it in effective ways. One of the greatest sins in Open Source communities is forking (Raymond 1998) where ideas break off from each other and start on two completely different trajectories. Organization allows members of a community to move toward a syn-thesis of research lines that pushes collective thinking forward. Differen-tiation helps in the development of nuanced infrastructure for maintaining the informational integrity of the community, such as trusted user systems that organically lead to a dynamic core of trusted users who will help protect the integrity of the working group.

The role of Open Source Intelligence becomes more apparent when understood as a logical extension of the ideas of fluid and crystallized intelligence. When Cattell first defined fluid and crystallized intelligence (Dewey actually made the initial differentiation in *Democracy and Edu-cation*, 1916) he described them as sequential – at least in a societal context. Fluid intelligence mirrors our earliest experiences with the world and our relationships to the information we discover. Humans reach out for whatever information is interesting without worrying about long-term implications or consequences. New ideas can drift out of a person's thinking just as easily as they drift in – the importance is in the search that opens the individual up to new engagements with the world. It is possible to compare fluid intelligence to a child swimming in the ocean, reaching out to any organisms that float by and then releasing them as he or she moves on to the next adventure (this is a logical extension of Cattell's metaphor of crystallized intelligence as coral formations, 1963). This early fluid exploration is conducted primarily at the individual level – there is little role for community in these initial thinking processes.

Crystallized intelligence comes later as we move our children toward a productive place in society – the appropriation of socially vetted knowledge through formal education, apprenticeship, or some other teaching/learning process. To continue with the coral/ocean metaphor, crystallized intelligence is discoveries over time that merge and harden into a protective, barrier reef for the social group – protecting the community against the vagaries of a chaotic world. Fluid intelligence does not disappear but moves to secondary status in the everyday life of the individual. Most attention and energy is devoted to crystallized knowledge that is developed and promoted by the social group.

It is difficult for those consumed with developing crystallized intelligence to engage in activities leading to innovation and invention. Innovation is by definition a threat to the status quo. Open exploration is still possible, but it often takes either a special status within the social group or a willingness to act independently of and even contrary to the established community (Rogers 1995). The Internet promotes a third type of intelligence that has the potential to combine the discovery qualities of fluid intelligence with the stability of crystallized intelligence – the new type of intelligence of the scientist as explorer that Bush envisions in his discussion of the mind making intuitive leaps, taking chances in the search for new information – as Bereiter might suggest, an intelligence that does not so much look for an answer as attempts to expand understanding so that we can see, if not take the next step in the development of, relational understanding and building knowledge. Open Source Intelligence extends Cattell's metaphor – the ability to stand on top of a hardened reef that has been so carefully formed over time and throw nets out into the passing waves looking to pull in new ideas – creating pathways for both individual and collective thinking into a larger universe of possibilities. Pathways that support search for solutions that are not yet known, along with abilities to differentiate signal from the noise so as not to spend too much time on trails that as Bush suggests "are prone to fade," and abilities to quickly organize this new-found information into meaningful questions. Perhaps most important is a willingness to give up the concept of ownership of information/know-ledge. Predetermined expertise is an anchor to innovation. Every node in the information universe has a right if not an obligation to grab hold of information in productive ways and add their own thinking while being open to the thinking of others in the ongoing process of knowledge building.

The intelligence of complexity and the complexity of intelligence

How we understand intelligence in Web-based activity will be critical in developing approaches to Internet-infused education going forward. The distributed intelligence of e-learning is probably the most direct and the easiest for both teachers to implement and students to access. But it is also the most limited and often restricted to more positivist, direct instruction models of pedagogy. It is far from clear how effective and sustainable these distributed learning platforms are and how limiting they might be for community building. For distributed models of col-lective intelligence the picture is far more complex. The relationships between collaborative/hypermedia intelligence, swarm intelligence, and collective agency/Open Source intelligence are intricate and in many ways nonlinear. How do we use social connectivity to bring students together into productive, sustainable communities?

Collaborative/hypermedia intelligence probably comes closest to re-creating the types of collaborative knowledge-building communities Engelbart and Licklider envisioned and English tried to (re-)create through the complex networking of individual computer work stations. But this type of intelligence treats the idea of deep exploration of an interconnected information universe as mostly secondary. The know-ledge building community already exists – has already established a purpose offline. These communities can still be partially limited by preexisting relationships. The community works together to solve prob-lems and create new (relational) understandings, but the community does not come together to specifically solve a problem. Organization and differentiation of new information/knowledge are already shared tasks. Governance structures are already assumed.

The effectiveness of swarm intelligence should not be underestimated, especially for difficult to reach and/or marginalized populations. Individuals acting as a part of problem-solving communities can recognize capabilities that they might never have even considered on their own. There is something to be said for the urgency and sheer force of spontaneous collective action. But swarm intelligence has no built-in function for helping the individual and/or the community organize and differentiate information/knowledge. It can easily go off the rails, and even at its best it is difficult for a swarm to evolve into an ongoing collaborative community with long-term goals and governance structures; often few opportunities exist for participants to recognize the limitations of swarm intelligence, and making adjustments is an important component of sustainable collective intelligence.

Collective agency/Open Source intelligence as found in Open Source communities is an excellent educational context in the ideal but – at least at this point – very difficult to develop in the concrete. Students often lack the motivation and sense of belonging that helps propel the type of agency critical for development of a sustainable, knowledge-seeking community forward. Many Internet-infused education models work at developing the types of forums where social connectivity can lead to a sense of social capital and collective efficacy of the participants – attempting to reverse engineer the intrinsic motivation at the heart of so many successful online communities. Whether this is possible through either system design or careful facilitation of relevant online activities remains to be seen.

All of these types of collective intelligence have been important in the development of human thinking and action during the Internet age. One is not superior to the other. We are still in the process of understanding what all three mean to each other and the human condition.

References

Abbate, J. (2000). *Inventing the Internet*. Cambridge, MA: MIT Press.
Bandura, A. (2001). Social Cognitive Theory of Mass Communication. *Media Psychology*, 3(3), 265–299.

Baran, P. (1962) *On Distributed Communications Networks.* Santa Monica, CA: RAND Corporation. http://www.rand.org/pubs/papers/P2626

Bereiter, C. (1991). Implications of Connectionism for Thinking about Rules. *Educational Researcher,* 20(3), 10–16.

(2002a). Emergent versus Presentational Hypertext. In *Writing* Hypertext and Learning. Conceptual and Empirical Approaches. Advances in Learning and Instruction Series. (R. Bromme and E. Stahl, eds.), 73–78. Bradford, U.K.: Emerald Group Publishing.

(2002b). *Education and Mind in the Knowledge Age.* New York: Routledge.

Bonabeau, E., Dorigo, M., and Theraulaz, G. (1999). *Swarm Intelligence: From Natural to Artificial Systems* (No. 1). Oxford: Oxford University Press.

Bush, V. (1945a). As We May Think. *Atlantic Monthly,* 176(1), 101–108.

(1945b). *Science, the Endless Frontier: A Report to the President.* OCLC 1594001. Washington, DC: U.S. Government Printing Office.

Cattell, R. B. (1963). Theory of Fluid and Crystallized Intelligence: A Critical Experiment. *Journal of Educational Psychology,* 54(1), 1–22.

Clark, A. (2004). *Natural-Born Cyborgs: Minds, Technologies, and the Future of Human Intelligence.* Oxford: Oxford University Press.

Clemens, E. S. (2013). Commentary: The Many Paths from Protest to Politics. *Journal of Civil Society,* 9(1), 111–115.

Dewey, J. (1916). *Democracy and Education.* New York: Macmillan & Co.

Garrison, D. R., and J. B. Arbaugh. (2007). Researching the Community of Inquiry Framework: Review, Issues, and Future Directions. *The Internet and Higher Education,* 10(3), 157–172.

Glassman, M. (2013). Open Source Theory .01. *Theory & Psychology,* 23, 675–692.

Glassman, M., and Kang, M. J. (2012). Intelligence in the Internet Age: The Emergence and Evolution of Open Source Intelligence (OSINT). *Computers in Human Behavior,* 28(2), 673–682.

Gordon, D. (2010). *Ant Encounters: Interaction Networks and Colony Behavior.* Princeton: Princeton University Press

Gould, S. J. (1996). *The Mismeasure of Man.* New York: W. W. Norton.

Hafner, K. (1997). The Epic Saga of the WELL. *Wired,* 5(5), May.

Hakkarainen, K. (2009). A Knowledge-Practice Perspective on Technology-Mediated Learning. *International Journal of Computer-Supported Collaborative Learning,* 4(2), 213–231.

Houston, R. D., and Harmon, G. (2007). Vannevar Bush and Memex. *Annual Review of Information Science and Technology,* 41(1), 55–92.

Huang, Y. M., and Liu, C. H. (2009). Applying Adaptive Swarm Intelligence Technology with STRUCTURATION in Web-Based Collaborative Learning. *Computers & Education,* 52(4), 789–799.

Jenkins, J. J. (1974). Remember That Old Theory of Memory? Well, Forget It. *American Psychologist,* 29(11), 785–795.

Johnson, S. (2001). *Emergence: The Connected Lives of Ants, Brains, Cities and Software.* New York: Scribner.

Kreijns, K., Kirschner, P. A., Jochems, W., and Van Buuren, H. (2004). Measuring Perceived Quality of Social Space in Distributed Learning Groups. *Computers in Human Behavior*, 20(5), 607–632.

Kreiss, D., Finn, M., and Turner, F. (2011). The Limits of Peer Production: Some Reminders from Max Weber for the Network Society. *New Media & Society*, 13 (2), 243–259.

Licklider, J. C., and Taylor, R. W. (1968). The Computer as a Communication Device. *Science and Technology*, 76(2), 1–3.

Matei, S. A. (2005). From Counterculture to Cyberculture: Virtual Community Discourse and the Dilemma of Modernity. *Journal of Computer-Mediated Communication*, 10(3).

McClelland, J. L., Rumelhart, D. E., and PDP Research Group. (1986). Parallel Distributed Processing. *Explorations in the Microstructure of Cognition*, 2.

Mitra, S. (2005). Self Organising Systems for Mass Computer Literacy: Findings from the 'Hole in the Wall' Experiments. *International Journal of Development Issues*, 4(1), 71–81.

Nelson, T. H. (1992). *Literary Machines 93.1: The Report on, and of, Project Xanadu concerning Word Processing, Electronic Publishing, Hypertext, Thinkertoys, Tomorrow's Intellectual Revolution, and Certain Other Topics Including Knowledge, Education and Freedom.* Sausalito, CA: Mindful Press.

(1974). *Dream Machine*. Chicago: Hugo's Book Service.

(1973). As We Will Think. Online 72: Conference Proceedings of the International Conference on Online Interactive Computing. Uxbridge, England: Online Computer Systems, 439–454.

Nyce, J. M., and Kahn, P. (1989). Innovation, Pragmaticism, and Technological Continuity: Vannevar Bush's Memex. *Journal of the American Society for Information Science*, 40(3), 214–220.

Putnam, R. D. (2000). *Bowling Alone: The Collapse and Revival of American Community*. New York: Simon and Schuster.

Raymond, E. S. (1998). Homesteading the Noosphere. *First Monday*, 3(10).

(1999). The Cathedral and the Bazaar. *Knowledge, Technology & Policy*, 12(3), 23–49.

Rheingold, H. (1993). *The Virtual Community: Homesteading on the Electronic Frontier*. Cambridge, MA: MIT Press.

(2007). *Smart Mobs: The Next Social Revolution*. New York: Basic Books.

Rogers, Everett M. (1995). *Diffusion of Innovations*. New York: Simon and Schuster.

Rovai, A. P. (2002). Sense of Community, Perceived Cognitive Learning, and Persistence in Asynchronous Learning Networks. *The Internet and Higher Education*, 5(4), 319–332.

Scardamalia, M., and Bereiter, C. (1994). Computer Support for Knowledge-Building Communities. *Journal of the Learning Sciences*, 3(3), 265–283.

Semet, Y., Lutton, E., and Collet, P. (2003, April). Ant Colony Optimisation for e-Learning: Observing the Emergence of Pedagogic Suggestions. In *Swarm*

Intelligence Symposium, 2003. SIS'03. Proceedings of the 2003 IEEE (pp. 46–52). New York: IEEE.

Surowiecki, J. (2004). *The Wisdom of Crowds: Why the Many Are Smarter than the Few and How Collective Wisdom Shapes Business. Economies, Societies and Nations.* New York: Anchor Books.

Verdegem, P., and Fuchs, C. (2013). Towards a Participatory, Co-operative and Sustainable Information Society? *Nordicom Review*, 34(2), 3–18.

Wolf, G. (1995). The Curse of Xanadu. *Wired*, 3(6), June.

3 Concepts of educational psychology applied to the internet

The Internet as a tool with the potential to dramatically change our conceptions of teaching and learning has not emerged in a vacuum. The Internet from its earliest rumblings was meant to adapt understandings and activities of the human mind and its relationships to information to the extraordinary changes and technological developments of the twentieth (and now the twenty-first) century. The idea of extending human thinking beyond the individual, beyond the local community, beyond even historically driven cultures into new spaces provided by interconnected computers was key for early pioneers such as Bush, Engelbart, and Licklider. At the same time while the tools the human mind is using are changing quickly and in dramatic fashion, it is far less clear how this is affecting the cognitive, social, or even physical architectures that help determine processes of teaching and learning, including the brain. (There is actually some argument about the malleability of the human brain in response to input; Maguire et al. 2000.) How qualitative are the changes the Internet is causing in our relationships to information, to each other, to the world – and how much of this (perhaps seeming) information revolution is simply a variation on a theme? Are we still in the end the same humans learning in the same ways?

At this point it makes little sense to throw out all or even some of the dominant educational theories as they have evolved over the last century while we try to sort out approaches to Internet-infused education. And, indeed, many of today's theorists and researchers trying to make sense and give meaning to the Internet in educational contexts have leaned on some of the most important educational theories and concepts of the twentieth century as underpinnings for new, Internet (or at least hypertext) explorations into teaching and learning. The publications of John Dewey, L. S. Vygotsky, and Albert Bandura as well as more recent information-processing theorists have already played important roles in Internet-focused education research. There is a paradox, however, in current Internet-infused education research: Most current educational researchers cut their teeth working within frameworks that predate the Internet, and in some cases the computer, sometimes by decades. To what degree are the current generation of education researchers attempting – sometimes clumsily – to pour old wine into the new, very differently shaped bottles provided by the Internet?

This chapter will focus on some of the most common applications of preexisting educational frameworks to the Internet's augmentation/community technological frame, especially the roles played by multi-access, problem-solving communities, and hyptertext/hypermedia in knowledge building.

Information processing and the internet

An influx of new Information: cognitive load and controlling information input

One of the most controversial aspects of hypertext environments including the Internet (it is important to remember that although the Internet and hypertext have roots in the same Vannevar Bush article, they evolved along different theoretical/research trajectories, eventually merging in the creation of the Web) is how the human mind might react to sudden floods of fast-moving, nonlinear information where inter-linked and sometimes simultaneous strands of knowledge often have relatively obscure relations to each other. Will the mind quickly adjust and use the new flows of information to its advantage (as Nelson suggests), or will it be overwhelmed, at best unfocused and at worst paralyzed? (Recognizing the relevance in differentiating between hyper-text information that has its own internal logic and the more general category of interlinked information sources that many times do not.) The difficulties associated with cognitive load in human-Internet interaction are one of the earliest problems studied by researchers concerned with how humans might learn, or have their abilities to process information inhibited, in linked information and hypertext environments.

Cognitive load theory (Sweller 1988) is based on the idea of working memory – dating back to a concept of memory proposed by George Miller (1956) in the 1950s. The basic idea is that short-term or working memory, our immediate source of actionable information, can hold only a limited number of informational items at any one time. When a new piece of information is introduced into the problem-solving process it will push out another piece of information from working memory. If this new piece of information is less relevant to the problem, adding it into working memory at the expense of more worthwhile information will actually detract from the individual's abilities to focus on the task at hand, limiting abilities to develop a directed solution, or at the very least a better understanding of the problem. Over the decades a number of studies have suggested that control of information in working memory enhances learning because it allows learners to focus their attention on the targeted problem or text (e.g., Baddeley and Hitch 1974).

Before continuing it is important to understand the different meanings of hypertext and hypermedia and the ways in which they are used in memory and education research. I believe Nelson was using "hyper" in its original Greek meaning of above or beyond; one of the best ways to understand Nelson's meaning is through his definition of "hyper-man" as "Protean, capable of infinite changes in appearance and style, a magician, a Balthazar bringing gifts" (Nelson 1974, p. 3). As discussed in the previous chapter the original concept of hypertext was based on Bush's vision of a continuously evolving dynamic information universe and explicated through Nelson's focus on the role(s) of the user in being able to understand the evolution of the current information choice and where to take it next as part of their own (problem-based) explorations. The processes of finding an information source along a web of trails, adapting it to current circumstances through annotation, and then leaving both the information source and its developmental history for the next user is central to the concept of hypertext. A transactional relationship exists between all users who access information – the information is constantly changing not just because of hyperlinked access, but also because once users are engaged online with an information source they become potential participants in the development of that source: There is not only an invitation but also an expectation that the user will leave an intellectual footprint.

The definition of hypermedia/hypertext as often used in educational research (as well as other Internet-related fields) can be far more broad and unidirectional than the original definition – sometimes interpreting hyper – as excessive rather than as above or beyond. Basically hypermedia is portrayed as any environment using hyperlinks and/ windows that allows users to move quickly between different information sources (suggesting that hypertext is defined by the linking structure rather than the other way around). This second definition of hypermedia is obviously based on the most basic level of Nelson's original outline of hypertext, but there is also a qualitative difference: Nelson's original hypermedia/hypertext focuses on the user as agent in development of information, while later conceptions often treat the user as an almost passive information consumer. As mentioned in the previous chapter the modifier "chunk" will be used to signify linked data at their most basic, proto-hypertext level, where hypertext is defined based on the linking structure of the information.

Web-based activity, by definition (remember that Berners-Lee was influenced by Bush and Nelson), puts individuals at the very least into chunk hypertext environments, creating obvious problems for controlling cognitive load (in this chapter synonymous with mental load). New technologies offer users easily realized capabilities, and indeed enticements, for using multiple windows and links to jump quickly and effortlessly between different frames of reference and/or pieces of information – a major factor in Engelbart's development of windows and Berners-Lee's creation of the Web. The question many researchers in memory and teaching and learning processes, including cognitive load theorists, ask is this subtraction by addition: Does the lure of new and better information at the moment take us further away from immediate and long-term directed goals of thinking (DeStefano and LeFevre 2007)?

To take a simple example: You are reading this chapter on the Internet with another window open containing your e-mail. You are trying to follow the argument about cognitive loads and the Internet and are slowly arranging different pieces of information in your working memory as you process the ideas. All of a sudden you hear the "bing" of your e-mail and switch windows to see who wrote you an electronic message – driven by curiosity or the natural romance of the unknown. You find, in another window, an e-mail asking you a question about a topic that has nothing to do with cognitive load or the Internet, or for that matter anything to do with memory teaching and learning (it is important to point out that this is not hypertext in any form). To respond to this e-mail, or even make a decision about whether you want to respond, you must replace items in your working memory that are helping you process immediate concepts and problems with other items related to your possible response to the new cognitive task posed by the message. When you return to the window (figuratively or literally) containing ideas and problems raised by this chapter you have a new catalog of ideas in your working memory that you would have to replace again as you continue your attempts to follow the argument. Not only do you lose time – cognitive load theory would argue that there is no ancillary to simultaneous windows in our mind that we can easily switch between – you will not be as (re)focused reading until you rebuild the relevance of your short-term memory. But what if you ignore the "bing"? What if you have well-developed, perhaps scaffolded, self-regulatory skills and are able to place the "bing" on the mind's proverbial backburner? The interlinking structure of windows/Web is a cruel task master; you still have to stop and make a decision not to respond that impacts the relevance of items in your short-term memory. This is an obvious and simplistic example, but we are constantly confronted by more subtle versions of interruptions to our thinking, especially when doing research on the Web – through, for instance, embedded links. Even if we don't click on the link, we are still distracted in our thought processes by the blue, underlined sequence of words that might unlock some new, important trove of ideas – "Balthazar offering gifts."

A recent comprehensive review of the relationship between cognitive load and (chunk) hypertext (DeStefano and Lefevre 2007) suggests that increased links may lead to increased cognitive load for readers. But the impact on the comprehension of the text were variable depending on other factors such as the structure of the links (whether they were hierarchical within the target text – meaning links moved from superordinate categories to subordinate categories, which also meant there were relatively few links – or more randomly networked in that linking is based on semantic or cause-effect relationships, which usually led to higher numbers of links), the working memory capacity of the user, and/or the users' prior knowledge in the immediate domain. Two ideas stand out from the review: (1) Most of the research does not actually use hypertext, at least based on Nelson's definition. The initial information and the links in most of the experiments are controlled by the researchers and not the user. The researchers establish projected end points to the link-based activity. Very little user agency is based on intuitive inquiry looking for responsive information sources. (2) Relatedly, readers' interactions with hypermedia/text are variable, those with less knowledge in a domain having a more difficult time with comprehension in these chunk hypertext environments, especially as the amount of links increases and appear more randomly structured. Less knowledge generally means less interest, which means lower levels of user agency.

This research may have important implications for the Internet as an educational tool – suggesting it is important to make primary educational sites and destinations highly structured, especially for students with limited knowledge in a given field (e.g., introductory courses). This might be especially true for younger students who have limited domain knowledge or students who already have difficulty in applying working memory to their comprehension tasks. The level of structure in Internet-based resources is a salient issue. Part of the genius of the Internet is that it can increase individual agency by allowing students to take control of their own problem solving (Glassman et al. 2013). Cognitive load theory and research suggests that this intellectual freedom must at least be balanced with development of highly structured Internet learning environments where teachers can guide students through their experiences with linked data by maintaining control over types and amounts of links and/or abilities to switch between windows. The relationship between the natural centrifugal forces of the Internet on human thinking and the more centripetal learning goals of traditional education is and will continue to be a major question in Internet-infused education (and this book).

One more issue shows up across research scenarios exploring the effects of linking structures on thinking/learning: There seem to be individual differences in users' abilities to engage in productive Internet learning activities. These differences may at least partially be the result of Internet-based experience. Users with strong Internet literacy skills (Leu et al. 2004) such as search and differentiation of information tend to be able to overcome deficiencies in specific knowledge domains in their reading for understanding on the Internet (Coiro 2011). The ability to overcome environments that increase cognitive load might be as much about the student's targeted Internet literacy skills and/or the types of intelligence they are using in their task (e.g., crystallized vs. Open Source) as it is about the human mind's abilities to organize working memory.

Sociocognitive theory and internet learning contexts

Albert Bandura's sociocognitive theory (1982) has had, and continues to have, a major influence on research into Internet-infused education. Human-Internet interactions and transactions promote and are in many ways dependent on user agency. Bandura's sociocognitive approach is designed to examine the individual's sense of agency and perceptions of efficacy in activity. Bandura's (2001) own writings on the Internet are short but interesting and forward looking, suggesting how and why sociocognitive theory can and should have important implications for human-Internet interactions. Bandura saw the Internet as being able to change the channels of communication bringing more individuals into the processes of innovation and discovery. It is the "transactions that occur within social relationships rather than the ties, themselves, that explain adoptive behavior." It is the "psychosocial determinants and mechanisms which govern the rates at which adoptions are acquired" (2001, p. 17). Bandura suggests we perhaps have to explore a new class of determinants for individual (and community) behavior – presumably centered on issues similar to if not the same as everyday activities such as motivation and self-regulation – trying to understand the role the Internet plays in everyday life.

The development of a sociocognitive approach to Internet-based education can be seen in many ways as a response to Bandura's challenge – what are the determinants and mechanisms that allow learners to access these new information (and collaborative) sources, "adopting" their behavior to Web-based activities? Experience is of course primary, but what types of experience and how can educational activities best be manipulated to take advantage of possibilities available through the Internet in teaching and learning – and what type of capabilities should these experiences promote? To this point the research into Internet-infused education has focused on two sociocognitive "mechanisms:" the broader mechanism of self-efficacy and the more (educationally) focused mechanism of self-regulated learning.

Internet self-efficacy

Internet self-efficacy has been to this point one of the most researched ideas based on a psychological theory/ideas that predates the Internet. In the sociocognitive framework self-efficacy refers to individuals' perceptions of how well they can do in accomplishing tasks – especially their preconceived abilities to overcome expected and unexpected barriers. These perceptions are developed through domain-specific experience (positive experience, especially mastery experience in activities increases self-efficacy). One of the reasons self-efficacy is such a resonant concept in the information age is that for many computers and the Internet represent new domains of activity – with a great deal of variation in the type of experiences users have within those domains (e.g., the digital divide). Willingness and motivation of students to use the Internet in their learning activities is highly dependent (at least theoretically) on perceptions of success in using the Internet as a tool for learning, which in turn is based on previous experience (Kim and Glassman 2013). This can be especially important in formal education contexts because even students who have had success in their traditional classroom-based studies may not have had the same types of experiences in online contexts. Similarly, even (or perhaps especially) if students have been successful in other online activities (e.g., role-playing games, extended activity on social network sites) both teachers and students may be frustrated by more directed, goal-oriented online activities with specific demands and/or high levels of teacher guidance.

There has actually been a slow (in Internet time) evolution from conceptions of computer self-efficacy to Internet self-efficacy. The earliest computer self-efficacy scales focused on perceptions of undertakings with stored program computers and had little if any relationship to hypertext-based activities in particular or the Internet in general. In a relatively recent review of research done on the concept of computer self-efficacy (Moos and Azevedo 2009) almost all the studies reported were based on hardware-and/or software-focused scales. One of the earliest, most well known of these scales, and the scale that shows up the most in the review, is the *Computer Self-efficacy Measure* developed by Compeau and Higgins (1995). What may be most important about this particular scale is that it was one of the first[1] attempts to apply sociocognitive theory to computer-based activity – but it also has little to do with any type of educational activities.

---

[1] This is not the first computer self-efficacy scale. At least one scale preceded it (Murphy et al. 1989).

Three different Internet self-efficacy scales emerged in close succession at the turn of the millennium, all more or less predating issues raised by the popularization of the readable/writable Web through editing/ What You See Is What You Get Applications. An Internet self-efficacy scale developed by Eastin and Larose (2000) was the first in the sequence and probably the most similar to the computer self-efficacy measure, focusing for the most part on software troubleshooting. Next was a scale developed by Torkazdeh and Van Dyke (2001) that is more directly concerned with Internet-specific activities such as "surfing" and "downloading," but the emphasis is for the most part on the individual as an information consumer – in other words not really concerned with the development of mechanisms relating to new channels of communication as suggested by Bandura.

The last of the three is a more education-related, chunk hypertext-based Internet self-efficacy scale developed by Tsai and Tsai (2003). This scale is the most closely aligned of the three with Bandura's vision of the relationship between sociocognitive theory and the Internet. It currently is one of the most widely used in Internet-infused education studies (especially in Asia). The scale has gone through a number of alterations and revisions (both by the original authors and by researchers looking to explore specific issues) allowing for the integration of readable/writable Web technologies as they have become more available and important in everyday uses of the Internet. The initial scale focused on ways in which users might be able use the Internet as a way to find information for individual problem solving. The first version of the scale was divided into two subcategories, exploration and communication. This represents one of the first times an Internet research tool explicitly recognized that the Web is not monolithic but can be used for multiple purposes. The first efforts at using the scale suggested strong correlations between self-efficacy and success in searching strategies – pointing to important relationships between relevant, positive Internet experiences and Internet literacy (Leu et al. 2004).

This early version of the Internet self-efficacy scale eventually evolved into the functional part of the more targeted *Web-based learning self-efficacy scale* (Cheng and Tsai 2011), which includes more focused items such as "I believe that I can e-mail instructors to make queries from an online learning system." This was combined with the development of a general scale assessing students' perceptions of how well they believe they can learn in Web-based teaching environments, with items such as "I believe that I can master the learning materials in Web-based courses." Researchers using the Web-based learning self-efficacy scale have found reciprocal relationships between experience, confidence, and willingness to engage in online education scenarios (as indicated by students' willingness to go online and find help about their courses). The evolution of the Tsai and Tsai Internet self-efficacy scale speaks to the evolving multidimensional nature of Web-based activities as well as the idea that general Internet experience does not necessarily translate into specific types of Internet self-efficacy (the concept of digital natives can be misleading in educational contexts).

A more recent Internet self-efficacy scale that concentrates in particular on human-Internet interactions/transactions in the context of readable/writable Web applications was developed by Kim and Glassman (2013). This scale attempts to push Internet self-efficacy further toward Bandura's vision of the Internet as opening new channels of communication and allowing for important avenues for diffusion of information leading to innovation. This Internet self-efficacy scale includes categories similar to the Tsai and Tsai scale such as communication and search, but also factors that focus on agency and the Internet's abilities to promote collaborative learning contexts. In particular a number of items measure the abilities of users to organize large amounts of information and to differentiate between different sources of information, and especially abilities to react to and generate information on the Internet as part of collective endeavors, attempting to address emerging issues such as student engagement and collaboration.

One of the most important issues in exploration of Internet self-efficacy is that self-efficacy, as Bandura (1982) suggests, is based on domain-specific experience. In the context of online education this would mean not just experience in general Internet activity (which many in the current generation of students have) but the types of experience that are designed to foster success either in Internet-based, goal-driven directed learning experiences and/or complex collaborative environments where users often face initial logical and conventional barriers to success (e.g., finding and differentiating difficult information sources, becoming a respected member of an online community). For instance, students' self-efficacy in generating and reacting to information was shown to increase in courses that emphasized independent blogging as part of a shared online/offline community (Kim et al. 2013). The role of experience in helping to develop motivation and self-efficacy for individuals from different economic circumstances, availability of Internet portals (e.g., computers, mobile devices), and broadband access are critical questions in preparing students for life in the twenty-first century.

The role of self-regulated learning

The concept of self-regulated learning in relation to Internet-infused education has drawn a good deal of attention from the research community. The importance of self-regulation in (chunk) hypertext environments is partially an extension of ideas suggested by cognitive load theory. If students do not develop strong self-regulatory skills they become susceptible to "lose their way in hyperspace" (Narciss et al. 2007, p. 1127). Development of self-regulatory skills may be especially important in formal education contexts that promote in-depth exploration of single topics, both because of possibilities of distraction and because casual users in informal, everyday Internet activities are often used to getting answers quickly and moving on to other subjects.

Self-regulation in the context of hypertext environments, especially those looking to promote collaborative learning communities, can lead to contradictions. On the one hand the work of Engelbart and Nelson suggests that willingness and abilities to follow a web of (thinking) trails to fruition should lead to emergent, functioning collaborative learning communities (as more users become contributors and owners of the developing information/knowledge). The regulation of these communities is inherent to the system, and it is not clear that individual attempts to control intake of or use information would be positive and may even be detrimental to this process. On the other hand hypertext-based activities can create a rich but potentially overwhelming information environment – the learner is constantly faced with decision points about which trajectories to follow, which intuitive leaps to make – indeed, if it is wise to make a leap at all at the moment. Perhaps most important, those following a web of trails need to be able to recognize when the trail has faded and move in new directions no matter the time and effort invested. Users need to develop new regulatory skills to successfully navigate environments if they are not to get lost in them.

Researchers exploring the issue of self-regulation in Internet-infused education suggest that students should be taught metacognitive strategies for stepping back from hypertext environments when necessary to control content before cognitive trouble ensues (e.g., being taken off task). The idea of metacognition has a long history in theory building and empirical research and seems an important topic for human-Internet interactions, especially when considering the open, nonlinear nature of the Internet as an information source. (Does the user control the Internet, or does the Internet control the thinking of the user?) The psychologist Roger Azevedo (2005) says as much in explaining why he sees an important fit between metacognition and the Internet as a tool in education.

A number of (nonexclusive) models of self-regulated learning have been developed by researchers such as Pintrich (1999), Zimmerman (1990), and Winne (1996), but at the core of all is the ability of the learner to focus on and complete tasks even when presented with (sometimes) difficult barriers to maintaining that focus. Basically the learning agent engages in an ongoing process of self-observation, reflection on those observations, and adaptation through necessary reinvention of task-related behavior. The self-regulated learner is able to engage in an internal dialogue about relative levels of success in completing the task at hand and then readjusts their behavior toward a more positive trajectory based on the that dialogue. However, a subtle difference seems to exist between self-regulation in traditional learning activities and human-Internet interactions/transactions. In traditional educational contexts individuals must learn to focus on the relevant activity at hand – distractions are alien to the immediate activity and can often easily be recognized as such; Internet-based studies are often more concerned with self-regulation as a means for avoiding degradation of the task at hand by nonrelevant information sources that are a natural part of and Internet-infused landscape (the embedded hyperlink, the aforementioned e-mail bing).

One of the earliest attempts at tying sociocognitive ideas of self-efficacy and self-regulated learning to Internet activity was conducted by Joo and colleagues (2000), at a time when editable Internet applications were just starting to draw attention across a larger online population. The timing is relevant because the Internet self-efficacy scale used was very basic, focusing on issues such as search, downloading information, and finishing Internet programs. Still the findings and research implications are important both because of the historical moment and the ways it impacted sociocognitive research on Internet-infused education going forward. The researchers found positive relationships between self-efficacy for self-regulated learning and academic self-efficacy, search strategy, and Internet self-efficacy. The focus was on the student/user as an active agent and the role(s) their perceptions of abilities to regulate their Internet activities (in learning) might play in using Web-based tools to accomplish academic goals.

More recent research into self-regulated learning in Internet activity has taken two trajectories: one that treats the Internet as a tool and/or tutor in helping to increase self-regulation strategies (and is often intermingled with the sociocultural concept of scaffolding, discussed later in the chapter), and one that focuses on the user being an effective agent in using the Internet as part of learning processes.

Using hypermedia/hypertext to teach self-regulatory behavior

The idea that hypermedia/hypertext can be used as a tool for increasing and/or enhancing self-regulated learning has strong ties back to theories developed in more traditional (pre-Internet) contexts. Research and theory development in this area is exemplified by Roger Azevedo and his colleagues (e.g., Azevedo and Cromley 2004; Azevedo et al. 2005). (Azevedo uses the term *hypermedia* rather than hypertext, which as the previous chapter suggests is technically correct but can be misleading. The definition Azevedo seems to be following falls into the broadest category of chunk hypertext: Nelson, who was mostly against computer/ Internet tutoring programs, might argue that these types of intelligence tutoring systems do not involve hypertext at all.)

The framework for the research trajectory of Azevedo and his colleagues is partially based on a set of assumptions about self-regulated learning and its relationship to chunk hypermedia including that "self-regulated learners are active and efficiently manage their own learning in many different ways" and that "SRL is a constructive process whereby learners set goals for their learning and then attempt to plan, monitor, regulate and control their cognition, motivation, behavior and context" (Azevedo 2005, p. 205). The working assumption is that chunk hypermedia learning contexts in particular and the Internet in general requires advanced self-regulation for students to function effectively. This suggests education in complex subjects based in hypermedia environments (such as Web-based scientific inquiry) should focus first on experiences that increase self-regulation skills in (relatively) autonomous learning activities.

Early research has focused on the effects of using chunk hypermedia interventions to teach users' self-regulatory skills (which they can apply to other learning tasks in similar environments). An intelligent tutor or media intervention is used primarily to teach metacognitive strategies that help learners regulate their relationships/learning processes with the new hypermedia environment. A set of studies published together in the journal *Educational Psychologist* in 2005 explored this topic in depth. Two of the articles explored abilities to enhance learning strategies through computer-generated learning systems. Quintana and colleagues (2005) looked into the idea of developing metacognitive strategies for skills critical to Internet-based inquiry projects such as search, information evaluation, and synthesis through computer-generated scaffolding interventions. Just-in-time commentary on student actions as they go through the processes of computer inquiry pull the metacognitive-developed strategies forward so that students have a more advanced relationship with the a broader, online information environment. Graesser and his colleagues (2005) focus primarily on traditional metacognitive/self-regulation strategies: They describe two interventions, AutTutor, which offers continuous questions on a particular topic helping students refine their understanding, and iSTART, which uses online characters to help students increase their metacomprehension capabilities through a three-step process. In a third study Mathan and Koedinger (2005) suggest possibilities of more complex feedback loops in cognitive tutoring where the program attempts to detect errors in process and to help learners redirect their own thinking rather than driving them toward the correct answer. At the heart of this research is the idea that offline learning strategies can be directly mapped on to online experience through what might be termed soft augmentation strategies – users' minds are engaged in dialectical relationships with chunk hypermedia (again, very broadly defined) in an effort to extend thinking skills.

One the most sophisticated of these "intelligent tutoring" initiatives has been developed by Narciss et al. (2007) and the *Study 2000* program. *Study 2000* uses both embedded instructional tools (e.g., tutoring links) and nonembedded instructional tools (e.g., guidance-oriented table of contents), direct instructional tools (classroom instruction), and indirect instructional tools (note taking and highlighting) – all designed to increase in-depth study of a single topic in a chunk hypermedia environment. In spite of the availability of tools, students used the more superficial tools such as highlighting and note taking only 13 percent of the time and barely used the tutoring tools at all. They did not use the links to search for more in-depth information at all. The findings suggest it may be difficult to manipulate self-regulation of even chunk hypertext in formal, traditional education contexts.

Self-regulated learning and epistemic beliefs about the validity of internet information

An interesting and potentially important line of research that has emerged over the last few years is the relationship between epistemological beliefs about the origins and validity of knowledge and how these beliefs might impact self-regulated learning in Web-based activities. Epistemology is of course the philosophy of knowledge. Epistemological beliefs (Schommer 1990) describe an individual's personal perspective or philosophy of knowledge integrity and knowledge acquisition, which (at least according to this particular theory) are relatively independent of each other. There are sophisticated perspectives of knowledge integrity where individuals/students see knowledge as being more valuable and/or worthwhile when it is fluid, highly interrelated, and originating from interaction. Simpler, less advanced perspectives of knowledge integrity can be identified where knowledge is seen as more valuable and/or worthwhile when it is fixed, basically an accumulation of isolated facts, and emanating from an external authority or expert. So, for instance (from an education perspective), some students see knowledge as more valuable when it emerges out of more active learning where they are challenged to develop their own understandings, and other students see learning as more worthwhile when they have a fixed syllabus, a textbook, and a series of fact-based quizzes and tests over the course of the year or semester. The idea that there are within individual differences between philosophy of knowledge integrity and knowledge acquisition is illustrated by instructors who teach courses on experiential learning from a textbook and have multiple choice quizzes to test appropriation of knowledge. Or the more everyday experience of the teacher telling their students they cannot use Internet pages as reliable information sources and then getting into an argument with a colleague and pointing to a Wikipedia page as evidence.

A number of studies have suggested a correlation between epistemological beliefs about potential knowledge sources and completing a task, especially in the preparatory phase of defining a task and laying out a strategy to reach a goal (Muis 2007). Various studies have also suggested a relationship between epistemological beliefs and individual Web-based search (Mason et al. 2011; Tu et al. 2008). Although research in traditional contexts shows strong correlation between sophisticated epistemic beliefs and advanced self-regulated learning, this does not necessarily transfer to the same students implementing successful search strategies in Internet environments (Bråten et al. 2008; Tsai et al. 2011). A particularly interesting study by Chiu et al. (2013) presents three findings that may help in developing a better grasp of learning, and individual attitudes toward learning, through Web-based activities: (1) Individuals with more sophisticated beliefs about justification of information they find on the Web (in other words they see information they find on the Web as being fluid and interrelated) are more likely to use the preparatory stage of self-regulation to set their own strategies and goals for the task at hand. (2) Individuals who question the validity of facts found on the Web are less likely to engage in preparatory strategies for Web-based searches – suggesting they are less willing to treat the Web as a valuable information source – creating a self-fulfilling prophesy in abilities to use the Web for research purposes. (3) Individuals who have more sophisticated perspectives on knowledge in traditional contexts are more doubting of knowledge they find through Web-based search and are less likely to engage in any self-regulated learning strategies while using the Internet.

This is a potentially important topic for understanding the development of Internet literacy and Open Source intelligence skills, and especially why some individuals who are highly successful offline may have difficulties or even rebel against using online tools to find or expand information/knowledge. Individuals who are highly self-regulated in traditional learning contexts may show little interest in planning and/ or organizing their thinking for online searches because they have little or no confidence in the information they might find. The Internet is a good tool for finding quick, superficial information or perhaps even a starting point for an inquiry, but true in-depth research takes place in libraries, or through personal relationships and not on Web sites. To tie this idea to some of the self-regulation studies mentioned earlier, these learners (dubious of acquiring high integrity information through Internet activities) don't use their metacognitive skills to develop questions and strategies for developing well-founded solutions when beginning their Web-based research – not because they don't know how to, or are not capable in some other way, but because they believe the quality of information they will find is not sophisticated enough to deserve invested time and effort.

It might be worthwhile to offer an illustrative example. David Carr (2013), media writer for the *New York Times* (who also has written a book on the Internet that among other things explores the issue of cognitive load in Web-based reading activities), discusses two types of journalists: one type of journalist who sees the Internet as being basically untrustworthy in the development of reliable information (without integrity) and one type of journalist who sees the Internet as a source of reliable information. The more traditional journalists often have very complex beliefs about traditional knowledge development, but they question the validity of information they might find through Web-based search – which impinges on their abilities to conduct a well-planned online inquiry. They take haphazard or dismissive attitudes toward Internet-derived information and are unwilling to engage in the types of metacognitive planning strategies that might help them develop online literacy skills (Leu et al. 2004) or better organization or differentiation strategies (Glassman and Kang 2011). Journalists who are more comfortable with information they find on the Internet might have trouble understanding why this first group is willing to completely jettison their research and knowledge-building skills (which they use to great effect in more traditional contexts) simply because the information is found on the Web.

What do the differences between self-regulated learning in traditional education environments and Web-based contexts mean? There are any number of possible interpretations. It could be that those with more sophisticated perspectives of knowledge and information integrity in traditional contexts (field research, institutionally vetted information sources such as universities, and top-flight newspapers/magazines/journals) question the Internet's efficacy in coherently solving problems.

It could be that those with more sophisticated perspectives are so successful in traditional environments that they never bother to develop higher levels of literacy and/or self-efficacy in using the Internet as a knowledge-building tool because there is (currently) no need. It could be generational where younger learner cohorts with greater Internet experience are more willing to accept information they find through Internet research as reliable and are willing to implement self-regulation skills in using the Web effectively as a knowledge-building tool to find trusted solutions to those problems. Or it could be that traditional conceptions of self-regulated learning simply do not fit the Internet learning environment. What may be most important about findings in this line of research is the potential havoc it can play with the more traditional mapping of self-regulated learning and patterns of research on Web-based teaching and learning processes.

The internet and coregulation

Akyol and Garrison (2011); Garrison and Akyol (2013) suggest metacognitive strategies in Internet activity might be more socially oriented than in traditional, hierarchical, linear teaching/learning processes, proposing a perspective on regulation that focuses more on collaborative learning contexts than individual planning. Two general ideas are found in the early development of their concept of coregulation, based in Garrison and Arbaugh's (2007) Community of Inquiry model (which will be discussed more in depth in Chapters 4 and 5). One is that the collaborative activities of a shared community of inquiry can naturally lead to development of metacognitive skills among its participants. The shared discourse among community members encourages participants to take a step back and reflect on their learning processes. This part of the Community of Inquiry model is almost Piagetian in nature (although Piaget is not mentioned),[2] suggesting that posts and comments of community participants will push other members of the community toward a social version of reflective abstraction

---

[2] Piagetian theory is rarely mentioned in Internet research – at least not nearly in the same way as theorists such as Bandrua, Vygotsky, or Dewey. It is difficult to know if this is because Piaget has fallen so far out of favor or if his ideas are less applicable to education on the Internet.

(e.g., "Why did they say that?" "That's a possibility I didn't think of"). The second aspect of the community of inquiry model related to meta-cognition is development of a coregulation community ethos – which according to Garrison and Akyol (2013) goes beyond simple coconstruction of knowledge in positing specific shared regulatory strategies similar to those of self-regulation but based on communal rather than individual reflection. Students within well-functioning knowledge development communities have responsibilities to ensure that other members have a good understanding of what they are trying to say and how it adds to (or detracts) from the task/conversation at hand. Participants readily take turns as teachers/facilitators in online discussion (taking on the teacher/facilitator role is part of what the community of inquiry model refers to as teacher presence), but to do so they must step back from the discussion and reflect on what they wish to accomplish and how they will accomplish it.

Self-determination theory: autonomy and connectedness

Little research has been done to this point in self-determination theory in Web-based activity, and in particular self-determined learning and the Internet – perhaps partially because of the complexity of the combined subject. But the ideas underpinning self-determination theory in many ways reflect the open-ended, exploratory nature of the Web better than most independent psychological theories. One could even argue that Bush was promoting the idea of self-determined pursuit of new ideas and possibilities as key to creativity and innovation in his article (of course, the article was written long before the theory emerged). Self-determination theory may potentially be one of the richest veins of research into Internet-infused education. The theory is relatively new (although it has a number of theoretical roots in the field of education), developed by Edward Deci and Richard Ryan (2008). It suggests that individuals develop more intrinsic motivations for their activities (including learning) when pursuing goals in situations that promote higher levels of autonomy, connectivity, and competency. The Internet very obviously offers novel opportunities for autonomous and/or highly interconnected learning environments in new and dynamic ways.

However, to this point relatively little research has explored this idea (self-determined learning in Internet-based educational contexts) (Chen and Jang 2010). Complexities are encountered in actually measuring a concept like autonomy in hypertext/Internet environments because of issues such as individual differences (what role does Internet literacy and/or epistemic beliefs about knowledge on the Internet play?) and programming differences (does reliance on intelligent tutors increase or decrease autonomy?).

Interesting preliminary findings related to self-determination theory and Web-based activities have been made. A study of an online teacher certification (Chen and Jang 2010) supports the idea that Internet-infused education that promotes autonomy and competency positively affects students' perceived autonomy, relatedness, and competency. The authors concluded, "In order for online instructors to better understand their students' needs, and adopt appropriated strategies to support their students, we suggest that online instructors create an *open, interactive, and learner centered atmosphere to freely express their feeling, thoughts, and concerns*" (p. 750, emphasis added) – something that is more likely to happen in an advanced augmentation/community technological frame where students are treated as knowledge workers in a collaborative problem-solving community.

Constructing the social online

Other than Bandura, the two pre-Internet education (or education-related) theorists who seem to have had the most impact on Internet-infused education to this point are L. S. Vygotsky (and the sociocultural theorists and activity theorists that are indebted to his work) and John Dewey (in particular his ideas on reflection, process-based learning, and inquiry). One of the reasons these two theorists have had an early impact is that the Internet is an inherently social medium – helping to create new types of human connectivity. Vygotsky and Dewey have socially oriented views of human activity where learning is often dependent on the connections the student/neophyte makes to relevant others. Vygotsky sees well-defined, interconnected community as both the source of crucial information for everyday activities and the chief provocation for learning (i.e., the community invests in teaching neophytes because they want them to serve as productive members of the social group). Sociocultural theories indebted to Vygotsky's world view such as limited peripheral participation (Lave and Wenger 1991) and community of learners (Brown and Campione 1994) are a natural fit for especially the community focus of the augmentation/community frame. Activity theory, which many see as an outgrowth of Vygotsky's work (along with the work of his student and colleague A. N. Leontiev), focuses on the systems of interrelationships and the ways in which they define and redefine tools, ideas, and perspectives.

The Vygotskian or more broadly defined sociocultural framework is used to inform (at least) two general areas of research into Internet-infused education: scaffolding and social collaboration in the development of community. The more tightly focused activity theory explorations address the ways everyday activity integrates the individual, the object, and the community in dialectically based learning practices (sociocultural theory and activity theory are not mutually exclusive, but currently there is also little communication between them in Web-based research). Dewey's ideas on the democratic classroom (1916), reflective learning (1910), and the logic of inquiry (1938) stress a nonhierarchical, often nonlinear approach to group problem solving, offering theoretical heft to some of the practical uses of the Internet for knowledge building suggested by Engelbart and Licklider.

The internet, education, and scaffolding

The concept of scaffolding was first introduced by Wood et al. (1976) and is based in the primacy of expert-novice teaching relationships in development of (socially defined) critical knowledge. Scaffolding is sometimes directly attributed to Vygotsky because of its similarities with his concept of zone of proximal development and the shared overarching concept of teaching leading development (Griffin and Cole 1984) (the degree of similarity is a debatable point); but Vygotsky's work does not actually appear in the initial article introducing the concept of scaffolding. The expert-novice teaching relationship is attributed to an unpublished dissertation by Kaye (1970).[3] One of the attractive qualities of the

---

[3] Roy Pea (2004) who was working in the same lab at Oxford at the time suggests that Vygotsky was one of the authors being read and the seeds of his ideas on zpd were in the volume of

scaffolding concept is that it offers a very visual metaphor for learning, or more particularly moving from lower order (thinking) skills to higher-order skills (which fits particularly well with self-regulated learning skills such as planning). The expert, recognizing what the novice needs to learn to be successful, develops an intellectual scaffolding (such as surrounds a building) so that the novice can safely and correctly build new skill sets. As the novice becomes more competent the expert slowly removes the scaffolds (or allows them to fade) so that the learner becomes independent. The key to successful scaffolding approaches (and where the concept is most closely aligned to Vygotsky's zone of proximal development) is in the personalized interaction between the expert and the novice. It is up to the expert to determine what skills the novice needs to establish independent capabilities, what type of scaffolding will most directly benefit this development, the dynamic relationship that allows the correct scaffolding to be applied at the right moments, and when to allow the scaffolding to be removed.

The expert-novice dynamic suggests that the optimum learning environment for scaffolding is the dyadic or one-to-one relationship. Unfortunately this is difficult if not impossible in large classes (Davis and Miyake 2004). The Internet presents both dangers and possibilities for extending the concept of scaffolding from a one-to-one to a one-to-many model. The dangers are in the open-ended nature of the Internet, putting more pressure on the learner to quickly develop higher-order thinking skills to navigate rich information-learning ecologies. The possibilities are in chunk hypertext environments that might quickly recognize and adjust to the needs of larger populations of neophytes through generalized, preprogrammed dialectical response dynamics (whether dialectical processes can be preprogrammed is an important consideration – one that some early pioneers of the Internet might not be that sympathetic to).

In the most direct forms of chunk hypertext scaffolding environments students must react to a succession of screens posing questions or offering prompts as they are engaged in problem-solving tasks (Bannert 2009). The intelligent tutor in these scenarios is similar to an omniscient

---

Thought and Language currently being read (along with a number of other authors), but the actual concept did not become broadly known until 1978. The historical relationship between scaffolding and zpd seems mostly post hoc.

narrator/expert guiding the student through complex problems, choosing when they are ready to move toward more complex thinking strategies based on their previous responses. The prompts or other enhancements are specifically planned input designed to get students to step back from and reflect on their tasks before continuing with the activity. The scaffolding-based self-regulated learning/metacognitive line of research suggests that through the right types of general manipulations individuals can learn to make these decisions efficiently within the context of the ongoing activity (rather than having students go through the experience and then reflect on it later – what usually happens in nonhypertext environments). Of course, the learning systems themselves are controlled (chunk hypertext–based scaffolding demands some type of omniscient expert control) and often part of closed Web (or software) systems (e.g., Dabbagh and Kitsantas 2005; Raes et al. 2012). At least some findings also suggest that while these technological enhancements can help, for some aspects of learning inclusion of teacher enhancements is often a significant factor in overall learning, including knowledge acquisition, especially for students with limited prior knowledge (Azevedo et al. 2008; Raes et al. 2012). Perhaps a personalized aspect to scaffolding exists that cannot be replaced by a machine.

The research on scaffolding in self-regulation as it currently stands (taking into consideration that Internet research on the whole is in its nascent stages) suggests two complexities that will have to be worked out through exploratory research: the difficulties of applying self-regulated learning to human-Internet transactions, especially for those who have been highly successful in offline educational contexts (both teachers and students), and the limited nature of scaffolding cognitive capabilities (which are inherently individual) within a larger sociocultural and/or collaborative learning environment. Scaffolding is basically interactional, but both human-human and human-Internet relationships are transactional and demand open rather than closed feedback loops – perhaps one of the reasons it might be important to include teacher enhancements in the process.

Vygotsky, sociability, and the internet

Vygotsky's theory has also been used as part of the larger ideas of sociability as a key attribute of successful cooperative/collaborative

Internet activity (Preece and Maloney-Krichner 2003). The development of online community is considered by many to be an important component of student engagement – the ability of students to trust and feel comfortable in the online social spaces provided by the targeted course/instructor. The general idea is that collaboration increases learning effectiveness as students become more adept at supporting each other within a larger community of learning (Sloep 2009). This sociability or social ability can lead to what many consider important features in online learning such as social presence, social navigation, and social connectedness – factors that can lead to increased motivation (Yang et al. 2006). Sociability has also been tied to Lave and Wenger's concept of communities of practice (Preece 2001). Online communities offer the possibility of serving as virtual communities of practice far less limited by boundaries of time and space where students can easily join the learning process, starting out as peripheral learners (e.g., lurkers, participants without trusted user status), seeing how dialogue and knowledge-building practices evolve through asynchronous observation and/or directed trusted users communications to neophytes, and appropriate successful community practices in their own time.

Using existing sociocultural theories as frameworks for sociability is not as well researched as scaffolding but may speak more directly to Vygotsky's larger theoretical trajectory (as will be discussed in Chapter 5, Vygotsky is often mentioned in sociability studies, but his actual ideas are rarely used). Much of Vygotsky's work certainly suggests we learn about the world primarily from other members of our community, and the more engaged we are in shared, goal-driven activities, the more likely we are to understand and appropriate knowledge about those activities into our everyday lives. But Vygotsky's work also poses some challenges to Internet-based education that have yet to be broached, or if they have, it has been only tangentially. At the core of Vygotsky's ideas on social engagement and learning is the extraordinarily important role that culture and history play in the learning process. As some of the theorists focusing on sociability recognize the learning context is essential. It is the local culture that develops this context over time through mediating tools for sharing of knowledge – from member to member, from mentor to neophyte – that are part of both the product and the process of that community.

These mediating tools are easily recognized by all members of the community because of their shared history, so it is natural for new members to recognize and appropriate them. The most pervasive and important tool of course is language, but a number of shared artifacts and cultural practices integrate learning as a social experience into everyday activities. Internet learning communities can be distributed and transient. The members of the learning community have far less shared history and therefore limited access to culturally developed mediating tools that might help along the teaching process. How do you develop socially infused learning environments with these types of transient communities where participants have no prior history together and few, if any, shared activities outside of the focused goals of the online group? Can this be done artificially, or must educators looking to integrate the Internet into their teaching/learning processes find some way to bring local history and culture online and merge it with the more transient activities of Web-derived communities?

The internet and activity theory

Activity theory is a modern interpretation/extrapolation of or addition to Vygotsky's baseline theory (depending on who you read). Activity theory is traced back to Vygotsky's student A. N. Leontiev (1981), but much of the current, Internet research is based in Engeström's (2014) more recent explications. These models take seriously Engeström's (2009) warning that introduction of new technologies is by itself not enough to create innovative learning practices. Engeström, in taking an activity theory approach, argues that we need to move from conceptualizing introduction of new technologies in terms of how they change the learning environment to how they might impact the (educational) activity system as a whole (and move from focusing on specific implementation strategies to development of expansive learning among system participants). The focus should be on the dialectical relationship between the new learning environments created as result of introduction of Internet technology into the classroom and the (often local) social practices of knowledge building (Hakkarainen 2009). A key assumption in an activity-based approach is that in the right circumstances introduction of new technologies will lead to contradictions for participants in the larger activity system pushing their thinking into dialectical tension. The only way to resolve this tension is by expanding the horizons of all participants in the thinking of the education system, setting them on a path to necessary innovation. Engeström (2009) makes the point that many times simple introduction of the possibilities offered by computers (and/or Internet applications) does not in and of itself create the dialectical tension in activity systems necessary for changes in thinking and practice. Teachers are still the same teachers and administrators are still the same administrators and students are still the same students, and introduction of new Internet applications, no matter how well designed, is not going to change that. The roles of the new tools need to be understood and experimented with as part of the larger activity system – a process that must be overtly designed and implemented, or else the social landscape will simply fall back in on itself.

Activity theory has been applied to Internet-infused education by a few researchers to this point. Hakkarainen and Paavola's trialogical approach (2009) is probably the most complex, focused activity theory–influenced program for Internet-infused education. Their development of a trilogical approach combines Scardamalia and Bereiter's theory and practice as integrated into the *Knowledge Forum* with Engeström's ideas on activity theory, suggesting a model for long-term integration of hypertext/Internet tools into ongoing educational activity systems by expanding the ways members of education systems think about the tools as a result of their experiences in using them. The trialogical approach will be discussed at some length in Chapter 4.

A second course of study looking to apply activity theory comes from the (relatively) early work of Hung et al. (2006). Interestingly Hakkarainen and Paavola's work and that of Hung et al. work start with attempts to apply the *Knowledge Forum* in diverse social/cultural settings (Finland for Hakkarainen and Singapore for Hung) and then trying to understand what turned out to be disappointing initial results. Hung and his fellow researchers quickly realized that the collaborative, knowledge-building nature of the *Knowledge Forum* did not fit the activity system of the Singapore school (administration, teachers, students) where they were attempting to implement it. Teachers and students were already well trained and psychically invested in practices that met the needs of their static curriculum. They engaged in these new knowledge-building activities with some interest but without any "buy in." Students entered into the prescribed learning activity because that is it what their teachers told them to do (when the students figured out what they were doing was not what the researchers wanted to hear they changed their answers to please the researchers but did not change their actions). The teachers assigned projects because they were part of the preexisting curriculum.

It doesn't really matter how well designed the *Knowledge Forum* or for that matter any Internet application or system of applications is, or how well developed the theory/philosophy behind it. If it is not integrated into the ongoing system of the school it is going to be subverted to the goals of the existing system, not the other way around. The new hypertext tool could easily wind up working against its original intent. There was really no opportunity for the learning community to develop into a social cultural learning environment with the qualities that might allow it to evolve as part of a collaborative effort where students looked for more advanced understandings (Bereiter 2002) – qualities such as situatedness (rich, goal-oriented contexts that engender self-reflection and discussion) and interdependence (where community participants engage each other based on their own particular knowledge levels and experience) (Hung and Chen 2001).

Hung and his colleagues were forced to reconsider their approach, moving to one that focused more on the students' authentic interests, but then found themselves colliding with another activity system – that promoted national education guidelines (which have become more important, in not only Singapore, but also numerous industrialized countries with high levels of Internet penetration). The researchers needed to pursue their authentic problem sets outside of traditional educational settings, during a three-day holiday camp. The interrelationships of different activity systems and their conflicting goals complicate both planning and implementation of Internet-infused education. But recognition also opens up pathways for what Ritella and Hakkarainen (2012) refer to as "instrumental genesis," the chance for users to develop new understandings of the tool.

Liaw and colleagues (2007) have also attempted to examine Web-based learning through an activity theory lens. They examined the interaction between a multimedia environment, student autonomy, teacher assistance, and Web-based learning as a problem-solving environment. This approach can be roughly translated into an activity system comprised of tools (multimedia instruction) leading to a change in rules systems (greater teacher autonomy) based on reinvention of division of labor (teachers acting as tutors to students in their Web-based learning environments). The researchers found that these interactions worked together (but not separately) to create innovation within the problem-solving community. Liaw and colleagues emphasize the importance of all factors acting in concert in the development of effective Web-based learning, reinforcing the idea that Internet learning tools should be considered as only one aspect of a larger education activity system.

The internet, John Dewey, and inquiry as an online activity

The application of Dewey to Internet education focuses on the unique social aspects of the Web – especially the ways in which it is capable of simultaneously integrating multiple perspective into the learning as an inquiry-based process. Internet-infused education has the potential to reflect and even extend the nonhierarchical, nonlinear problem-solving processes of Dewey's democratic classroom in ways that are often difficult, if not impossible, in place-based classes (Glassman and Kang 2011). These types of democratically based, problem-solving communities, mirroring Dewey's vision of education, sometimes emerge spontaneously online in noneducation activities, especially within Open Source communities.

The Internet provides ongoing, asynchronous communications, allowing potential members of learning communities to engage each other over time and across distances. This provides new possibilities for strategies that lead to more open, honest, and efficient learning situations where individual circumstances and perspectives are continuously available and respected, given a well-developed communication infrastructure (Hung and Chen 2001). The multilateral, multiperspective communications that Dewey promotes as central to human inquiry (1938) are based on the types of collaborative activities he places at the heart of his democratic classroom (1916): Timothy Koschmann (2002) suggests these ideas set the stage for a new paradigm for learning in computer-supported collaborative environments, writing "Dewey, in his description of the processes of inquiry, laid the groundwork for a distinctive vision of learning and human problem solving" (p. 19). Students must move from passive learning of (predefined) knowledge to being active, engaged agents in their own knowing. Dewey suggests this can be accomplished in place-based classrooms over time and with high levels of commitment on the part of all participants, but so many factors are working against nonhierarchical, multilateral problem solving in traditional teaching/learning contexts that attempts at democratic education are often set up for failure. Computer-supported collaborative learning models suggest unique qualities offered by the Internet might help alleviate many of the most difficult issues facing democratic classrooms.

The Community of Inquiry model put forward by (Garrison and Arbaugh 2007) also uses Dewey's work and in particular his ideas on inquiry (active problem solving) as a central, organizing principle for their model – but based more on his earlier work, in particular his outline of *How We Think* (1910). The cognitive presence aspect of the Community of Inquiry is modeled on Dewey's ideas of human learning as a step-by-step reflective process. There is no real dividing line between doing and knowing how to do. Inquiry into the problem is a joint, community endeavor in which participants bring in their prior knowledge and compare and contrast different possibilities as they develop possible solutions. There is a merging of thinking with social relationships – what the Community of Inquiry model refers to as cognitive presence and social presence in an online community. Asynchronous communications offered by Internet-based applications and the chance to continuously fine tune the relationship between social presence of community members and cognitive presence (learning tasks of the members) give new urgency to Dewey's educational philosophy in online education.

As with Vygotsky, Dewey's theory also presents challenging questions for Internet-based education. Dewey is very clear that the everyday lives of students outside of the formal educational context is critical to the learning process (Dewey 1916). Students learn best from problems in which they have a natural interest, and these types of compelling problem sets cannot and should not be separated from the relevant issues of their everyday lives. In fact, a continuum of interest from everyday life to classroom learning is one of the elements for successful or vital educational experience. This does not mean you teach students only what they want to learn (a common mistake with Dewey) but that teachers must be aware of the experiences of their students' lives outside of the classroom and interweave them with new and important ideas and possibilities as part of the educational process. Internet educational contexts, especially those that are more distributed, tend to take students and teacher away from their everyday experiences in creating transient online communities – potentially more alienating than inviting. Online learning needs to find overt strategies for having students reach back into their offline world and/or other compelling online experiences (e.g., gaming) and bring them into the conversation if they are going to meet Dewey's vision. And this reaching outside the community has to be done without the advantage of informal engagement (side conversations, offhand comments) of placed-based educational or other offline contexts.

Chaos/complexity theory

A theory that has become more popular in Internet-based education is chaos/complexity theory. One of the biggest concerns in Internet-based education scenarios is the establishment of dynamic, organic learning communities. How and why do they emerge? Researchers focusing on student engagement suggest that emergence of community is the result of careful planning of teachers and facilitators in preestablishing social and cognitive attributes for a vibrant community – the better planned the community, the more successful the learning experience. But perhaps there is a danger in being too controlling and thereby sacrificing some of the qualities of the Internet that might be most unique and productive in teaching/learning processes – there was no real controlling authority in many of the successful bulletin board/conference system communities or the Open Source communities that followed; rules, situational ethics, and division of labor are developed on the fly. Perhaps the Internet itself, left to its own devices, can best bring together different strands of thinking and/or online activity, creating true, democratic learning environments.

Complexity theory is not an educational theory or even one that is used much (or at least successfully) in analyzing proactive learning behavior. Yet because of its focus on emergent phenomena and non-linear dynamics it can be used as a framework for understanding education on the Internet. Complexity theory was first developed in describing physical and biological systems. The theory suggests that under the right conditions new, more complex, problem-solving systems can emerge out of constituent, connected elements (Mason 2008). These emergent systems develop bottom up – there is no predetermined plan or executive controlling function in their development. The right context includes rich information flows, high levels of connectivity between elements/ agents, and high levels of diversity between agents (Stacey 1996) fitting the transactional nature of the Internet. The idea is that the emergent whole will be greater than the interconnected parts, at least in terms of the relevant problem at hand.

The use of complexity/chaos theory has been used both overtly and as subtext in Internet-infused educational discussions. One of the most interesting examples is the research of Sugata Mitra and work derived from his naturalistic "hole in the wall" experiments (Mitra 2005) – one of the more interesting and controversial examples of the role(s) the Internet can play in reinventing education for diverse populations. Mitra placed Internet portals (embedded touch screens the size of small television sets) into kiosks in play areas in a slum neighborhood in India and just left them there for children to experiment with and explore – what Mitra and his colleagues would come to refer to as minimally invasive education. The children who played in the area had negligible literacy capabilities of any kind, yet researchers found the children in the play area were capable of self-learning computer applications through self-organizing cooperative learning groups. Mitra has worked to re-create this phenomenon of self-organizing learning systems in more traditional, middle-class educational contexts. The primary idea is that the combination of open information systems, possibilities for collaborative interest, and user agency sets up the circumstances for the development of students self-organizing into productive, collaborative problem-solving groups using naturally developing swarm intelligence.

The same principle is used in early conceptions of massive open online courses (Kop et al. 2011). A conceit of first generation massive open online courses – which have come to be referred to as "connectivist" – is that distributed populations will be able to self-organize into learning communities based on much the same principles as suggested by Mitra, but on a much larger scale. There have recently been attempts to tie chaos/complexity theory to the idea of interconnected massive open online courses (Carreño 2014; de Waard et al. 2011). The application of self-organizing dynamic learning systems to education is happening in the shadow of the Internet, but it is nowhere nearly as developed an idea as the other theories mentioned in this chapter and currently shows few signs of becoming central to self-sustaining research programs.

So how valuable are existing theories for understanding the internet?

This chapter started with the question of whether it was productive or even possible to apply educational psychology theories developed prior to (sometimes long before) the Internet. A number of difficult questions emerge, chief among them whether human learning is the same activity in human-Internet transactions as it is in traditional human classroom interactions. The question is much more difficult than for computer/Internet-human interactions because these activities often are designed to reflect traditional human interaction – hierarchical, linear, and focused. The Internet potentially opens the mind to new possibilities – extending rather than reflecting human thinking. One of the questions we need to ask in the twenty-first century is if the new information landscape demands new types of literacies and intelligence – and do existing theories help us in these tasks or bias us against them?

Information processing, sociocognitive, sociocultural, and Deweyan theory have helped at the very least to put Internet-infused education into some type of educational context – providing important starting points for new explorations – the first step in coming explorations of interlocking webs of trails. Later chapters will go deeper into some of the research mentioned in this chapter and the ways it has moved to take on its own Internet character. But each of these starting points creates its own problems and frustrations. Perhaps as Bush suggested in his predictions of an Internet-type system, researchers must be willing to make their own imprints on these ideas and be ready to branch off into unforeseen directions. It is important not to get stuck in protecting particular theoretical trajectories, especially because right now there is relatively little to protect.

References

Akyol, Z., and Garrison, D. R. (2011). Understanding Cognitive Presence in an Online and Blended Community of Inquiry: Assessing Outcomes and Processes for Deep Approaches to Learning. *British Journal of Educational Technology*, 42(2), 233–250.

Azevedo, R. (2005). Using Hypermedia as a Metacognitive Tool for Enhancing Student Learning? The Role of Self-Regulated Learning. *Educational Psychologist*, 40(4), 199–209.

Azevedo, R., and Cromley, J. G. (2004). Does Training on Self-regulated Learning Facilitate Students' Learning with Hypermedia? *Journal of Educational Psychology*, 96(3), 523.

Azevedo, R., Cromley, J. G., Winters, F. I., Moos, D. C., and Greene, J. A. (2005). Adaptive Human Scaffolding Facilitates Adolescents' Self-Regulated Learning with Hypermedia. *Instructional Science*, 33(5–6), 381–412.

Azevedo, R., Moos, D. C., Greene, J. A., Winters, F. I., and Cromley, J. G. (2008). Why Is Externally-Facilitated Regulated Learning More Effective than Self-Regulated Learning with Hypermedia? *Educational Technology Research and Development*, 56(1), 45–72.

Baddeley, A. D., and Hitch, G. (1974). Working Memory. *Psychology of Learning and Motivation*, 8, 47–89.

Bandura, A. (1982). Self-Efficacy Mechanism in Human Agency. *American Psychologist*, 37(2), 122.

(2001). Social Cognitive Theory of Mass Communication. *Media Psychology*, 3(3), 265–299.

Bannert, M. (2009). Promoting Self-Regulated Learning through Prompts. *Zeitschrift für Pädagogische Psychologie*, 23(2), 139–145.

Bereiter, C. (2002). *Education and Mind in the Knowledge Age*. New York: Routledge.

Bråten, I., Strømsø, H. I., and Samuelstuen, M. S. (2008). Are Sophisticated Students Always Better? The Role of Topic-Specific Personal Epistemology in the Understanding of Multiple Expository Texts. *Contemporary Educational Psychology*, 33(4), 814–840.

Brown, A. L., and Campione, J. C. (1994). *Guided Discovery in a Community of Learners*. Cambridge, MA: MIT Press.

Carr, D. (2013). War on Leaks Is Pitting Journalist vs. Journalist. *New York Times*, August 25. www.nytimes.com/2013/08/26/business/media/war-on-leaks-is-pitting-journalist-vs-journalist.html?pagewanted=all&_r=1&.

Carreño, I. D. V. G. (2014). Theory of Connectivity as an Emergent Solution to Innovative Learning Strategies. *American Journal of Educational Research*, 2(2), 107–116.

Chen, K. C., and Jang, S. J. (2010). Motivation in Online Learning: Testing a Model of Self-Determination Theory. *Computers in Human Behavior*, 26(4), 741–752.

Cheng, K. H., and Tsai, C. C. (2011). An Investigation of Taiwan University Students' Perceptions of Online Academic Help Seeking, and Their Web-Based Learning Self-Efficacy. *The Internet and Higher Education*, 14(3), 150–157.

Chiu, Y. L., Liang, J. C., and Tsai, C. C. (2013). Internet-Specific Epistemic Beliefs and Self-Regulated Learning in Online Academic Information Searching. *Metacognition and Learning*, 8(3), 235–260.

Coiro, J. (2011). Predicting Reading Comprehension on the Internet Contributions of Offline Reading Skills, Online Reading Skills, and Prior Knowledge. *Journal of Literacy Research*, 43(4), 352–392.

Compeau, D. R., and Higgins, C. A. (1995). Computer Self-Efficacy: Development of a Measure and Initial Test. *MIS Quarterly*, 19, 189–211.

Dabbagh, N., and Kitsantas, A. (2005). Using Web-Based Pedagogical Tools as Scaffolds for Self-Regulated Learning. *Instructional Science*, 33(5–6), 513–540.

Davis, E. A., and Miyake, N. (2004). Explorations of Scaffolding in Complex Classroom Systems. *Journal of the Learning Sciences*, 13(3), 265–272.

Deci, E. L., and Ryan, R. M. (2010). *Self-Determination.* New York: John Wiley & Sons.

DeStefano, D., and LeFevre, J. A. (2007). Cognitive Load in Hypertext Reading: A Review. *Computers in Human Behavior*, 23(3), 1616–1641.

Dewey, J. (1910). *How We Think.* Lexington, MA: D. C. Heath & Company
  (1916). *Democracy and Education.* New York: Macmillan & Co.
  (1938). *The Theory of Inquiry.* New York: Holt, Rinehart & Winston.

Eastin, M. S., and LaRose, R. (2000). Internet Self-Efficacy and the Psychology of the Digital Divide. *Journal of Computer-Mediated Communication*, 6(1).

Engeström, Y. (2014). *Learning by Expanding.* Cambridge: Cambridge University Press.
  (2009). From Learning Environments and Implementation to Activity Systems and Expansive Learning. *Actio*, 2, 17–33.

Garrison, D. R., and Akyol, Z. (2013). Toward the Development of a Metacognition Construct for Communities of Inquiry. *The Internet and Higher Education*, 17, 84–89.

Garrison, D. R., and Arbaugh, J. B. (2007). Researching the Community of Inquiry Framework: Review, Issues, and Future Directions. *The Internet and Higher Education*, 10(3), 157–172.

Glassman, M., Bartholomew, M., and Hur, E. H. (2013). The Importance of the Second Loop in Educational Technology: An Action Science Study of Introducing Blogging in a Course Curriculum. *Action Research*, 11, 337–353.

Glassman, M., and Kang, M. J. (2011). The Logic of Wikis: The Possibilities of the Web 2.0 Classroom. *International Journal of Computer-Supported Collaborative Learning*, 6(1), 93–112.

Graesser, A. C., McNamara, D. S., and VanLehn, K. (2005). Scaffolding Deep Comprehension Strategies through Point&Query, AutoTutor, and iSTART. *Educational Psychologist*, 40(4), 225–234.

Griffin, P., and Cole, M. (1984). Current Activity for the Future: The Zo-ped. *New Directions for Child and Adolescent Development*, 1984(23), 45–64.

Hakkarainen, K. (2009). A Knowledge-Practice Perspective on Technology-Mediated Learning. *International Journal of Computer-Supported Collaborative Learning*, 4(2), 213–231.

Hakkarainen, K., and Paavola, S. (2009). Toward a Trialogical Approach to Learning. In B. Schwcarz, T. Dryefus, and R. Hershkowitz (eds.). *Transformation of Knowledge through Classroom Interaction* London: Routledge. 65–80.

Hung, D. W., and Chen, D. T. (2001). Situated Cognition, Vygotskian Thought and Learning from the Communities of Practice Perspective: Implications for the Design of Web-Based E-Learning. *Educational Media International*, 38(1), 3–12.

Hung, D., Tan, S. C., and Koh, T. S. (2006). From Traditional to Constructivist
     Epistemologies: A Proposed Theoretical Framework Based on Activity Theory
     for Learning Communities. *Journal of Interactive Learning Research*, 17(1),
     37–55.
Joo, Y. J., Bong, M., and Choi, H. J. (2000). Self-Efficacy for Self-Regulated Learning,
     Academic Self-Efficacy, and Internet Self-Efficacy in Web-Based Instruction.
     Educational Technology Research and Development, 48(2), 5–17.
Kaye, K. (1970). *Mother-Child Instructional Interaction*. Unpublished doctoral thesis,
     Department of Psychology, Harvard University.
Kim, Y., and Glassman, M. (2013). Beyond Search and Communication: Development
     and Validation of the Internet Self-efficacy Scale (ISS). *Computers in Human
     Behavior*, 29(4), 1421–1429.
Kim, Y., Glassman, M., Bartholomew, M., and Hur, E. H. (2013). Creating an Educational
     Context for Open Source Intelligence: The Development of Internet Self-Efficacy
     through a Blogcentric Course. *Computers & Education*, 69, 332–342.
Kop, R., Fournier, H., and Mak, J. S. F. (2011). A Pedagogy of Abundance or a
     Pedagogy to Support Human Beings? Participant Support on Massive Open
     Online Courses. *International Review of Research in Open and Distance
     Learning*, 12(7), 74–93.
Koschmann, T. (2002, January). Dewey's Contribution to the Foundations of CSCL
     Research. In *Proceedings of the Conference on Computer Support for
     Collaborative Learning: Foundations for a CSCL Community* (pp. 17–22).
     International Society of the Learning Sciences.
Lave, J., and Wenger, E. (1991). *Situated Learning: Legitimate Peripheral
     Participation*. Cambridge: Cambridge University Press.
Leontiev, A. N. (1981). *Problems of the Development of the Mind*. Moscow: Progress
     Publishers.
Leu, D. J., Kinzer, C. K., Coiro, J. L., and Cammack, D. W. (2004). Toward a Theory of
     New Literacies Emerging from the Internet and Other Information and
     Communication Technologies. *Theoretical Models and Processes of Reading*,
     5(1), 1570–1613.
Liaw, S. S., Huang, H. M., and Chen, G. D. (2007). An Activity-Theoretical Approach
     to Investigate Learners' Factors toward E-Learning Systems. *Computers in
     Human Behavior*, 23(4), 1906–1920.
Maguire, E. A., Gadian, D. G., Johnsrude, I. S., Good, C. D., Ashburner, J.,
     Frackowiak, R. S., and Frith, C. D. (2000). Navigation-Related Structural Change
     in the Hippocampi of Taxi Drivers. *Proceedings of the National Academy of
     Sciences*, 97(8), 4398–4403
Mason, L., Ariasi, N., and Boldrin, A. (2011). Epistemic Beliefs in Action:
     Spontaneous Reflections about Knowledge and Knowing during Online
     Information Searching and Their Influence on Learning. *Learning and
     Instruction*, 21(1), 137–151.
Mason, M. (2008). Complexity Theory and the Philosophy of Education. *Educational
     Philosophy and Theory*, 40(1), 4–18.

Mathan, S. A., and Koedinger, K. R. (2005). Fostering the Intelligent Novice: Learning from Errors with Metacognitive Tutoring. *Educational Psychologist*, 40(4), 257–265.

Miller, G. A. (1956). The Magical Number Seven, Plus or Minus Two: Some Limits on Our Capacity for Processing Information. *Psychological Review*, 63(2), 81–97.

Mitra, S. (2005). Self Organising Systems for Mass Computer Literacy: Findings from the "Hole in the Wall" Experiments. *International Journal of Development Issues*, 4(1), 71–81.

Moos, D. C., and Azevedo, R. (2009). Learning with Computer-Based Learning Environments: A Literature Review of Computer Self-Efficacy. *Review of Educational Research*, 79(2), 576–600.

Muis, K. R. (2007). The Role of Epistemic Beliefs in Self-Regulated Learning. *Educational Psychologist*, 42(3), 173–190.

Murphy, C. A., Coover, D., and Owen, S. V. (1989). Development and Validation of the Computer Self-efficacy Scale. *Educational and Psychological Measurement*, 49(4), 893–899.

Narciss, S., Proske, A., and Koerndle, H. (2007). Promoting Self-Regulated Learning in Web-Based Learning Environments. *Computers in Human Behavior*, 23(3), 1126–1144.

Nelson, T. H., (1974). *Dream Machine.* Chicago: Hugo's Book Service

Pea, R. D. (2004). The Social and Technological Dimensions of Scaffolding and Related Theoretical Concepts for Learning, Education, and Human Activity. *Journal of the Learning Sciences*, 13(3), 423–451.

Pintrich, P. R. (1999). The Role of Motivation in Promoting and Sustaining Self-Regulated Learning. *International Journal of Educational Research*, 31(6), 459–470.

Preece, J. (2001). Sociability and Usability in Online Communities: Determining and Measuring Success. *Behaviour & Information Technology*, 20(5), 347–356.

Preece, J., and Maloney-Krichmar, D. (2003). Online Communities: Focusing on Sociability and Usability. In J. Jacko and A. Sears (eds.) *Handbook of Human-Computer Interaction.* Mahwah, N.J.: Lawrence Erlbaum and Associates, 596–620.

Quintana, C., Zhang, M., and Krajcik, J. (2005). A Framework for Supporting Metacognitive Aspects of Online Inquiry through Software-Based Scaffolding. *Educational Psychologist*, 40(4), 235–244.

Raes, A., Schellens, T., De Wever, B., and Vanderhoven, E. (2012). Scaffolding Information Problem Solving in Web-Based Collaborative Inquiry Learning. *Computers & Education*, 59(1), 82–94.

Ritella, G., and Hakkarainen, K. (2012). Instrumental Genesis in Technology-Mediated Learning: From Double Stimulation to Expansive Knowledge Practices. *International Journal of Computer-Supported Collaborative Learning*, 7(2), 239–258.

Schommer, M. (1990). Effects of Beliefs about the Nature of Knowledge on Comprehension. *Journal of Educational Psychology*, 82(3), 498–504.

Sloep, P. B. (2009). Fostering Sociability in Learning Networks through Ad-Hoc Transient Communities. In *Computer-Mediated Social Networking* (pp. 62–75). Berlin: Springer.

Stacey, R. D. (1996). *Complexity and Creativity in Organizations*. San Francisco: Berrett-Koehler.

Sweller, J. (1988). Cognitive Load during Problem Solving: Effects on Learning. *Cognitive Science*, 12(2), 257–285.

Torkzadeh, G., and Van Dyke, T. P. (2001). Development and Validation of an Internet Self-Efficacy Scale. *Behaviour & Information Technology*, 20(4), 275–280.

Tsai, M. J., and Tsai, C. C. (2003). Information Searching Strategies in Web-Based Science Learning: The Role of Internet Self-Efficacy. *Innovations in Education and Teaching International*, 40(1), 43–50.

Tu, Y. W., Shih, M., and Tsai, C. C. (2008). Eighth Graders' Web Searching Strategies and Outcomes: The Role of Task Types, Web Experiences and Epistemological Beliefs. *Computers & Education*, 51(3), 1142–1153.

de Waard, I., Abajian, S., Gallagher, M. S., Hogue, R., Keskin, N., Koutropoulos, A., and Rodriguez, O. C. (2011). Using mLearning and MOOCs to Understand Chaos, Emergence, and Complexity in Education. *International Review of Research in Open and Distance Learning*, 12(7), 94–115.

Winne, P. H. (1996). A Metacognitive View of Individual Differences in Self-Regulated Learning. *Learning and Individual Differences*, 8(4), 327–353.

Wood, D., Bruner, J. S., and Ross, G. (1976). The Role of Tutoring in Problem Solving*. *Journal of Child Psychology and Psychiatry*, 17(2), 89–100.

Yang, C. C., Tsai, I., Kim, B., Cho, M. H., and Laffey, J. M. (2006). Exploring the Relationships between Students' Academic Motivation and Social Ability in Online Learning Environments. *The Internet and Higher Education*, 9(4), 277–286.

Zimmerman, B. J. (1990). Self-Regulated Learning and Academic Achievement: An Overview. *Educational Psychologist*, 25(1), 3–17.

4 | Developing agency on the internet

The successful bulletin board/computer conferencing systems virtual communities, in particular the Whole Earth 'Lectronic Link (WELL) and the later evolving Open Source communities suggest two critical aspects of well-functioning, sustainable discussion forums: agency (based on interests) and a sense of social connectedness. This is no surprise for educators: As will be discussed in the next chapter, theorists such as Dewey and Vygotsky suggest that the critical components of well-functioning, sustainable social communities in general include shared goals and a willingness to recognize other members of the group as participants in a common project. Those looking to create dynamic, goal-oriented education-based online communities are often in a position of trying to create workable combinations of the two. Some researchers focus more on agency, using the interest and motivation fostered through Internet connectivity to try to create and establish social bonds that engender trusting and supportive relationships between members. Other researchers focus more on creating environments where students cultivate a strong sense of social engagement thinking, believing that an increase in quantity or quality of interactions will lead to the development of shared community purpose. Many times we do not really find a bright line between the two (such as in the Community of Inquiry model). This chapter will examine models that are more agency oriented, and the next chapter will focus on social engagement.

Developing user agency

The success of Internet-infused education is based to a great extent on users' abilities and willingness to be agents in their own knowledge-building activities – from the most basic acts of logging on and typing key words into a search engine to the much more complex actions of joining and participating in online communities. This can be different from some traditional educational models, especially direct instruction approaches where students are treated more as passive consumers of information. Creating a sense of agency, including a willingness and the unique literary skills of the Internet to pursue new ideas through active inquiry, motivation to engage in complex online activities, and self-efficacy in Internet-based activities are important for online education in an augmentation/community technological frame. Gilly Salmon (2004) suggests a five-step process in the development of (individual) agency in an online educational ecology – a proactive process driven by well-trained e-moderators using what she refers to as e-tivities (2013) to help guide (or push) users through the five increasingly complex stages. Stage 1 is access and motivation to log in to the community; Stage 2 is the development of a personal online identity, including making connections to other users; Stage 3 is the introduction of learning processes, including engaging in tasks that facilitate online support systems; Stage 4 is the willingness to engage in conferencing, to treat information as dynamic, to form a community in the service of problem solving; and Stage 5 is the ability to take new-found knowledge and capabilities back out into the larger information universe. Arguments can be made about the linearity of these stages or the value in having a strong e-moderator as a guide, but it is a good outline of the types of agency important to successful online educational experiences.

A difference can be seen between online education in a communicative/service technological frame and in an augmentation/community technological frame when considering the role of user agency. In communicative/service e-learning scenarios users often need only the earliest stage of agency, the willingness to log on to the Internet and request an already known web page. The motivation is already assumed and often based on extrinsic rewards (e.g., to get credit for completing an online course), and the role of a user support system is often negligible. The asynchronous nature of the communications can allow the users to pick and choose times when they log on to get information or respond to requests. And yet in many circumstances it is difficult to get distributed user populations to engage in even these early-stage activities – apart from whether communication frameworks create optimum educational environments. Various models have attempted to increase basic user agency in communication/service initiatives, including attempting to merge communication with collaboration, which will be discussed in the second half of the book.

In the augmentation/community framework user agency plays a much more prominent and complex role – stretching – or attempting to stretch – online human activity in new directions. Augmentation is basically an ongoing process of reaching out and engaging with the thinking of other users. Individuals need to act as agents in finding information and ideas that extend their current understandings in unforeseen directions – perhaps by looking for individuals, groups, or communities that are exploring similar issues and/or ideas. Productively engaging these individuals/communities means being willing and able to judge the validity, reliability, and efficacy of their knowledge and relationship systems. And if they judge the community as not meeting their needs or taking their thinking in unproductive directions – engaged in a web of trails that they think will fade – they need to be able to take more active roles in guiding the trajectory of collaborative thinking or be willing to leave these communities (no matter what the initial investment) and find others. Early attempts have been made to develop concepts and learning ecologies that might help us understand and extend a burgeoning sense of agency as part of the educative process.

A definition of collaboration

One of the themes of this chapter is the role of collaboration in learning, and by extension the difference between simple cooperation and the complexities of collaborative, goal-directed activity. This difference is one of the more important but less discussed issues in online education. We can identify three general levels of successful online community-based activity: supportive, cooperative, and collaborative. In supportive communities individual participants pursue their own goals for their own reasons but are willing to answer questions and/or share information with other community members. In cooperative communities individuals are willing to engage with other participants on a shared problem or project, follow rule systems, bring whatever they are able to the shared activity, but make little investment in the sustainability of a cohesive problem-solving community: When participants have achieved whatever they as individuals joined the community to achieve, they move on. For example, an individual wants to learn a particular political polling technique. The individual finds an online community that is engaged with projects using this technique. The individual joins the community, cooperates with other members of the community involved in projects who are willing to share their thinking (also to gain knowledge and/or new ways of knowing), and when the participant has learned what he or she was looking to learn, moves on to another community and/or project.

Collaboration is the most complex community-based activity. The work of John Dewey has had an important impact on at least two of the major models focusing on agency through collaboration discussed in this chapter: Computer Supported Learning Environment (CSLE) and Community of Inquiry (CoI). Interestingly, neither discusses Dewey's definition of collaboration through communication, which is in many ways directly applicable to the type of collective agency intelligence researchers working within these models are attempting to develop: Timothy Koschmann (2002) suggests that the Computer Supported Collaborative Learning initiative use Dewey's *Logic: The Theory of Inquiry* (1938), whereas the Community of Inquiry model focuses more on the problem solving that Dewey outlines in his book *How We Think* (1910/1997). Even though the concept of collaboration is often used when discussing Internet-infused education as both a process and a goal, it is rarely defined to any great extent – sometimes being confused with cooperation.

Dewey devotes an entire chapter to the concept of collaboration as a result of human communication capabilities in his book *Experience and Nature* (1925/1958). Even though it was written years before the Memex machine was even a gleam in Vannevar Bush's eye, it may offer a prescient description of collaboration on the Internet. In starting with communication Dewey points out that all animals are capable of responding to signals. Humans have special abilities to use signals to communicate their intention to use a shared tool/instrument to achieve a future consequence for their action (this is a simplification). Collaboration is the ability of two (or more) individuals to come to an understanding about the subjective meaning of a separate (third) object so that they can use that object as a stable instrument to achieve a consequence that they both want (and both know they want). Dewey uses the example of person A and person B walking together. Person A points at a flower. Person B recognizes the meaning of the communication and its intended consequence. Person B picks up the flower (perhaps bargaining for it with a merchant) and gives it to person A, who then carries it for the rest of the journey. Person A and B are involved in a collaborative effort. Consider an alternative (noncollaborative) scenario. Person A points to the flower. Person B looks and comments that, yes, it is a pretty flower and keeps walking (cooperation). Later person A screams at person B, "You never buy me flowers." Or person A points to the flower and person B responds, "I think that is the type of flower that grows at higher altitudes." (individual/supportive). Person A finds somebody else to walk with. The building of mutual understandings of objects through social relationships that will aid in successful collective action is the key to collaborative activity and satisfying experience.

The knowledge forum

Perhaps the most well developed and complex of the learning ecologies looking to establish user agency leading to collaboration as an integral part of the educational process is Scardamalia and Bereiter's Computer Supported Intentional Learning Environments (Scardamalia and Bereiter 1994) and subsequent *Knowledge Forum* (Scardamalia and Bereiter 2006). The development of Computer Supported Intentional Learning Environments attempts to explore the possibilities in using a combination of discrete and collateral hypertext where students can engage nonsequential writing communications to develop shared understanding of educational objects and a community database, an approach with ties to Nelson's vision of hypertext in educational settings but more focused and more concrete. The early generations of the Intentional Learning environment used intraconnected computer (conference) ecologies; later generations of the *Knowledge Forum* looked to integrate some major Internet applications such as the web, browsers, and search engine pages.

Scardamalia and Berieter originally developed the concept/context of Computer Supported Intentional Learning Environments in the time frame between the development of Ethernet technology at the Palo Alto Research Center and the popularization of the Web. The collaborative teaching/learning initiative merges three lines of research:

1. Intentional learning, where the student acts as an agent in attempting to attain some type of cognitive object (agency)
2. Expertise, where there is a reinvestment of cognitive resources into an ongoing issue/problem leading to a spiral of progressive understanding/problem solving (augmentation); and

3. Restructuring of classrooms and schools as knowledge-building communities – moving the focus from transmission of static individually
   oriented first-order knowledge (similar to Catell's crystallized intelligence) to more dynamic, community-oriented second-order knowledge, based primarily on making and sharing contributions to
   collective knowledge inquiries – basically the use of hypertext to
   teach and extend knowledge (collaborative communities).

All three have parallels to Engelbart's reasoning behind the oNLineSystem. (Scardmalia and Bereiter do not reference Engelbart. The assumption is they came to the same conclusions using the same interventionist
technologies in different contexts.)

Scardamalia and Bereiter use the term *knowledge building* to describe the
process of second-order knowledge learning (again similar to Engelbart's
identifier *knowledge workers,* which he used to describe members of his
oNLineSystem community). The original Computer Supported Intentional
Learning Environment was an interconnected note-writing environment –
where students used computers to write discussion notes to each other based
on active problem solving and then leave them for other students to read
and comment on – re-creating the oNLineSystem for a K-12 population.
There are also multiple entry points into the online conversation so students
of different ages and ability levels can become productive participants in
the hypertext-based processes. The asynchronous nature of communication
allows for open peer commentary and removes difficulties in turn taking
(shared discourse does not have to be dominated by the most aggressive
and/or garrulous students). The students also write self-diagnostic state-
ments questioning their own relational understanding of the issue and its
trajectory at the moment using an "I Need to Understand" (INTU) note. The
INTU note is an interesting addition to an (educationally salient) concept of
hypertext suggesting the possibility of a preparatory phase where students
recognize inherent limitations to information they already know. The
teacher and members of the knowledge-building community are aware
not only of the shared problem, including a collective understanding of
where they are in the problem-solving process at the moment and how they
got there (all notes are archived), but also of where their individual understanding is in relation to other members of the community.

The most important material component of Computer Supported Intentional Learning environments is the intranetworking of the shared learning

(e.g., the specific class). This reflects the workings of the original, interconnected collaborative communities at ARC; the critical breakthrough was not the interconnections per se, but the oNLineSystem and hypertext that interconnected computer systems enable. Bill English, who headed the group developing Ethernet technology, was not only an important researcher in the early days of ARPANET but was Engelbart's primary collaborator at ARC. It was English who initially questioned the efficacy of time-sharing models (a primary impetus for early internetworking initiatives) for successful collaborative online activities. He believed the emphasis needed to be on the community of problem solvers and their abilities to easily develop relationships leading to shared understanding – to collaborate as a cohesive unit (Bardini and Friedewald 2003).

The *Knowledge Forum* is a Web-based learning environment developed out of some of the early successes of the Computer Supported Intentional Learning Environment emphasizing student agency and connectivity in second-order knowledge learning. The *Knowledge Forum* combines developing collaborative activities of local classroom communities with Internet-based capabilities for interconnecting with a larger information universe. One of the most interesting characteristics of the *Knowledge Forum* is what might be referred to as layered knowledge-building communities – which in a sense splits the difference between an oNLineSystem and Internet capabilities made possible through the web. Flexible, locally evolved *Knowledge Forum* databases are (or should be) capable of interconnecting with other databases to create larger, more encompassing Knowledge Society Networks (Hong et al. 2010). A local community can enter into relationships with other linked communities anywhere in the world to explore common problems from sometimes very different perspectives. This potentially takes the idea of collaborative/hypertext intelligence to another level, where communities not only work together to solve problems, but community developed trajectories are augmented by the collaborative work of other communities. There is not only shared understanding of objects between members of a collaborative community, but shared understanding between different collaborative communities. The opportunities for interconnections can also motivate intraconnected collaborative communities to develop more advanced resource pools – both to establish stronger connections with other knowledge-building communities and to increase standing and trust within the larger information network.

Computer-supported collaborative learning

The *Knowledge Forum* and Computer Supported Intentional Learning Environments can be seen as falling under the larger theoretical umbrella of Computer-Supported Collaborative Learning (CSCL). Stahl and his colleagues (2006) trace CSCL back to three long-term projects in education: the ENFI program at Galludet University, which allowed deaf students to use interconnected computers so that they could develop "voice" in the context of audience presentation; the Laboratory of Human Cognition's Fifth Dimension project, which attempted to coordinate participation among participants at different ability levels in an after-school reading program; and Scardamalia and Bereiter's Computer Supported Intentional Learning Environments. The authors distinguish between e-Learning approaches and Computer Supported Collaborative Learning approaches, although not on the basis of difference between the communication/service technological frame and an augmentation/community frame. They also distinguish between cooperation and collaboration (a common theme in the literature), although their definition of collaboration is more limited than the Dewey definition provided earlier. The authors focus on collaboration as a synchronous process of negotiating and sharing meanings – but do not extend this to the reasons why groups of individual would do this, the ability to engage in coordinated actions of future consequence (this, however, may be implicit in their definition).

Stahl (2006) in his own research focuses on a sociocultural approach that focuses on shared meaning making – suggesting that this type of activity becomes more accessible to students (and teachers) and transparent when using online tools that help in the creation of small, intensely active learning communities. This intense interaction between local agents can lead to emergent group understandings that surpass any individual knowledge in efficiency and efficacy in (math-related) problem solving. Stahl suggests a Knowledge Building Environment where software interventions enable members of a community to come together, compare perspectives in asynchronous discussions forums, negotiate different positions, and emerge with a group perspective with more complex and/or more nuanced understanding. These new meanings become conceptual artifacts that can be used for various purposes, but there does not seem to be any expectation that the group will become an ongoing, problem-solving community.

Stahl's Knowledge Building Environment seems to use the same type of local, intranetworking methodology as the *Knowledge Forum* but is more focused on the processes of swarm intelligence (with ties to chaos theory) for meaning making.

Community of inquiry

The Community of Inquiry model (Garrison and Arbaugh 2007) is probably closer in nature to virtual communities such as the WELL than to the augmentation-based initiatives of Engelbart and English. The model looks to establish the same type of interactive conferences, but in a more directed and defined manner that meet predetermined educational expectations. Community of Inquiry involves what Garrison, Arbaugh, and their colleagues see as three interconnected elements of online learning: social presence, cognitive presence, and teaching presence, or, more colloquially, students' abilities to project their selves online, the establishment of a dynamic problem-solving community, and a strong, dedicated moderator. The starting point of the model – at least from an evolution of research perspective – is social presence, which has been a major topic in computer-based education for a few decades. The most important part of social presence is student engagement online and the willingness of peers to reach out to each other and form a proactive, supportive community. Social presence will be a major topic of the next chapter. This chapter will focus primarily on cognitive presence and teaching presence.

Cognitive presence

Garrison (2003) sees the central component of cognitive presence as "rooted" in Dewey's ideas on Pragmatic learning, in particular the ways in which he outlines human thinking processes in his book *How We Think* (1910/1997). This book comes relatively early in Dewey's body of work when he was still focused directly on education and students' agency in the classroom – how and why we should educate them in the service of active inquiry – focusing in particular on productive reflection based on empirical evidence. Participants exhibiting cognitive presence engage in three levels of inquiry – recognition of the problem, exploration of the problem in the context of developing a solution, and integration and application of developed information (Dewey lays out a similar pattern for problem solving in his book on inquiry [1938] but for a collaborative community). Garrison and his colleagues (2001) argue that in traditional education students rarely make it past the points of problem recognition and early exploration; well-functioning problem-solving groups do not easily coalesce and move into the integration/ resolution stages. Maintaining online cognitive presence of learners then demands well-designed learning activities that can move the students through the entire cognitive process (it can be argued the idea of designed learning activities moves away from Dewey's [1916] larger education project, which suggests students often stop the exploration process where solutions to problems are preordained or the students aren't particularly interested in the problem).

Social interactions on their own are not enough to ensure cohesive community problem solving leading to effective online learning – there needs to be (certain) content and opportunities for students to be metacognitively aware of where they are in and proceeding through the problem-solving process (recognition, exploration, or integration/solution). Content and metacognitive awareness should be orchestrated by the teachers through learning activities design. The question of how much guidance a teacher or some authority figure gives to students in the learning process has become a big issue in not only online education but education in general (Kirschner et al. 2006) (although the self-directed nature of Internet activity has brought the issue more to the forefront). How important is learner agency and who or what controls that agency? Community of Inquiry falls on the side of limited agency that is controlled by teaching presence – where the moderator of the conference takes a strong hand in the types and trajectory of learning activities.

Teaching presence (with the definition of teacher fluid within the Community of Inquiry model) involves three responsibilities: (1) Instructional design and organization – the teacher should be able to facilitate discourse among students in ways that develop problem-solving communities as well as individual reflection (actually integrating the two) so that participants are "sharing meaning, identifying areas of agreement and disagreement and seeking to reach consensus" (Garrison et al. 1999, p. 101). (2) Direct instruction when needed – the teacher is more than a facilitator but acts as a local knowledge check for community discourse, helping to determine accuracy and injecting new sources of information when necessary. The teacher is also tasked with recognizing knowledge/ understanding levels and developing scaffolding initiatives to help learners move forward. (3) Development of a clear and consistent course structure that students can use to maintain a sense of stability in their inquiry-based activities – these might include creating online Power-Point presentations or developing online video lectures (e.g., lecture capture). The Community of Inquiry model sees strong teaching presence as critical to maintaining a cohesive, active problem-solving commu-nity – without teaching presence online, discourse might easily devolve into a series of individual monologues with little integration or chance for resolution.

Community of Inquiry is at its strongest when social presence, cogni-tive presence, and teaching presence are integrated into a single course trajectory. All three should support and complement each other. A poorly conceived course can result in students talking past each other. A well-conceived online course can create opportunities for learning through problem solving that are very often not available in traditional class-room settings.

Learning presence

Peter Shea (Shea and Bidjerano 2009) attempts to introduce a fourth component into the Community of Inquiry model: learning presence. Learning presence focuses more directly on the role of socially determined perceptions of individual learners in online education ecologies, in particu-lar the (individual) sociocognitive qualities of self-efficacy and self-regulation. Shea hypothesizes that a student's perceptions of success (self-efficacy) in online learning (serving as a predictor of self-regulation) could have a positive impact on their cognitive presence in online courses. In other words students who have positive perceptions of their abilities to accomplish educational goals in an Internet-based learning environment will be more likely to not only adopt but continue to engage in Community of Inquiry cognitive processes, pursuing solutions to problems even when encountering difficulties/obstacles. Shea also suggests important relation-ships between learning presence and teaching presence. Teaching presence – especially the way the teacher designs the course – needs to be coordinated with the learner's level of self-efficacy in being a vibrant, effective member of the online learning community. A teacher working with students with low levels of self-efficacy may need to keep the design of the course very basic, with transparent facilitation of discourse and easily solvable problems, while students with high levels of self-efficacy can be led into more complex types of inquiry.

The original developers of the Community of Inquiry model have expressed some concern with the introduction of learner presence as an additional central component to the model (Akyol and Garrison 2011). They don't see any theoretical rationale for bringing sociocognitive concepts such as self-efficacy into the equation. More important, at least from their point of view, they see little value in positing a static differentiation between teacher and student. One of the goals of Community of Inquiry is to reach a point of co-regulation where all the members of the learning community are responsible for gauging and dealing with differences in understanding and willingness/capabilities to participate in the shared problem-solving process: "The basic premise of a CoI is that learner agency is shared" (Azykol and Garrison 2011, p. 189). Roles and responsibilities in teaching and learning are dynamic and nonhierarchically shared among all participants. There is no reason to consider a separate learning presence, and this points to what might be considered a theoretical inconsistency in the Community of Inquiry model. The proximal goal of Community of Inquiry initiatives is creating environments conducive to online learning – but to accomplish this the learning must be relatively directed. The distal goal though is co-regulation, where participants move easily in and out of teaching and learning roles. This type of co-regulation demands high levels of autonomy among participants, which can be more difficult to achieve in directed learning environments. The addition of learning presence does seem to take the Community of Inquiry away from its distal goal of co-regulation, but is this a better fit for the theory as a whole? Building self-efficacy and online self-regulation fits well with development of a consistent course structure that helps maintain a sense of stability within the learning community.

What role the learners?

One thing that Community of Inquiry (at least without the learning presence component) and many models of Computer Supported

Collaborative Learning don't deal with (at least overtly) are the differences among learners. The development of environments that enhance collaborative learning are enticing, and Internet-infused education offers new possibilities for turning students into active agents in their own learning; but how much burden can (or should) educators put on Internet-based tools, treating student populations as if they are monolithic in their reactions to course design. Two areas that put more emphasis on the role of learners are the development of Constructivist Internet-based Learning Environments and the exploration of differences between students who function better in more autonomous learning environments and those who are more comfortable in controlled learning environments.

Developing a constructivist internet-based learning environment

Chuang and Tsai (2005) use the student as entering a new (online) educational environment, rather than the technology or curriculum implementation, as a starting point in the development of Constructivist Based Learning Environments, focusing on the qualities students might prefer in their Internet-infused learning environments. The underlying assumption is that students are more likely to take an active role in their own learning and be successful in environments where they feel more comfortable (this is certainly an underpinning of much constructivist-inspired education).

In the initial article exploring this idea the researchers used scales to measure (Taiwanese) high school students' perceptions of what they (the students themselves) consider environments conducive to Internet-based learning. These scales included items measuring the extent to which students perceive they have the ability to explain and modify their ideas to other students (student negotiation scale), the extent to which students perceive opportunities to produce self-reflective thinking (reflective thinking scale), and the extent to which students perceive the Internet learning environment as "authentic" and representative of real-life situations (relevance scale). Perhaps surprisingly it was the relevance scale that had the highest mean scores of any preference, while student negotiation had the lowest mean scores. In discussions researchers had with students as an addendum to their survey results comments supported the findings that relevance was the most important issue for their participation. The phrase "perhaps surprisingly" is used because many early attempts to design and/or develop curricula for Internet-infused education have focused on the critical roles of negotiation (e.g., development of relational understanding) and reflection (e.g., cognitive presence).

In a follow-up study with adults Chu and Tsai (2009) again found that perceptions of relevance to their (everyday) own lives – along with opportunities for reflective thinking – were perceived as the most important components of an Internet learning environment. The findings suggest that agency in Internet learning environments is, or at least could be, driven by the relationship between course content and the everyday lives of the targeted learners. The idea of relevance is especially important because so much energy has been devoted to issues of peer-to-peer communication and negotiation. As will be seen, for instance, in the chapter on massive open online courses, most of the energy has been devoted to developing forums that (attempt to) foster student negotiation, but participants who finish these courses may actually do so more because they find relevance in the content of the course to their everyday lives.

One important caveat must be made to the work on constructivist-based Internet learning environments: To this point research has been conducted only in Taiwan. It is difficult to know how much culturally/ socially based preferences might play into the larger equation of developing successful learning environments (it could be, for instance, that Taiwanese students rarely have chances to engage in negotiated learning and do not initially view it as a highly valuable part of the learning experience). Still the work to this point has important implications for how and why students buy into online learning initiatives, suggesting that Internet learning environments need to be authentic and meaningful for participants to have a sense of agency – an issue that is complex but worth exploring further. Course design/instruction needs to be dynamic and find multiple ways to deal with relevance of content across even highly distributed populations.

Autonomous and controlled learning environments

Rienties and colleagues (2012) also focus on the role students play in the development of their own agency in Internet-infused learning. The work is again preliminary but has important implications for course design and/or teacher/student relationships from the perspective of the student as a unique actor. The researchers divide potential student participants in Internet-infused learning into two categories – autonomous learners and control-oriented learners. They then studied two Internet-based learning environments: a more open, problem-based learning environment, and a more structured learning, scaffolding-dependent learning environment (referred to as Optima). In the problem-based learning environment autonomous oriented students contributed a (much) higher level discourse (both quality and quantity) than the more controlled oriented students. The type of discourse that a number of Internet-infused learning models suggest leads to community building Scardamalia and Bereiter 2006, emergent intelligence Stahl 2006, and/or co-regulation, Akyol and Garrison 2011. The Optima (-controlled) design led to more balanced discourse between student populations, but this was in large part because the autonomous students were contributing less high-level discourse. This preliminary study highlights one of the most perplexing issues in developing the types of online agency within an Internet-infused environment that might lead to collaborative learning – and very likely a coming education battlefield (if we are not there already). What should be the emphasis in online education, and how should it impact course design and teacher-driven activities? Should educators worry more about establishing higher levels of discourse wherever they might find it – believing that a well-functioning social community will develop its own momentum and bring other students along with it? Or should the focus bring all students together forward as members of a cohesive virtual community?

The basic conceit of Internet-infused education – at least in the augmentation/community frame – is that curriculum should serve to introduce students to a new type of learning and intelligence created by and through the burgeoning information age, based on the qualitative changes in humans' relationships to knowledge systems and their meanings in everyday life. At the heart of this new learning is increased reliance on agency in the use and development of information sources, including collaborative/hypertext intelligence, swarm intelligence, and collective agency/Open Source intelligence – all dependent to some extent on willingness and abilities to engage in collaborative learning activities. But this may be dependent on deemphasizing content learning in favor of teaching students *how* to learn through the Internet. New types of process-based learning has to coexist and in some cases override teaching based on crystallized intelligence. There may be times when teachers and the larger educational infrastructure need to choose between the development of agency-based intelligence and the surety of content-based knowledge. The work of Rienties and his colleagues suggests that ways may be found to balance the two – autonomous learning environments that stress agency in the learning processes combined with the control offered by structured scaffolding. But this problem has all the earmarks of a new Gordian knot for education.

Knowledge forum redux: the trialogical approach

One of the biggest questions in introducing the Internet-infused education as an important choice for (or demand on) teachers is whether it makes any sense to introduce a new, dynamic tool into a system of static educational practices with vested interests and belief systems about what teaching and learning is (or should be). Teachers in their classrooms, administrators in their schools, the larger educational system, and perhaps the political system – all need to buy into the benefit of the new technology for it to gain a foothold. The stored program computer never had the impact on education that many predicted (Cuban and Cuban 2009). Some suggest that the reason for this was because the educators themselves were not really ready, willing, and/or able to accept and experiment with the computers as part of their everyday practices. The same might be even truer for the Internet, where traditional teaching and learning practices can be challenged to a far greater extent than the standalone computer ever could. This is combined with the social backdrop of teachers fearing that Internet technologies will be used to take their place in the classroom.

Kai Hakkarainen and Sami Paavola (2009) look to expand Scardamalia and Bereiter's idea of knowledge building into more concrete knowledge creation (through the development of artifacts) based on what they refer to as the trialogical approach. They suggest it is not enough to create programs that help students build new ideas through collaborative interplay. For Internet-infused education to have a real impact the collaborations must change social practices by turning the products of this collaboration into lasting material artifacts capable of challenging more traditional practices. Hakkarainen (2009) (having studied with Bereiter) offers a gentle critique of Scardmalia and Bereiter's *Knowledge Forum*, suggesting that the teaching/learning model does not go far enough in helping to understand, and implement, possibilities for transformation through Computer Supported Intentional Learning Environments. Hakkarainen reinvoices Bereiter's notion of building ideas through collaboration in hypertext-rich educational environments. Students within interconnected systems become capable of knowledge building by commenting on and annotating existing, shared knowledge. Hakkarainen and Paavola (and Bereiter) refer to these new ideas as "conceptual artifacts," more focused on the processes of the ongoing collaborative work than the outcomes.

The question for Hakkarainen and Paavola is whether students are in a social (and cognitive) position to realize the potentials of these new capabilities, and whether teachers are in the social positions to lead them, or even let them engage in these new types of twenty-first-century learning activities. While agreeing that the conceptual artifacts are important, forward-looking educational endeavors, Hakkarainen (2009) recognizes that these accomplishments often do not bring with them any lasting changes in the social practices of students, teachers, or the educational infrastructure as a whole. It is all too easy, and likely, for participants in, and administrators of, educational processes to fall back into traditional activity patterns once the process is complete – or even during the process. Although the *Knowledge Forum* learning environment can lead to immediate success in knowledge building, there is a very good chance it will not lead to the more long-term encompassing educational transformation that Bereiter and Scardamalia hope for. You can provide a well-designed knowledge-building environment, but there is no way to make teachers and students continue to engage in non-hierarchical, nonlinear activities in sustainable ways; in other words a well-designed program like the *Knowledge Forum* might be able to win the battle for a collaborative hypertext knowledge approach to education, but it is not equipped to help in the war against socially prescribed educational practices.

Hakkarainen and Paavola base their concerns about the limitations of the *Knowledge Forum* at least in part of their own experiences attempting to introduce the program into classrooms in Finland – finding that even students at more elite schools used knowledge-building tool sets primarily for copying and finding and making lists of preexisting facts. Rather than adapting their learning processes to the new possibilities offered by the *Knowledge Forum*, the students adapted the technology to traditional, preexisting social practices of learning. These authors argue that if the *Knowledge Forum* is going to have a lasting impact on education, it must set its goals beyond proximal knowledge-building processes to the creation of material, knowledge-laden artifacts that can then be used as ongoing tools in inquiry – tools that will push both students and their teachers to recognize the long-term value of the technologically enhanced learning processes. Conceptual artifacts need to evolve into what they term "epistemic" artifacts – external knowledge that exists as material tools independently of specific processes of inquiry. These epistemic artifacts are then instrumentalized by the knowledge-building community as tools for further/future inquiry, exhibiting lasting value and serving as a continuous illustration of the power of Internet-infused learning. The evolution toward externalization and instrumentalization occurs through an ongoing, interactive process of "instrumental genesis" (Ritella and Hakkarainen 2012).

Hakkarainen and Paavola (2009) offer an interesting illustration of the possibilities of a trialogical approach in extending the classrooms and the learning of students within a computer-supported collaborative context. Using Scardmalia and Bereiter's *Knowledge Forum* as a (augmentative/community) technological framework, they organized a learning initiative – "The Artifact Project – the Past, the Present, and the Future." In the first phase of the project students from different classes at an elementary school (fourth and fifth grades) worked together to build an exhibition of artifacts. In the second phase of the project students worked together investigating the physical properties of the artifacts they were studying such as creation of light through tools and the characteristics of different metals. In the third phase the students, with the help of professional designers, designed new lamps but also "outlined and visualized artifacts of the future." Students worked together over time to build knowledge about artifacts (especially light-giving artifacts) and used that knowledge to create epistemic artifacts (new designs for lamps) that could be carried forward separately from the particular lessons of the classroom. There was a shared object of study. Knowledge about that shared object developed over time (using the technological capabilities offered by an intraconnected computer network) leading to what Bereiter might term more advanced relational understanding. But the trialogical approach took the knowledge building further, creating contexts where students actually created their own independent artifacts.

This trialogical perspective is one of the most complex, wide-ranging approaches to Internet-infused education that combines micro-genesis of specific knowledge-building activities with the macro-genesis of the social practices of teaching over time. There are, however, two possible difficulties with the trialogical approach – one minor (and what some might actually consider a positive) and one that may pose larger problems. The minor difficulty is that a trialogical perspective is difficult to study in any systematic way. The iterative process of instrumental genesis and the hit-or-miss development of epistemic artifacts (it is almost impossible to know which concepts student will be willing to tenaciously pursue) suggest that the trialogical approach cannot really be studied through traditional, short-term, controlled experimentation. It is impossible to know, even from the point of new conceptual artifacts, that a student or group of students would be able to push their newfound understanding into the realm of instrumental genesis – and that the larger educational activity system would see this as valuable. The students in the example earlier may have easily lost interest in the artifacts they were studying and moved on, or worse become bored or frustrated. The trialogical approach demands very high levels of agency to come to fruition. Any research would probably need to be historical/retrospective.

Some might consider historical/retrospective methods a better approach in general for understanding the role of the Internet in educational pro-cesses – or for that matter everyday life. The character of the Internet may be forcing us into new modes of exploration and understanding of the ways in which we teach and learn. There is an old story in research about a person who comes out of a bar to see a drunk searching for house keys. The person, worried about what will happen to the drunk, joins in the search. Then a couple more people join in. They search for fifteen minutes and find nothing. One of the searchers becomes frustrated and asks, "Can you remember exactly where you dropped the keys?" The drunk points out into the darkness, "Oh, I'm pretty sure I dropped them somewhere out there." The person asks, "Then why are we looking here?" The drunk points to the streetlight above them and says, "Because this is where the light is." We may have to venture into the darkness to truly understand the Internet.

A second difficulty with the trialogical approach poses greater diffi-culties. It is an educational method that demands long-term agency of students that is both driven by and driving the development of epistemic artifacts through the process of instrumental genesis. What is the logic behind this type of student agency? It can be difficult to keep students engaged in online educational communities for even short periods. One reason students used the *Knowledge Forum* environment for copying and making lists might have been because they just weren't interested in any further personal investment in their assigned tasks. Hakkarainen and Paavola don't specify what it is that would give students the agency to engage in the hard work of iterative development of new artifacts over relatively long periods.

Engelbart's Augmentation Research Center is in many ways a good case study for the potential positives and negatives of the trialogical approach. The members of the Center might be considered an optimum collaborative group for knowledge creation and instrumental genesis. They developed and used the oNLineSystem to engage in ongoing col-laboration in which conceptual artifacts quickly evolved into epistemic artifacts. Instruments such as windows and hyperlinks changed social practices in numerous ways that are still playing out today. But even with high levels of interest and what some might consider extraordinary success, the community soon started to devolve. Knowledge creation is a difficult and frustrating process that can test the patience of even the most committed researchers. What would happen if you put teachers and students with limited interest and resources into this type of situation? Can something like the trialogical approach be sustained?

Agency in connection

Stephen Downes has had a long career in online education – partially in the tradition of Engelbart, Licklider, and Taylor – as an Internet pioneer (or perhaps pirate) who is broadly expanding out our understanding of the role(s) the larger information universe will play in education. His work combines Bush's conception of an increasingly interconnected universe acting as a strong centrifugal force on human thinking with the possibilities of building emergent learning communities based on found connections. He is also one of the originators (along with George Siemens) of the first massive open online courses, which came to be known as MOOCs (discussed in-depth in Chapter 9). Downes is also as far as I can tell the only person in this book to reference *Star Trek* (any book on the Internet worth its salt should have at least one person who references *Star Trek*).

Downes (2010a) thinks of the Internet as an extension of the human mind in almost a material sense. He sees the interconnections that an individual is capable of making with other nodes as mimicking the fast-moving interconnections between neurons – the Internet as re-creation of the physical workings of the human brain. Just as neurons interconnect to constantly re-create knowledge schemes that not only enable but also help frame the way we understand information in the world, the network nodes interconnect to create new merged knowledge schemes that enable the same type of framing at a more expansive level. Mitra's "hole in the wall" experiment can serve as a tangible (offline) illustration. None of the children playing in the slum area had any existing knowledge about how the Internet connections provided through the kiosks worked. But the children came together over the problem of how to get the interesting new tool to meet their needs and desires, interconnecting with other children in their local network to create knowledge and understanding that were beyond their individual reach.

Downes (2010b) takes this concept of emergent knowledge (based in swarm intelligence/complexity theory – connected nodes merge to create communities that are capable of superseding the intelligence of any individual participant) and applies it to asynchronous Internet connections. The Internet opens possibilities for any person to tap into any available network – making the Internet connections a natural extension of their own thinking networks so that the move from individual thinking to network thinking (and back again) is seamless. If a person trains as an engineer they begin to develop the types of neural connections that help us recognize and assimilate new information we encounter related to the problems engineers might face. If a network of engineers come together through a series of Internet connections to merge their thinking, they can form an external, expansive model of the thinking of each of those individual engineers. Participation in these networks helps build processing capabilities both for the individuals and for the network itself.

The increased power of the network through participation of more nodes, more minds, is fairly obvious (arguments are to be made against the idea of more equaling better, such as Brooks 1995, *The Mythical*

Man-Month). The more difficult questions are how participation in these networks actually helps the individual participants and, of course, in the spirit of this chapter's theme, why the individual nodes would want to participate in this type of connective community. Downes suggests that the benefit to the individual for participating in the network is basically selfish – the chance for members of (what Downes refers to as) the *Connective* to strengthen their individual thinking capabilities by exercising them. Downes compares participation in one of these external thinking networks to going to a gym to work out. Participation in these external networks pushes users to stretch and challenge their own thinking schemes. This would be especially important for individuals with limited access to the types of classroom experiences that engender development of strong and lasting neural networks. To this point Downes is really not that different from even a number of communication/service technological frame e-learning proponents.

Where Downes's thesis is radical is his emphasis of connectivity and the processes of interconnected thinking rather than any type of content. He believes there should be little defined content (outside of the general topic that brings the participants together) and no defined end point for the interconnected community. The primary purpose of the community should be in exercising individual capabilities in problem solving going forward. If this sounds familiar it is because it reflects John Dewey's vision for education in *Democracy and Education* (1916) (which Downes might have acquired naturally by participating in networks of educators). There are (at least) two important implications for Downes's perspective on interconnected learning. The first and perhaps most important is that Downes places almost no importance on content learning – it is enough that nodes in the network are participating in relevant problem-solving activities – the goal of the teacher/facilitator of the educational initiative (e.g., course) then is not only creating a community that potential participants would want to connect into, but building a series of continuous interconnections among the participants. In the age-old battle in education between content and process, for Downes there is no battle – the sole (or at least very primary) purpose of connectivity-based education is to immerse the individual mind/brain within an ongoing, encompassing activity-based network. For example, in the "hole in the wall" experiment it is not important that the children learned how to use Microsoft Paint per se – it is important that they exercised their minds so they would be stronger in framing Internet connectivity problems, capable of moving on to the next educational experience.

Second, Downes sees these networks as completely nonhierarchical. Like the Community of Inquiry vision of co-regulation, no distinction is made between teacher and student – we find only a community of potential problem solvers (although Downes might dispense with some of the more directive aspects of Community of Inquiry). And like the *Knowledge Forum*, individuals with different schemes (levels and types) can enter the network and be productive participants. A neophyte can challenge the thinking of much more experienced members of the network with a single, unique question or posed problem.

The issue of agency in Downes's conceptualization is more difficult. Potential participants can increase the strength of their neural schemes in a given area of problem solving, but why would they? Downes's answer is one of the most straightforward and philosophically sophisticated of those working in Internet-infused education (his intellectual history is in philosophy of education). Downes sees the whole of a network as being greater than the individual minds that compose it (how else could it strengthen thinking?) with new types of problem-solving capabilities creating an emergent intelligence that supersedes anything individuals could experience on their own. However, because he does not see value in content or defined endpoints of network activity (he also places little importance on collaboration), no object of inquiry really draws the community together, let alone sustains it. Instead he sees participation in connected networks as being based in utilitarianism, directly quoting John Stuart Mill, "Each person pursuing his or her own good in his or her own way." Each member of a network participates in that network because they get satisfaction and a good feeling from building up their capabilities – in much the same way somebody might find satisfaction and a good feeling from building up their muscle tone. Downes does believe that participants need to cooperate in the development of an interconnected community but defines cooperation as "an exchange of mutual value between autonomous individuals." The interconnected network is basically a means to a self-defined end.

It may seem paradoxical that Downes uses a very individualistic philosophy in explaining behavior on highly connected networks. Downes seems to be arguing against the type of collaboration proponents of computer-supported collaborative learning are attempting to promote. From Downes's perspective because members of a collaborative community (if it is even possible on a large scale) give themselves up to the community goals, they lose their autonomous identity in the process. If one of the great strengths of Internet-infused education is its ability to create autonomous teaching-learning processes, are educators working against the natural, connective structure of networks by encouraging collaborative groups? It is a stronger, more well-grounded explanation of agency than most other researchers to this point provide, but does it make long-term sense in Internet-infused educational design? There is little doubt that many Internet pioneers and entrepreneurs outside of education can take a similar utilitarian approach – but is this a reflection of the Internet or a reflection of current society? (Downes, it seems, would also have little use for the next chapter on social engagement.)

At what price agency

Another reason can be given why Stephen Downes's ideas on connectivism are included in this chapter. As mentioned, Downes sees agency as being primarily utilitarian. Users log on because they believe Internet activity will in some way lead to satisfaction and happiness at an individual level. Many of the most popular applications on the Internet do seem to have a utilitarian undercurrent, especially those based on the communication/service technological frame: Facebook allows users to maintain relationships, to express their likes, to declare their status; YouTube allows individuals to retrieve enjoyable videos; Pinterest allows users to share media content, to name just a few. Even most games (including role-playing games) are utilitarian in nature. Most applications survive (or not) based on the level of utilitarian value; when users feel that accessing the site no longer offers a minimum level of utility for achieving satisfaction or happiness, they will stop logging on. One can even make the argument that Internet applications offer possibilities for a hedonistic utilitarianism. Others face very little consequence by your engaging in activity for your own enjoyment on the Internet (there are, of course, limits).

The question is how much of a trade-off do educators make between the types of agency that come with utilitarian use of the Internet and the exigencies of educational processes – a question made more difficult by the point Downes seems to be making: Individual utility does not have much of a relationship with and is in some ways antithetical to collaboration. It is perhaps also important to remember that even though much current use of the Internet has utilitarian purposes, that was not its original intent, at least within the augmentative/community technological frame. Early visions of the Internet were more pragmatic in nature, more focused on helping individuals understand how to navigate a new, fast-moving information universe, to solve problems through collaborative intelligence. Vannevar Bush, Douglas Engelbart, Ted Nelson, and even Tim Berners-Lee were really not that interested with individual satisfaction (Engelbart actually seemed to think individual utility was detrimental, while Nelson championed the role that frustration and confusion play in creativity). To what degree do we see learners on the Internet as consumers, and to what degree do we see them as adventurers? This distinction is made more difficult by the emergence of Internet-based for-profit educational organizations.

Agency plays a defining role in all Internet activity, and education is no exception. But at the heart of the decisions and discussions are whether educators focus on user agency as the defining issue (in which case it might be best to take a utilitarian approach), or whether agency is one issue among others that needs to be nurtured within a larger integrated activity framework. Three (at least) critical issues are central to this discussion: (1) whether educators are looking for cooperation or collaboration as a goal of their learning communities, (2) whether a focus on agency creates a new digital divide, and (3) whether a utilitarian approach leads to progress and creativity in thinking.

The *Cooperation versus Collaboration* issue is perhaps the most interesting and most consequential issue in examining the trade-off between agency and sustainable learning environments. Downes (2010b) in his discussion of *Connectives* and Stahl et al. (2006) in their history of computer-supported collaborative learning define both cooperation and collaboration almost exactly in the same way but from opposite perspectives. For Downes "cooperation is an exchange of mutual value between autonomous individuals" and collaboration is individuals "subsumed under a common goal." For Stahl and colleagues cooperative learning is "conducted by individuals" who contribute their "individual results" to a group project, whereas in collaborative learning "participants do not go off to do things individually, but remain engaged with a shared task that is constructed and maintained by and for the group as such." Both Downes and those encouraging the development of computer-supported collaborative learning environments agree that cooperation and collaboration are possible in Internet-infused learning initiatives (although Downes does not think collaboration is possible with large groups) and that cooperative Internet learning communities are easier to develop than collaborative ones. But Downes also suggests that cooperation is more beneficial for learning because each participant can remain autonomous, choosing the type and trajectory of participation that will meet their educational/thinking needs. Stahl and colleagues see cooperation as limited, more mimicking traditional education settings than exploring the new possibilities for collaborative learning environments offered by the Internet. Most approaches in the augmentation/collaborative frame tend to focus on the development of collaborative learning environments – but is this asking too much of the Internet and the learners? Is it the case where, as Hakkarainen and Paavola (2009) suggest, the social practices do not match the projected impact of the technology?

The issue of *a new type of digital divide* poses a second difficulty. If we depend on utilitarian motivations for learning on the Internet, are we using new forms of education to reinforce rather than meliorate educational differences? Downes's utilitarian perspective, especially in the context of his larger connectivist framework, suggests that people join online learning communities to strengthen thinking abilities they already have and want to extend. This increases possibilities for individuals who already have rich experience opportunities, and success in a certain type of thinking, for finding communities that can help them learn in new and interesting ways – but offers almost no possibilities for potential learners with little or no successful experiences in these areas. Only somebody who already has some interest in engineering is going to want to become a participant in, let alone learn from, an online engineering education community – creating a digital Matthew effect (Merton 1968). Those that know have the greatest capabilities for knowing more. In an interesting and important study by Neuman and Celano (2012) researchers observed the ways in which children from affluent neighborhoods were using library-installed computers as compared to children from neighborhoods of concentrated poverty. What they observed over several years was that the children from the affluent neighborhoods were able to use the computers to far greater intellectual advantage – leading to bigger differentials in development of knowledge/information sources. It was (it can be assumed) experience and prior knowledge that guided learning choices. In a situation like Mitra's "hole in the wall" experiment the children were able to develop computer skills, but again for very utilitarian purposes with the most popular sites Disney's Blast and MTV. One could make the argument that if the Internet is going to level the playing field, it will be through learners joining collaborative communities, where other members of the community are willing to not only engage new members but also draw then into a supportive online ecology – a learning community where neophyte members are unexpectedly taken in new directions of thinking through the momentum of community problem solving – a much more difficult proposition requiring long-term efforts, and again changes to the social practices of formal education institutions.

The third issue, education that in some way encourages *development of new and creative ways of thinking,* is related to the first two. The primary idea behind hypertext (Nelson 1974) and the motivations for the Internet is that the human mind benefits from open, transactive relationships with other minds. The development of new ideas is not the product of a single way of thinking but the efforts of multiple minds building toward new solutions to pressing or just interesting relevant problems (Dewey 1916). It is the willingness of individuals to give up part of their thought process and the ownership of ideas to a larger community effort. This can happen from a utilitarian perspective: The ability to bring together dynamic communities around a single problem is in many ways more easily accomplished when individuals believe they will be getting something out of their initiatives – at least initially. But as discussed in the earlier chapter on intelligence and the Internet the type of swarm intelligence that emerges from fast-developing connective communities can be limiting, or even go off on unforeseen and sometime destructive trajectories. Internet-based cooperation can offer emergent solutions to immediate problems, but the ability and/or willingness to participate is based on previous experience with the problem, and solutions can be derived out of that experience. The ability to address problems over time necessitates sustainable communities that develop shared meanings more relevant to the online community than experiences outside of the community: This requires collaboration and a willingness to become a participant for the sake of the community more than for the needs of the self. Rather than allowing students to find their niche through new types of connectivity, should Internet-based educational activities teach students the joys (and the frustrations) of engaging in a nonlinear, nonhierarchical problem-solving communities where every voice is of worth? This may be why so many models focus on agency for collaborative work.

Of course, this leads to a problem – which is if you take away the natural and obvious utility of Internet activity in the lives of individual students, how do you convince them to engage to the point of collaboration? Is it possible to establish this through the strength of community?

References

Akyol, Z., and Garrison, D. R. (2011). Assessing Metacognition in an Online Community of Inquiry. *The Internet and Higher Education*, 14(3), 183–190.

Bardini, T., and Friedewald, M. (2003). Chronicle of the Death of a Laboratory: Douglas Engelbart and the Failure of the Knowledge Workshop. *History of Technology*, 23, 191–212.

Brooks, F. P., Jr. (1995). *The Mythical Man-Month, Anniversary Edition: Essays on Software Engineering.* New York: Pearson Education.

Chu, R., and Tsai, C. C. (2009). Self-directed Learning Readiness, Internet Self-efficacy and Preferences towards Constructivist Internet-Based Learning Environments among Higher-Aged Adults. *Journal of Computer Assisted Learning*, 25(5), 489–501.

Chuang, S. C., and Tsai, C. C. (2005). Preferences toward the Constructivist Internet-Based Learning Environments among High School Students in Taiwan. *Computers in Human Behavior*, 21(2), 255–272.

Cuban, L., and Cuban, L. (2009). *Oversold and Underused: Computers in the Classroom.* Cambridge, MA: Harvard University Press.

Dewey, J. (1910/1997). *How We Think.* New York: Courier Dover Publications.

(1916). *Democracy and Education.* New York: McMillan.

(1925/1958). *Experience and Nature.* New York: Dover.

(1938). *Logic: The Theory of Inquiry.* New York: Holt, Rinehart & Winston.

Downes, S. (2010a). Learning Networks and Connective Knowledge. In H. Yang and S. Chi-Yin Yuen (eds.), *Collective Intelligence and E-Learning 2.0: Implications of Web-Based Communities and Networking.* Hershey, PA: IGI Global.

(2010b). Connectivism and Transculturality. Talk delivered to Telefónica Foundation, Buenos Aires, Argentina. Posted on *Stephen's Web,* May 16, 2010, www.downes.ca/post/53297.

Garrison, D. R. (2003). Cognitive Presence for Effective Asynchronous Online Learning: The Role of Reflective Inquiry, Self-direction and Metacognition. *Elements of Quality Online Education: Practice and Direction,* 4, 47–58.

Garrison, D. R., Anderson, T., and Archer, W. (1999). Critical Inquiry in a Text-Based Environment: Computer Conferencing in Higher Education. *The Internet and Higher Education,* 2(2), 87–105.

(2001). Critical Thinking, Cognitive Presence, and Computer Conferencing in Distance Education. *American Journal of Distance Education,* 15(1), 7–23.

Garrison, D. R., and Arbaugh, J. B. (2007). Researching the Community of Inquiry Framework: Review, Issues, and Future Directions. *The Internet and Higher Education,* 10(3), 157–172.

Hakkarainen, K. (2009). A Knowledge-Practice Perspective on Technology-Mediated Learning. *International Journal of Computer-Supported Collaborative Learning,* 4(2), 213–231.

Hakkarainen, K., and Paavola, S. (2009). Toward a Trialogical Approach to Learning. In B. Schwarz, T. Dreyfus, and R. Hershkowitz (eds.) *Transformation of Knowledge through Classroom Interaction* (pp. 65–80). London: Routledge.

Hong, H. Y., Scardamalia, M., and Zhang, J. (2010). Knowledge Society Network: Toward a Dynamic, Sustained Network for Building Knowledge. *Canadian Journal of Learning and Technology/La revue canadienne de l'apprentissage et de la technologie,* 36, 1–29.

Kirschner, P. A., Sweller, J., and Clark, R. E. (2006). Why Minimal Guidance during Instruction Does Not Work: An Analysis of the Failure of Constructivist, Discovery, Problem-Based, Experiential, and Inquiry-Based Teaching. *Educational Psychologist,* 41(2), 75–86.

Koschmann, T. (2002, January). Dewey's Contribution to the Foundations of CSCL Research. In *Proceedings of the Conference on Computer Support for Collaborative Learning: Foundations for a CSCL Community* (pp. 17–22). International Society of the Learning Sciences.

Merton, R. K. (1968). The Matthew Effect in Science. *Science,* 159(3810), 56–63.

Nelson, T. H., (1974). *Dream Machine.* Chicago: Hugo's Book Service.

Neuman, S. B., and Celano, D. (2012). *Giving our Children a Fighting Chance: Poverty, Literacy, and the Development of Information Capital.* New York: Teachers College Press.

Rienties, B., Giesbers, B., Tempelaar, D., Lygo-Baker, S., Segers, M., and Gijselaers, W. (2012). The Role of Scaffolding and Motivation in CSCL. *Computers & Education,* 59(3), 893–906.

Ritella, G., and Hakkarainen, K. (2012). Instrumental Genesis in Technology-Mediated Learning: From Double Stimulation to Expansive Knowledge

Practices. *International Journal of Computer-Supported Collaborative Learning*, 7(2), 239–258.

Salmon, G. (2004). *E-moderating: The Key to Teaching and Learning Online*. New York: Routledge.

(2013). *E-tivities: The Key to Active Online Learning*. New York: Routledge.

Scardamalia, M., and Bereiter, C. (1994). Computer Support for Knowledge-Building Communities. *Journal of the Learning Sciences*, 3(3), 265–283.

(2006). Knowledge Building: Theory, Pedagogy, and Technology. In K. Sawyer (ed.), *Cambridge Handbook of the Learnig Sciences* (pp. 97–118). New York: Cambridge University Press.

Shea, P., and Bidjerano, T. (2009). Community of Inquiry as a Theoretical Framework to Foster "Epistemic Engagement" and "Cognitive Presence" in Online Education. *Computers & Education*, 52(3), 543–553.

Stahl, G. (2006). *Group Cognition: Computer Support for Building Collaborative Knowledge*. Cambridge, MA: MIT Press.

Stahl, G., Koschmann, T., and Suthers, D. (2006). Computer-Supported Collaborative Learning: An Historical Perspective. In K. Sawyer (ed.), *Cambridge Handbook of the Learning Sciences*. New York: Cambridge University Press. 409–426.

5 Online social engagement

The relative importance of well-developed, well-defined social relationships in problem-solving communities has a long and complex history in education and human development in general. The famed Russian psychologist L. S. Vygotsky (1987) suggested that integrated community relationships are one of the primary driving forces in human teaching/learning processes. Humans learn because they naturally yearn to be participants in (well)-functioning social groups and to maintain their place of membership in those groups. John Dewey (1916) based much of his educational philosophy on the idea that learning is a community/social–oriented process – with the quality of that learning based very much on the value and relevance of the connections problem-solving group members have and use with each other and the world around them. More recent ideas such as Lave and Wenger's (1991) limited peripheral participation outline the ways in which neophytes are slowly integrated into community processes by observing relevant activities. Paolo Freire (1970) makes the argument that social systems control what we know and how we know for their own purposes, and the only ways to understand and change these (sometimes individually destructive) knowledge systems is by recognizing this.

The role of social relationships in online learning seems like a natural focus of study, especially considering the role communication and connectivity play in everyday Internet activity. It is almost axiomatic that the Internet can be used as a tool for developing communities where users support and complement each other in their efforts to gain new understandings and insights. Yet the development of socially cohesive learning communities where members feel a commitment to both the group and its goals has been one of the most difficult issues in Internet-infused education. Many Internet-based education initiatives pay little if any attention to student (or teacher) online social relationships, prioritizing communication, putting emphasis on transmission of information, many times through direct instruction or individual tutoring.

A smaller group recognizes the role that social relationships play in successful learning environments but relegate development of these relationships to secondary status. Also, some initiatives make the argument that social connection is a natural human want – we are all wandering nodes looking to tie into some larger network of activity if given the opportunity: The Internet (or a well-designed intranet) provides those opportunities.

As well, a nascent but growing body of research suggests that productive, online social communities can be nurtured into existence through either design (Preece 2001) or active facilitation (Salmon 2004). At the heart of much of this research is the concept of sociability. One of the difficulties with the research into the development of socially advanced learning communities is that there are two different ways of understanding sociability: (1) as an objective quality of the community that can be broken down into measurable components such as amount and quality of interactions over a given time frame and (2) as a subjective quality based in the human propensity to make connections and be part of well-defined social groups that can offer help and support in adaptive learning processes (usually in the service of the community itself). A second related issue is whether the development of sociability is a function of a well-designed (online) social ecology or whether individual users need to be mentored and coached through the process of productive online interactions. What are the relative roles of the teacher/facilitator and the software designer, individual course and educational institution, in the development of online social communities? This is an especially important question as many institutions invest in preassembled software packages.

This chapter starts with a discussion of two major theories on the relationship between social relationships and the development of viable, sustainable teaching/learning communities: L. S. Vygotsky and John Dewey. This is followed by two key early influences on the development of online social groups – Licklider and Taylor's (1968) project meeting/ conference based in computer communication and Rheingold's (1993) virtual community. It will then move on to the idea of sociability through design – including the development of "social spaces" that promote high-level participant interactions. This is followed by a look at attempts to develop sociability and "social presence" through overt efforts on the part of the moderator/teacher/facilitator of the online learning community.

It is important to point out that though there are two approaches to development of enhanced interaction among Internet community participants – course design and moderator facilitation, the two are not mutually exclusive (some researchers attempt to merge them) – the differences are in focus of approach.

Sociability in human development

Sociability is a central issue in research into the development of online learning communities. Most discussions of sociability in Internet-infused education focus on limited definitions involving (theoretically measurable) interactive communication of participants, but the larger concept of uniquely human social behaviors and the ways they help create and support adaptive groups/communities has been an important part of the study of human development for more than a century. The original idea of sociability stretches back to Darwin and his interpreters, especially the Russian sociobiologists of the late nineteenth and early twentieth century. Petr Kropotkin used Darwin's *The Descent of Man* (1871) to suggest that the human quality of sociability is a primary factor in survival and prospering of the species (Glassman 2000). In essence individuals have a natural desire to develop connections and relationships with others that engender the creation of flexible, highly adaptive working groups (broadly defined). Humans look to make and especially sustain connections with others as part of their natural activities. Once the group is formed and becomes meaningful for sustaining everyday life activities of the participants, group members will engage in almost any behaviors necessary to sustain the group's existence. This tendency toward sociability as a driving force in human activity runs deep and is a counterpoint to more egoistic, utilitarian views of participation in social groups (being part of a group primarily to meet an individual organism's immediate needs). It can be argued a number of educational theorists and researchers have developed their ideas based in a general context of this type of human sociability, Dewey and Vygotsky in particular (there are no direct ties between either Dewey or Vygotsky and Kropotkin, but it is relatively easy to make the argument that all were influenced by Darwin in similar ways).

From an educational perspective this means that a primary concern of the teacher/mentor is developing teaching strategies within the context of maintaining and extending the larger social group. The teacher acts as interlocutor for the social group, using learners' natural tendencies toward sociability to invite (and/or pull) the neophyte into the social cooperative as a full (or partial) member. Vygotsky (1978), for instance, suggests that mentors should be aware of, and when possible use, learners' inclinations to appropriate relevant community tools that (obviously) promote the general needs of that group (e.g., language and other shared mediating symbols) in ways that benefit both the individual and the larger community. These ideas have been partially incorporated into (or are reflected by) the work of more recent sociocultural theorists who focus on the natural relationships between learners and sociability such as Griffin and Cole's Zo-ped (1984), Rogoff and the concept of learning apprenticeships (1994), and Lave and Wenger and learning through limited peripheral participation (1991).

John Dewey takes a slightly different approach to sociability by suggesting that humans are not only ready but eager to develop impromptu problem-solving collaborative groups that might or might not last beyond the needs of the immediate situation. It is not that the individual desires just to solve a pertinent problem, but the interest and joy that comes from working within a well-functioning problem-solving group drives the human desire to make connections (1916). Acclimate individuals to the possibilities of working in groups by setting them on productive, problem-solving trajectories that are relevant to their every-day lives and a (democratic) community will emerge. Individual learning will meld into a problem-solving community, with members willing to subvert their individual desires to the satisfaction of finding solutions to shared problems, no matter where those solutions take them. Dewey offers a more rational model of sociability: A cohesive group never becomes independent of recognizable shared goals. There is always a logical purpose behind the joint actions of the individual and the community – when there is not, individuals are acting primarily out of habit and not vital intelligence.

Humans are constantly searching for social connections to relevant social communities. Pre-Internet that relevance was partially but important-antly determined by social and/or physical proximity – leading to ongoing cultural histories tied to place. The Internet's abilities to transcend traditional boundaries changes the sociability equation as it changes so much else. At this point it is difficult to know what directions these changes might take – but explorations should probably focus on the same human inclinations for social connections to relevant communities that in some ways meet the needs of the existent or emerging social group such as proposed by theorists such as Vygotsky and Dewey (there is a reason these two theorists are so often mentioned in Internet education models and research). Users are most likely to make connections to meaningful individuals and/or groups. Sociability is tied to maintenance and sustainability of groups that will provide them with a sense of ongoing belonging and survival (the two cannot be separated).

The project meeting and the virtual community

J. C. R. Licklider and Robert Taylor's article "The Computer as a Communication Device" (1968) set the stage for the use of networked computers (and networked individuals) in project development – the baseline for computer conferencing. Based on work done at (D)ARPA (including Engelbart's oNLineSystem) and the System Research Center in Palo Alto, Licklider and Taylor outlined how they saw collaborative project development changing through incorporation of new online possibilities. They believed that common interests would draw (distributed) sets of individuals together into central, computer-mediated project conferences when necessary. In a humorous and none too subtle dig at the world of elite expertise (almost certainly including academics) they suggest that the optimum problem-solving community was one where experts could stay apart as much as possible to create their own empires and devote "more time to the role of emperor than the role of problem solver" (p. 29). The working group would come together only for online project meetings when absolutely necessary, with each expert logging in remotely from their personal domains. Not only do members of the project meeting not have to have strong offline social relationships, they do not have to really like each other. It is the opportunity to work together for a common cause with like-minded thinkers that brings and holds the project group together into a cohesive enterprise.

This does not mean conference participants can act as independent nodes; social cohesiveness is critical for success of the conference.

Licklider and Taylor discuss the importance of reciprocal social relationships in computer conferencing, stressing the role of efficient and
respectful interactions. Communications between participants should
be on-point and relatively short – there should be no attempts to
dominate the (cyber) space created by the networked computers (e.g.,
filibustering). More complex analysis can and should be placed online
but separate from the immediate goal-oriented communications so that
participants can diverge their attention to examine the tangential information on their own without disturbing the flow of the meeting (perhaps
the first discussions of online multitasking). In the best of circumstances
the conferees bring back newly gained perspectives to the meeting,
helping push the agenda forward. Licklider and Taylor understood the
importance of individual members of the conference establishing and
following rule systems such as turn taking and willingness of participants to "listen" to each other, while at the same time allowing them to
take advantage of new abilities to quickly access relevant information
based on their own perspectives and needs of the moment.

One almost side idea in the Licklider and Taylor article would reemerge
almost half a century later as a tool for the development of online
educational social communities – the "online interactive vicarious
expediter and responder" or the OLIVER (named after artificial intelligence pioneer Oliver Selfridge). They proposed that the OLIVER would be
able take notes (or not take notes, the OLIVER will make the choice) on
material that users read online, the things they buy, and where they buy
them. It will use that data to connect users to potential friends, determine
who they might see as prestigious (and perhaps those they would like to
avoid), and with whom to share their files. The OLIVER would identify
the communities users might want to join, determine what information
should be shared with members of each of those communities, and help
the user develop an online identity in the different communities. In the
days of online advertising programs and surveillance the OLIVER can
seem simultaneously terrifying and fascinating.

Rheingold (1996) credits Licklider and Taylor with the first suggestions
of online communities – a distributed group coming together within a
synchronous/asynchronous social (learning) environment. But Rheingold based his own conception of the virtual community not on Engelbart's Augmentation Research Center but on his own experiences on the
Whole Earth 'Lectronic Link (WELL). In his descriptions of virtual

communities Rheingold is less concerned about targeted projects than basic human sociability in the more subjective sense – the desire to reach out through cyberspace and establish connections that play similar roles to the connections humans make (or are unable to make for a variety of circumstances) "in the real world." Rheingold saw the WELL of his own experience first and foremost as a place of "conviviality" where he could look in on friends and discuss what was on his mind. He suggests that a primary reason for the emergence of virtual communities around the world is the ability for users to increase their circle of friends, to extend their abilities to make contact with the shared human experience. In his discussions of the activities of the WELL (1993, 1996) he recounts sharing information and supporting members of his community because of the relationships he had built with them over years of online (and offline) communications. The emphasis on the more subjective definition of sociability and the role it plays for individuals engaging with each other over time is evident in the concept of virtual community (the activities of the WELL are discussed in depth in Chapter 6).

A similar (at least desired) role for sociability in online learning plays a central part for a number of researchers exploring the development of online learning communities – shared online spaces where participants will want to point each other in new and interesting directions, to support each other in their educational endeavors, to drop in when they have something to say or are just looking for some type of intellectual stimulation. The question is where did this sociability come from for Rheingold and his compatriots on the WELL and how might it be re-created in planned online learning environments?

Designing sociability

The objective (measurable) conception of sociability emerges out of the communications tradition and early research into telephone conferencing. The focus is on immediate production of interactive communications (level and quality) generated by community participants. This can cause some confusion. In more recent discussion and research, computer conferencing is often explored in the context of teleconferencing (e.g., concepts such as social presence), but even though both Licklider and Taylor had interests in psychoacoustics, their ideas and writings on computer conferencing were based primarily on the work Engelbart was conducting at the Augmentation Research Center. Original conceptions of computer conferencing and teleconferencing emerged from two very different lines of inquiry. Much of the research on sociability has its roots in teleconferencing research, giving it a design orientation – but goals for sociability in computer conferencing are often closer to the work of Engelbart, Licklider and Taylor, and Rheingold, which is more based on moderation and dependent more on human-human interaction in cyber-space (with design a secondary consideration).

Jennifer Preece (2000) suggests two major ways that platforms can influence the development of successful online communities, both design oriented: level of usability and level of sociability, with sociability as a possible subgenre of usability. Usability of platforms/programs is primarily concerned with issues such as ease of access, aesthetically pleasing information design, and social interaction support. Sociability, as mentioned, is level and quality of interactive communications, usually determined by a mixture of the types of *people* drawn to (or allowed to be part of) the online community, the *purpose* of the community (not only whether primarily goal oriented or convivial, but the particular topics/ issues guiding interactions), and the *policies* of the community. The reason that sociability can be considered a subcategory of usability is that interactions are at least partially a result of how the community was initially designed for potential users. How the community developers, for instance, limit access through registration and/or requisites for being an active participant will impact who joins, their reasons for joining, and their expectations of shared activities, all of which have important implications for type and sustainability of interactions. A course that is closed except to registrants of a particular class, university, or network is going to have very different interactions than a course that is open to all comers. The designers can also have an impact on the purposes of and policy of the community.

The WELL might serve as an example of how general usability can help determine sociability within an online community. The WELL was different from many other bulletin board/conference systems, UseNet-developed communities, and multiuser dungeons (for gaming on a number of levels), with many of the differences based in the ways design (some of it the result of conscious decisions, but most the conse-quences of unique circumstances) affected level and quality of online interactions. For instance, the WELL was made up primarily of individuals who had some relationship to the Whole Earth Catalog and its founder Stuart Brand, suggesting many of the users had similar worldviews and perhaps even social predispositions. Time spent on the WELL could be expensive (users had to pay a monthly fee), suggesting users needed to have at least some disposable income. The original program for the threaded discussions used for the conferences was complex and initially frustrating to use, limiting potential participants to those who were already familiar with or at least motivated enough to navigate the software. Users knew what type of people they would encounter in the specific conferences based on their purpose as suggested by their topic/title/moderator. For example, those joining the Grateful Dead conference (the most popular on the site at the time) could probably anticipate community affect and discussion trajectory. A moderator such as Howard Rheingold could draw participants based on his reputation in the larger WELL community as a moderator of conferences. The communally oriented policies (and nonpolicies) taken from the place-based social cooperative The Farm might have been confusing/frustrating for certain types of users, causing them to make early exits from the community; the WELL was not a space for those who desired/needed rules and order. It is true that many of these usability issues of the WELL were not part of any overt design, but this does not mean they did not have important effects on participant interactions.

The idea that larger transactional factors have important impacts on sociability may be a vital point for success in online courses. Sociability can be affected by the conscious decision making of the course designers, but it can also be heavily influenced by socioeconomic and/or cultural-historical circumstances that the course designers are not even aware of and never think to take into account. Although general issues of usability based on program design probably have implications for the quality of interactions, it is difficult to know whether it is the primary cause or simply serves as context for a larger host of variables. For instance, a number of conferences were held on the WELL with many of the same usability/sociability variables that failed. The differences could have easily involved less controllable issues such as conference moderators (one of the few shifting variables in the discussion forum), with those better able to project themselves online and bring others along in developing the discussion, creating more successful experiences for participants. The idea that some social variables are beyond design is apparent in a study comparing two blog-centric classes (Glassman et al. 2013). The blog as discussion forum had very similar conscious usability/ sociability design but different outcomes. The differences may have been based more on issues of participant ownership and a balancing of the relationship between cyberspace and the traditional classroom.

Designing constraints for an online community space

The idea of design for usability/sociability poses the question how much responsibility educators should give to system-wide innovations and design features in developing classes they hope will evolve into high-level virtual learning communities. Embedding usability/sociability-related technologies and/or strategies in design suggests educational experiences can be managed separate from the everyday activities of the particular course. Kreijns and his colleagues (e.g., Kreijns et al. 2002; Kreijns et al. 2013) discuss developing online environments that integrate social "affordances" that promote high levels of quality online interactions.

Affordances and constraints

Before continuing with the idea of online spaces that promote and sustain sociability in educational initiatives it is important to make a short digression delving deeper into the concept of affordances; the term *affordances* is often used in describing the relationship between the individual user and the ecology they are traversing in cyberspace. Affordances is a psychological/ecological concept first developed in the mid–twentieth century by J. J. Gibson (1977) – a concept that focuses on the role of the ecological setting in human-object interactions, integrating perception, movement, discovery, and engaged activity. Humans move through their ecological surroundings encountering physical objects that very obviously invite them into consequential activity. The affordance is a combination of where the human as active agent is at that moment in their journey through the ecological setting when they come across an inviting object, and what the object has to offer them in their attempts to move forward. I am walking across a field and I come to a stream I want to or need to cross. I see a plank that crosses the stream.

I gauge that the plank is wide enough for me to walk safely across and thick enough to hold my weight. These qualities are the plank's affordances for continuing my activities. (The fact that I have the right mobility and weight to accomplish this task are my abilities.)

Donald Norman applied Gibson's idea of affordances to object design (1988), suggesting that we can and often do develop everyday physical objects that provide affordances that help guide us through a complex, technologically oriented ecology that can make greater demands on our abilities to navigate movements. If we enter a dark, new hotel room and want to turn on the light we look for a switch and recognize its interactive value based on its (perceived) affordances (e.g., being within reach, a hard surface that is recognizable to the touch but also responsive to pressure from fingers.) In the context of a computer I sit down at my keyboard wanting to interact with the computer to navigate the information universe. I look around for something to help me extend my thinking on to the screen (Engelbart's original reason for developing the mouse). I perceive an object that fits my palm, moves easily in a restricted area, and correlates those movements with the cursor on the screen – these are its (perceived) affordances. In some circumstances the computer becomes so integrated into human activities that we stop thinking about it as a separate, technologically complex object much like we don't really think of the plank we use to cross the stream as a piece of wood cut from a tree but as a bridge that suits our purposes. Gaver (1996) applied the concept of affordances to more abstract computer-based technologies. He continued to stress that affordances were based on a combination of movement and perception of material qualities enabling successful interactions in current ecological circumstances, but stretched the idea to include more ethereal perceived "objects" such as e-mail and video communications systems.

What affordances do not do is act as decision points, overtly offering trajectories for ongoing activities, pushing individuals in specific directions. Norman (1999) suggests that what are many times defined as affordances are actually what Gibson refers to as constraints. These constraints are based on perceived relationships within the ecological setting, leading the actor to make logical or cultural inferences about what they should do next: If A is taken as a given within the ecological context, then the actor naturally assumes B and makes inferences about their own future activity based on these inferences. For instance, if a technological tool overtly connects a user to other individuals within the ecological cyberspace with whom they share perspectives and/or actions, then the user can easily assume those initial connections will lead to further successful communications/collaborations. Constraints can be physical (if I cannot move the cursor outside the boundaries of the screen, then I cannot engage in cursor-driven activity outside of the screen, therefore I infer that I must limit my cursor activity to what I can see on the screen), logical (I should engage in collaborative activities with those I have connections with), or cultural/conventional (a patriarchal gender-segregated group establishes a discussion forum focused on social, political, and/or financial models so users infer that the forum is only open to males). Inferences about this relationship will lead to specific behavioral trajectories (e.g., limiting participation, limiting collaborative activities, the need to hide gender or be attacked based on gender). Conventional constraints develop over history and are often arbitrary but paradoxically can have the largest impact on behavioral trajectories for specific populations. The different constraints may play an important role in the design of online tools and spaces, but they are not affordances in the original sense of the concept.

Very often when designers of programs discuss affordances of ecologies in cyberspace they are actually talking about constraints. It is an admittedly complex argument, and the broader version of affordances is now widely used in discussions of computers and the Internet. One reason to reestablish the difference is it might be important to hold on to the original concept of affordances as we move forward in integrating virtual reality and augmented reality technologies into educational initiatives where participants can actually move through ecologies and perceive virtual objects in their interactive tasks. A second reason is that a concept of constraints based in inferences from relationships may be more helpful in developing designs for usability/sociability than vague conceptions of affordances. Recognizing the concept of constraints may be especially important when designing courses/platforms that are meant to be inclusive of minority and/or oppressed populations. A third reason is a focus on constraints in design may give us better insight into how and why ecological settings in cyberspace promote behavioral trajectories: The theory/approach of cybernetics that has had an important impact on the development of both computers and the Internet is based on the idea of controlling behavior through negative feedback that constrains our range of choices (Bateson 1967).

Using constraints to create a social space

One of the more interesting and subtle discussions of usability/sociability can be found in attempts by Kriejns et al. (2002) to establish reciprocal social relationships between learning community participants and the learning environment – with the online ecology inviting but also guiding participants to initiate interactions with other community members. The authors suggest this can be accomplished by establishing what they refer to as "group awareness" – user perceptions that other members of the community exist who are interested in some of the same things they are interested in and/or engaged in similar or even parallel online activities. Once aware of these sympathetic/parallel community members, participants might infer possibilities for collaboration with these potentially connected others in joint problem-solving activities. This in some ways reflects the earliest conceptions of sociability (e.g., Kropotkin) – if we know that others are interested in the issues we are interested in, we are often motivated to interact with them and perhaps develop a joint project. The concept is so everyday that we sometimes forget the power it has over our actions. If I become aware of somebody talking animatedly about a show I watched the night before (perhaps by overhearing them at the water cooler) I might feel motivated to offer a comment and join the conversation even if I don't know the speaker. If I become aware of somebody liking a sports team I like in a hostile environment (e.g., by seeing that they are wearing a jersey with the team's insignia), I might be motivated to make a connection, have a beer with them to continue talking about our shared passion. Individuals may or may not act on these spontaneous motivations for connection and potential collaboration, but new possibilities for social interaction suddenly emerge.

Group awareness

The types of chance encounters described earlier are much rarer in online environments (especially when there are no preestablished relationships or relationship contexts such as the Whole Earth community was for the WELL). Group awareness in traditional online courses often has to be part of either the curriculum or consciously designed constraints within the shared ecology of the course. Kreijns and colleagues (2002) suggest development of specific tools that promote tapping into natural inclinations toward sociability with those with whom we share relevant commonalities. They offer as an example of this type of tool a (proposed) *group awareness* widget, or what have more recently been termed Group Awareness Tools. The group awareness widget can be seen as a (bounded) modern version of Licklider and Taylor's OLIVER, using students' own data to make connections with others. The group awareness widget would basically function as a Web crawler, an Internet electronic (ro)bot that is constantly browsing through/examining activities of other members of the community looking for matches with predefined activities and/or perspectives. The group awareness tool can then point users to matches creating logical or conventional constraints for them, creating contexts where they can recognize possibilities of collaborative activity based on shared interests and/or perspectives.

Less complex group awareness tools have been implemented to this point, for the most part letting participants know how much other participants have contributed to the community (Kimmerlee and Cress 2008). These tools seemed to increase participation among students, but the question is at what cost? These are basically public comparison tools. Does surveillance of contribution have a deleterious effect on other components of sociability? This is one place where recognizing the difference between logical constraints and conventional/cultural constraints may be critical. The targeted comparisons made by participation group awareness tools can create constraints on how users view the participation of others but possibly in very different ways for different cultures with different conventions. In highly competitive cultures where individuals equate academic value with keeping up with or surpassing members of their cohort (e.g., elite colleges) it might constrain participation in ways that increase user collaborations with other highly competitive members of their shared, online community. In cultures where individuals are more circumspect and/or careful about their contributions it might actually constrain participants to make fewer connections or even take marginal positions within the network. This might be especially difficult in communities where participants are from different socioeconomic/cultural/educational backgrounds.

Cognitive group awareness and social group awareness

Jannsen and Bodemer (2013) break down group awareness into two categories – (1) cognitive group awareness where individuals have a good idea about the knowledge level of the other participants in their community and (2) social group awareness where participants know how much others are engaged with and contributing to the community – similar to the Kreijns et al. widget where participants are aware of each other's activities and online status (it can also be more broadly defined as the social status of other members of the group). Jannsen and Bodemer consider both types of group awareness to be important – while cognitive awareness leads to greater coordination in content space, social awareness leads to greater coordination in social space (the networks norms, values, beliefs, and ideas of the shared online space). They also suggest the two types of group awareness can, if used in the right way, complement each other in fostering online collaboration.

Group awareness tools are representative of both the potentials and the dangers of designing tools specifically for sociability. Information search engines were one of the turning points in the emergence of the Internet/Web as a major force in the information age – group awareness tools might take the next step in shifting the focus of connections from user to information to user to user, much as Licklider and Taylor prophesized – an idea the ubiquitous computing group at the Palo Alto Research Center considered the next step in human relationships with computer technologies (Weiser et al. 1999). But group awareness tools also run the danger of limiting collaborative human thinking rather than extending it. Would group awareness tools drive same to same, reinforcing users' thinking rather than challenging it? Is the purpose of collaboration simply to accomplish a task with others, or to use the new-found relationships to recognize new approaches to the task – or the possibilities of new tasks? Group awareness tool researchers are careful to point out that plugging into a group awareness tool is or would be a user's choice. A user gets advanced group information (and makes their information available) only if they want to – and then makes inferences based on the constraints presented by these choices. But even this can be a cultural/conventional constraint. What type of user chooses to plug into these tools and what type does not?

Development of mental models and social space

Group awareness tools present only one category of constraints (or affordances) that can lead to a sound social space creating a strong context for collaborative learning. Kreijns and colleagues (2013) also highlight the importance of individual mental models on learning outcomes. The mental models are developed through increased social interactions – allowing participants to develop internal schemes about whom they are dealing with and why (Walther 1996). Tapping into their own and others' internal schemas about online, collaborative participation helps members of the community to recognize and/or anticipate social interactions of others, increasing social presence (the sense of the other being there) (Tu and McIsaac 2002). Kreijns and colleagues hypothesize that perceived positive movement toward learning goals by members of the online community can reinforce social interaction among participants. This perceived movement seems at least partially dependent on positive mental models of community activity. The increased social interaction then works toward development of social space in a type of virtuous cycle: If participants think other members of the community see the community as successful, they are more likely to interact in the service of goals, increasing perceptions of success.

Social space as a set of social interrelationships

Kreijns and colleagues (2013) offer a framework for systematic research into computer-supported collaborative learning that is basically a set of interrelationships between social constraints, sociability, social presence, and social interaction. At the heart of these relationships is the idea that socially developed constraints influence sociability. This has ties to both Preece's argument about purposeful design (constraints) for sociability as well as arguments made by Vygotsky and other sociocultural theorists who followed: The social community acts to create (seemingly) productive constraints on human thinking, which naturally leads to sociability among social group members and potential members. The more participants perceive their community as successful the more they are willing to do to sustain it. Some aspects of the Kreijns et al. model are also reminiscent of Stephen Downes's utilitarian perspective (2010) of online education: Mental models and positive movement foster further social interactions, suggesting that individuals will remain involved with and help sustain the community as long as they perceive they are getting something important from it.

The Kreijns and colleagues model is probably the most advanced and comprehensive to date for exploring the development of sociability within a designed, online context. But it also raises important questions that stretch across discussions of social engagement. Is the desire and the willingness to make connections based on a desire to form communities, to establish ongoing relationships where problem solving is based in shared interest (as, for instance, Howard Rheingold suggests)? Or do our social interactions have a utilitarian foundation, based in attempts to engage the group to meet individual needs, and when users perceive the community is no longer meeting that need they drop out from it, perhaps to find another community, or to use the newly developed abilities to pursue individual goals (e.g., become a better and/or more employable engineer)?

Nurturing social presence: what role the teacher?

The previous chapter discussed Salmon's five stages of online learning. Although the overall goal of Salmon's five stages is to increase user agency, the middle three stages focus primarily on increasing social engagement to meet that goal. Salmon does not concern herself much with design, suggesting that online teaching platforms are more or less vessels that contain user activities. The driving force in increasing social engagement in online environments is productive activities, or e-tivities, as facilitated by an e-moderator, that open up users to recognizing possibilities in relationships. Salmon and her colleagues (2010) used the virtual world/ecological setting platform Second Life as an illustration for developing students' online learning capabilities through step-by-step processes. E-moderators first helped students to gain access to the evolving Second Life community through the creation of avatars – virtual projections that can move through the online world. The e-moderators then developed online activities for those avatars to help students create an identity, to feel as if they are inhabiting their Second Life projections as extensions of themselves. The e-moderators then moved from agency-based to social-based activities where the avatars traversed their virtual ecological settings much like their human counterparts might traverse their everyday worlds, meeting and communicating with other students/avatars as they begin to acclimate to living in an immersive, virtual social environment – in a sense learning to breathe online. Salmon and her colleagues relate a telling anecdote where one of the students became fearful because another person offered to transport her avatar to another virtual realm. On one level of course teachers don't want students to be afraid of their online learning ecologies, but on another level the incident suggests a growing recognition on the part of the student of the social presence of others in the shared, virtual community. The social projection of the other was actually capable of instilling fear that traveled from the virtual to the real self and back again – all this accomplished through the careful guidance of the moderators.

Social presence

What is social presence? Many researchers/theorists of online social engagement break down the components of sociability in different ways (or consider sociability itself a component); one of the most commonly used components is social presence, a subcategory of communication theory (Richardson and Swan 2003). The concept of social presence originates in work done on telephone communications by the Communications Study Group at the University College in London. Short and colleagues (1976) wrote a seminal book in which they defined social presence as communicators experiencing the other(s) in their communication scenarios who had the quality of "being there." The "salience" of the interpersonal communications is dependent on the "salience of the other" in that communication (p. 65). When humans are in face-to-face communications that salience is easily observable (and it can be disconcerting when it is not there). But communication occurs in so many different ways beyond verbal and written text (e.g., small gestures, facial expressions, body language, the use of secondary artifacts in the surrounding environment) that it is difficult to have a really strong sense of the other(s) involved in the interactions when face-to-face information is not available, especially when affective/emotional aspects are critical to understanding (which is often).

Before the Internet it was believed that physical distance necessarily reduced an individual's sense of belonging to a community and abilities of individuals to project their personalities out to create the combined sense of immediacy and intimacy that lies at the heart of social presence (Arrogan 2003). Daft and Lengel (1986), for instance, suggest that lack of nonverbal cues in telephone conversations results in short, straightforward communications; these types of command and control interactions do little to foster any sense of community among participants, or any sense of social presence between participants. Licklider and Taylor (1968) did not worry much about the issue of social presence (suggesting it is interest and relevance of the projects that draws the community together), but their suggestion that computer conferencing is a combination of face-to-face conferencing and telephone conferencing does seem to make it reasonable to extend the concept of social presence to computer communications.

Charlotte Gunawardena (1995) along with colleagues (Gunawardena and Zittle, 1997) were among the first to directly introduce social presence as a topic in (educational) computer conferencing. Their research suggests high correlations between learners' perceptions of social presence and their satisfaction with the course using computer teleconferencing (findings were based on Gunawardena's own social presence scale along with students' reported satisfaction with the course), suggesting that computer teleconferencing can offer unique capabilities for increasing social presence in non–face-to-face interactions in spite of lack of traditional immediacy variables in social interactions. Given enough time people would learn to compensate for the lack of nonverbal cues, or more likely social presence could actually "be cultured" among teleconferencing participants (by moderators/facilitators).

Social presence in the community of inquiry

In defining social presence in the Community of Inquiry framework Rourke and colleagues (2007) suggest it is dependent on the abilities of members of an online learning group to move beyond command and control communications (e.g., direct transmission of information, expectations, and requirements). It is important to offer affect-laden responses to inquiries and especially more personalized introjections that express emotions and feelings – the types of interactions that help nurture the humanness of the online, interactive space. Teachers/facilitators are able to foster and sustain more personalized communication contexts by using language that focuses on purposefully enhancing social interactions as opposed to simply conveying specific information. Some of the ways teachers might enhance social interactions is by promoting interactive responses that show support and encouragement for strong/relevant/interesting posts (e.g., participants responding to original posters with comments such as "great post" and "hey, that really made me think"). One difficulty with this strategy, though, is these types of directed-affect based responses can be highly dependent on the types of platform(s) being used – it is relatively easy for teachers and students to make targeted encouraging remarks meaningful to posters on blogs with a dedicated comments section, but much more difficult in threaded discussions because they move so quickly and it is difficult to make direct, sequential responses to contributions, or wikis where the focus is on editing and change rather than community.

Tu and McIsaac (2002), for instance, found that students often become frustrated with threaded discussions – they want to know whom they are talking to at any given (online) moment and why. The farther an encouraging response gets away from a contribution, the greater potential for its affective power dissipating and the communication becoming depersonalized. As discussed in later chapters, wikis are rarely successful in establishing an ongoing learning community in spite of their obvious benefits for collaboration.

Teachers/facilitators in online education can also enhance a nurturing social presence online atmosphere by encouraging participants to call out other participants by name when they respond to a post or a comment (one of the reasons so many posts and responding comments start with salutations such as "Hi Michael" and posters sign their names at the end). The communication is as much about the person writing the new contribution to the discussion as it is about any information that might be contained within it – virtual "shout outs" and salutations help community members recognize that the poster's text has ties back to their real-world presence. Teachers can also improve the online atmosphere by establishing the use of inclusive pronouns such as "we" and "us," suggesting greater possibilities for nonhierarchical relationships and shared ownership of the learning space among participants. The idea that there are no authoritative voices can be critical to sustaining a community (Rovai 2002).

Teacher immediacy, internet ecologies, and social presence

Some research suggests that interlocutors might be able to create a context for social presence rather than simple information transfer by cracking jokes and engaging in jovial back and forth with students (Rourke et al. 2007). This type of behavior has been referred to as teacher immediacy when it occurs in traditional educational contexts (based on Meribhian's concept of immediacy, 1977). Initially teacher immediacy was conceptualized in place-based classroom interactions and communicated primarily through nonverbal cues such as body language, smiling, and making eye contact (Andersen 1979), as a way of inviting students into more sociable communication patterns. Teachers use more relaxed communication styles to break down traditional barriers between the front of the classroom and the back of the classroom. For the most part these nonverbal cues are unavailable in online communications (it remains to be seen if Internet-derived replacements for nonverbal cues such as emoticons or emojis can compensate). Perhaps more applicable to Internet-based contexts, some research has been shown that verbal/text-based tools, especially humor, can be a powerful device in establishing teacher immediacy (Gorham 1988). The use of humor and good-natured repartee, though, can be something of an emotional minefield in online communications.

The balance between developing online contexts for increased social presence and transferring information in Internet-infused education will most likely be an important topic going forward. The time and energy that the teacher devotes to developing learning atmospheres that might lead to greater social presence among participants may mean less time for other teaching/learning tasks. Establishing immediacy through humor, for instance, can demand more time and attention online, especially if there are limited or no nonverbal cues to set the context; the teacher needs to be much more careful about miscommunication and misinterpretation. The promotion of affect-laden encouraging commentary such as "great post" and "thanks for making me think" may help establish social connections between students but often does little to drive substantive discussion of the topic forward and can even be frustrating for the instructor (how do teachers establish a balance between substantive and community-building posts?). For instance, arguments have been made that the Community of Inquiry framework by promoting social presence (sometimes through teacher presence) does not place enough of an emphasis on the types of cognitive presence activities that would lead to deep learning (e.g., students' abilities to integrate knowledge streams and bring problems to resolution).

Rourke and Kanuka (2009) suggest increasing cognitive presence by emphasizing three processes: assessment, reducing content of courses, and confronting misconceptions of students. Both assessment of students and confronting student misconceptions, however, can easily detract from the types of online atmospheres that nurture increased social presence, especially if done in a heavy-handed manner or through misapplication of teacher immediacy tools such as humor. Continuous assessment beyond simply measuring participation changes the role of the teacher and instructors' relationships with students. It is difficult to move from cracking jokes and engaging in off-topic banter with students to collecting evidence of student learning to inform their work and provide feedback (it is easy to see the benefits in the abstract, but in practice assessment protocols can be depersonalizing for the student, extraordinarily time consuming for the teacher, or both). It is also the case that teacher assessments are often formal, administrative educational acts – but it has been shown that informality is one of the qualities that decreases psychological distance (Tu and McIsaac 2002). As well, some teachers are able to strike this balance offline, but for reasons already mentioned and some not, it might be much more difficult to move back and forth between teacher immediacy activities and teacher assessment activities online.

Activities in which teachers or peers confront student misconceptions seem to work against positive emotional, affective interactions as well (or, worse, can lead to the types of emotional interactions that break a community apart). Students might be open to staying part of a learning community out of long-term trust in the other members and/or a willingness to put community above the self – but these are the types of interconnective qualities usually built over time. Students engaged in cooperative writing tasks using wiki technologies, for instance, have difficulties even editing each other's work. Blogs or even threaded discussions can quickly devolve into flame wars based on a single comment: If there is no underlying social structure to help quickly bring the community back to a positive trajectory, that impact on the community can be devastating or even fatal. Few opportunities are given for tapping into trust/community-building processes in quickly formed, modular classes (e.g., semester driven, assembled based on predetermined curricula necessities). The members of the WELL, for instance, were able to survive even major confrontations between community members because they had built up their community over many years, through generations of conferences and offline office parties.

Methodological issues in studying social presence

One of the difficulties in trying to understand, let alone capture, the phenomenon (or phenomena) of social engagement in online learning communities is methodological issues in attempting to define and/or study levels of social presence. Studying social presence in an online educational initiative can be extremely time intensive, large differences can exist based on topics, and level of discourse and/or size of the class studied come into play, as well as a plethora of individual differences among students and teachers. Development of social presence in a graduate psychology class may have very different characteristics and may need to be understood and measured in different ways, than social presence in a large, undergraduate mathematics class (indeed, they may be representative of diverse phenomena). This is aside from the complexity of assessing social presence as a reified, measurable entity. Gunawardena (1995) developed a short and very simple self-report survey for social presence, but the items seem more applicable to general communication research than to online education. Kim (2011) has developed a more intricate scale for social presence specifically designed for online educational contexts. The scale breaks down social presence into four major factors, including affective connectedness (related to intimacy and psychological distance), sense of community (e.g., willingness to work with others to complete tasks), open communication (willingness to openly exchange ideas), and mutual attention and support (e.g., empathy, interdependent support). Social presence, however, is a nuanced, hard-to-define concept – one difficult to completely capture in any general survey tool. For instance, as well designed as Kim's survey is, it really does not deal with sense of immediacy, one of the most important components in many researchers' conception of social presence. Rourke and colleagues (2007) developed a complex content analysis coding scheme for social presence that breaks down individual postings according to affective responses, interactive responses, and cohesive responses, but this seems most appropriate for smaller communities with high levels of social interaction (e.g., the graduate-level psychology class).

The classroom community

Alfred Rovai, one of the earliest voices in online education, focuses more on creating community as a whole than the specific components of an engaged community such as social presence or even sociability. Rovai (2002) takes a social constructivist approach to classroom community building that incorporates some aspects of the process-oriented human development perspective of sociability into more immediate measurable aspects of online social relationships, a view of community that mirrors Preece's components of sociability – purpose, people, and policy – but also reflects Salmon's e-moderator-driven model in that community is seen more as emerging out of facilitated online activities than general design in service of developing an advanced social space.

Rovai (2002) is careful to point out the obvious – that communities differ, defined by what people do together, and that classroom communities are of a specific type. He suggests various qualities that help define an evolving community, among them spirit – feelings of friendship and cohesion (really not that different from traditional conceptions of "school spirit"); trust – where participants believe other members of the group are at least intending to post credible information and there is a desire to assist others in understanding, similar to the mental models approach discussed earlier; interactivity – both task-oriented and affect-oriented (but where quality of interactions is more important than quantity for both); and common expectations – where members of a community see a common purpose to their activities (tying back to the human development conception of sociability).

Rovai posits seven positive correlates for establishing sense of community in an online course. These include the self-explanatory *small group activities* and the already discussed *social presence*; but they also include the following:

Transactional distance – Similar to the idea of teacher immediacy, the idea is that the smaller the psychological distance between learners and instructors, the greater the sense of community. But Roval (Rovai and Jordan 2004) also suggests grading/assessment as being important to online learning scenarios, which can increase distance between teacher and student, assessee and assessor (although for Rovai assessment is primarily for motivational purposes). The challenge is how to limit distance when community participants know they are (eventually) going to be assessed, and they know this assessment is going to be done by the online instructor(s).

Group facilitation – The instructor or some other member of the community acts as encourager, harmonizer, compromiser, and gatekeeper. Many educational models merge the roles of instructor and facilitator (suggesting a single person find some type of balance between the two), but no reason exists they have to be the same person(s). Especially in online courses, it might be worth experimenting with how these roles develop in Internet-based education as the community evolves – as suggested by the Community of Inquiry model.

Alignment between teaching and learning styles – This idea is important for educational initiatives in general, but it is especially salient for online education scenarios where students often don't have the buffer of other students to help negotiate real or perceived differences with course instructor(s) and/or the larger educational context (e.g., discussing difficulties with other students after class to gauge their reactions/understanding, joining study groups). Misalignment can also create complications for teachers of online courses who are attempting to teach diverse, highly distributed student populations. For instance, there may be important differences between students from high-context cultures that are more dependent on nonverbal and other contextual cues in interpreting information and students from low-context cultures who are less dependent on nonverbal and indirect cues (Hall and Hall 1990). Majority cultures tend to be low context, direct and assertive, whereas minority cultures may need greater context for making determinations about what is important and what they should focus on within particular course contexts. This can lead to difficulties in online environments where so much course context is based primarily on limited, static information sources such as posted text/notes, lecture capture videos, and assignments. Greater possibilities may be identified for miscommunication and misinterpretation between teachers and students, leading to even higher levels of alienation of marginalized students than in more traditional classes. The amount of context needed for understanding might also be historical-situational. A participant from a majority culture who has attended privileged institutions is more likely to be low context in an online ecology originating at Harvard or Stanford than an individual from a minority or distant culture who has little history with these types of institutions. Put the same two students in learning contexts that reflect the "other students'" culture(s) such as understanding whether a water supply is potable or navigating a violent neighborhood, and the need for higher levels of context for understanding and learning may be reversed.

Social equality – The emerging online community should be as nonhierarchical as possible with diminishing use of an authoritative voice by teacher/facilitator/moderator or other students. This may be one of the least appreciated but important elements in developing online educational communities, especially those that include distributed/heterogeneous members. Social equality is critical for compensating for other factors such as transactional distance and misalignment between teaching and learning styles.

Community size – Too small of a group is potentially limiting for consequential interactions, whereas too large a group might be overwhelming for participants. Research suggests that online educational communities function better when they reach a critical mass (Glassman et al. 2013; Walther 1996), but this is probably at least partially dependent on teacher and student expectations for participant activity in the course and individual issues such as students' Internet self-efficacy. More problematic is the upper limit for online learning communities. Rovai (2002) suggests that the upper limit on enrolment for optimum development of classroom community should be around thirty. Again this is situational and perhaps speaks to issues of facilitation rather than instruction (if the two can be separated). It might be possible, for instance, to break larger populations down into subgroups that communicate and augment each other's thinking as open resource pools guided by local facilitators contextualizing discussions and examining the same problem or problem sets from different perspectives based on immediate ecologies (e.g., Karno and Glassman 2013).

Scripting students for online community processes

Is it possible to influence students' perceptions and thinking about online activities, guiding them toward a more community/collaborative orientation? Can teachers/facilitators actually nurture individual schemas for online collaboration that lead to successful participant engagement? Script theory (Fischer et al. 2013) suggests that humans develop internalized patterns of activity that help us process and understand diffuse and at times overwhelming information, helping us to efficiently navigate the surrounding world. It is impossible to quickly process information every time we encounter a new situation – the complexity and enormity of the task would very quickly paralyze behavior. Humans then use a combination of experience and social cues to develop frameworks that allow for quick organization of information into workable schemes that can be easily followed (Neisser 1967). Internet education, as a new arena of activity for many students, seems especially fertile ground for the development and use of specific scripts that might guide and enhance learning processes. If users are unable to quickly organize and differentiate information, they can easily become frustrated or lost.

Fischer and colleagues (2013) suggest the development of two types of scripts in collaborative, online learning environments: internal scripts and external scripts. Highly flexible *internal scripts* help students entering into online collaborative activities to recognize what other members of the community are trying to accomplish (the play), lead them to try and access knowledge that is relevant to the task/discussion (the scene), and understand their particular part in the shared educational process (the role). The ability to understand role(s) in online learning communities is especially important when considering the different characteristics that many approaches to online social engagement/social presence look for from engaged community members (e.g., Community of Inquiry, Classroom Community). Sometimes a participant will need to be a leader in problem solving, sometimes they will need to be an encourager, sometimes they will need to be active group participants, and sometimes they will need to step back and decode available contextual cues, perhaps becoming an interpreter or short-term facilitator. *External scripts* are developed through course design, inhibiting or extending participants' scope of activity by integrating targeted constraints into the evolving shared cyberspace. This is perhaps one of the more intriguing methods for balancing community and social presence with topic instruction and/or targeted problem solving.

It should not be forgotten, however, that many times students (and teachers) bring their own scripts for online activities to nascent learning communities – scripts that they develop through activities separate from formal education using applications such as social network systems and short messaging services. These applications are often far more important to the students' everyday lives than any traditional education activities. One of the important questions for Internet-infused education is how much teachers and designers should integrate these existing scripts into course expectations and how much they should attempt to override them by establishing new education-centered schemes (e.g., should educational scripts be taken from Facebook activities, or should instructors/course designers attempt to establish scripts that are completely separate everyday online spaces so that the two don't become confused in students' activities?).

A more overt sociocultural approach to the development of online community

Most of the research discussed in this chapter focuses on developing Internet-infused education that reflects many of the time and topic constraints of traditional education settings. But it is difficult to specify any reason that online learning communities have to follow predetermined guidelines. The most socially engaged online communities evolve over time, adapting to multiple challenges. Is this a possible trajectory for the development of socially sanctioned, formal online learning communities? In their discussion of the Math Forum, Renninger and Shumar (2002; Renninger et al. 2004) suggest a model that taps into participants' inclinations to join with a meaningful learning community that supports and challenges its participants. The Math Forum (mathforum.org) is not about development of short-term classroom experiences, but it can offer a different type of lesson about online education–based communities. The Math Forum was started as the Geometry Forum in 1992 by an egalitarian band of educators at a small college. Little pressure was placed to develop a scalable or profit-making model of online education from their work. The original site was developed in the context of Dewey's ideas on democratic education (1916), and this philosophical base is still obvious more than two decades later. The Math Forum does not attempt to reify social interactions by creating forms, rules, or lists that participants are expected to adhere to. It includes various resource centers for participants, including *Ask Dr. Math* where students and teachers can ask questions about how to solve mathematics problems, a *Problem of the Week*, an interactive *Teacher2Teacher* forum where mathematics teachers can engage each other sharing materials and approaches, and an archive of participant contributions (e.g., lessons plans, past contributions). The *Ask Dr. Math* resource is the most used by students, but teachers also interact with the site both as facilitators and as learners. Interactivity is essential, but it is dynamic and based on the participants' relationship to the larger community and the way(s) the community meets their needs, with each potential participant being met where they are. Participants log on for different reasons, with different goals, and different perspectives on how the resources could be used, and then they form relationships based on interactions that are relevant to their needs.

About a third of visitors to Math Forum become what the authors refer to as "sticky" traffic, returning to the site again and again, their relationships to and understanding of the site changing over time. Those looking to become core members of the Math Forum go through a process of mentoring/tenuring (e.g., responding to questions with provocative, leading questions rather than specific answers that bring the inquiry to a conclusion). It is a variation of the trusted user systems developed by Open Source communities or the conference/moderator systems established by virtual communities such as the WELL – a cadre of committed users looking to sustain and expand the reach and capabilities of the community through asynchronous but community-oriented communications. Initial motivations for logging in/joining the community may be utilitarian, but at least some individuals recognize value in sustaining the community, both for themselves and for others.

The dynamic approach to community outlined by Renninger and Shumar opens up important questions for the relationship between social engagement and the development of educational communities. To this point most of the initiatives in online education, even those that see community and social engagement as primary, have focused on re-creating the general structure of the traditional, encapsulated course, where a group of students come together with an instructor/facilitator(s) for a defined period of time to achieve specific educational goals. The communities are necessarily transient and focused on particular end points (students should have appropriated a specific set of skills by a preset time point when the community itself will disappear) and predetermined assessments of success. Development of courses with high levels of social presence/sociability is dependent on finding the right design, curricula, media, and/or scripts for creating community within this specialized context – and we still don't know if this is possible. But there is really no reason that online education needs to work this way. Whether Dewey, or Vygotsky, or more modern conceptions such as limited peripheral participation or apprenticeships, compelling education models exist where individuals learn by being active participants in ongoing communities; interweaving relationships are built up over time and individuals know they can return when the need arises (WELL was not just an acronym – many members logged on to draw on social and intellectual sustenance; Rheingold 1993). Learners can come into these ongoing communities and leave them as they see fit, with a chance of becoming part of what Renninger and Shumar refer to as sticky traffic, part of the (trusted user) core of the community. Perhaps learners are able to change themselves and the community through their activities, perhaps they find little or no fit with the community and move on.

One of the reasons we moved to defined educational contexts such as walled classrooms, stand-alone schools, and separated subject periods/classes was because it was efficient and using a more community-oriented model can be cumbersome. The Internet offers the opportunity to change these equations, to bring a broader, more humanistic conception of sociability into an ongoing vision of education.

References

Andersen, J. F. (1979). *The Relationship between Teacher Immediacy and Teaching Effectiveness* (Doctoral dissertation, ProQuest Information & Learning).

Aragon, S. R. (2003). Creating Social Presence in Online Environments. *New Directions for Adult and Continuing Education*, 100, 57–68.

Bateson, G. (1967). Cybernetic Explanation. *American Behavioral Scientist*, 10, 29–29.

Daft, R. L., and Lengel, R. H. (1986). Organizational Information Requirements, Media Richness and Structural Design. *Management Science*, 32(5), 554–571.

Darwin, C. (1871). *The Descent of Man, and Selection in Relation to Sex*. London: John Murray.

Dewey, J. (1916). *Democracy and Education*. New York: McMillan & Co.

Downes, S. (2010). Connectivism and Transculturality. Talk delivered to Telefónica Foundation, Buenos Aires, Argentina. Posted on *Stephen's Web*, May 16. www.downes.ca/post/53297.

Fischer, F., Kollar, I., Stegmann, K., and Wecker, C. (2013). Toward a Script Theory of Guidance in Computer-Supported Collaborative Learning. *Educational Psychologist*, 48(1), 56–66.

Freire, P. (1970). *Pedagogy of the Oppressed*. New York: Continuum Press.

Gaver, W. W. (1996). Situating Action II: Affordances for Interaction: The Social Is Material for Design. *Ecological Psychology*, 8(2), 111–129.

Gibson, J. J. (1977). *The Theory of Affordances*. In R. Shaw, J. Bransford (eds.) *Perceiving, Acting and Knowing: Toward an Ecological Psychology*. Hillsdale, NJ: Lawrence Erlbaum Publishers.

Glassman, M. (2000). Mutual Aid Theory and Human Development: Sociability as Primary. *Journal for the Theory of Social Behaviour*, 30(4), 391–412.

Glassman, M., Bartholomew, M., and Hur, E. H. (2013). The Importance of the Second Loop in Educational Technology: An Action Science Study of Introducing Blogging in a Course Curriculum. *Action Research*, 11, 337–353.

Gorham, J. (1988). The Relationship between Verbal Teacher Immediacy Behaviors and Student Learning. *Communication Education*, 37(1), 40–53.

Griffin, P., and Cole, M. (1984). Current Activity for the Future: The Zo-ped. *New Directions for Child and Adolescent Development*, 23, 45–64.

Gunawardena, C. N. (1995). Social Presence Theory and Implications for Interaction and Collaborative Learning in Computer Conferences. *International Journal of Educational Telecommunications*, 1(2), 147–166.

Gunawardena, C. N., and Zittle, F. J. (1997). Social Presence as a Predictor of Satisfaction within a Computer-Mediated Conferencing Environment. *American Journal of Distance Education*, 11(3), 8–26.

Hall, E. T., and Hall, M. R. (1990). *Understanding Cultural Differences*. Yarmouth, ME: Intercultural Press.

Janssen, J., and Bodemer, D. (2013). Coordinated Computer-Supported Collaborative Learning: Awareness and Awareness Tools. *Educational Psychologist*, 48(1), 40–55.

Karno, D., and Glassman, M. (2013). Science as a Web of Trails: Redesigning Science Education with the Tools of the Present to Meet the Needs of the Future. *Journal of Science Education and Technology*, 22(6), 927–933.

Kim, J. (2011). Developing an Instrument to Measure Social Presence in Distance Higher Education. *British Journal of Educational Technology*, 42(5), 763–777.

Kimmerle, J., and Cress, U. (2008). Group Awareness and Self-presentation in Computer-Supported Information Exchange. *International Journal of Computer-Supported Collaborative Learning*, 3(1), 85–97.

Kreijns, K., Kirschner, P. A., and Jochems, W. (2002). The Sociability of Computer-Supported Collaborative Learning Environments. *Educational Technology & Society*, 5(1), 8–22.

Kreijns, K., Kirschner, P. A., and Vermeulen, M. (2013). Social Aspects of CSCL Environments: A Research Framework. *Educational Psychologist*, 48(4), 229–242.

Lave, J., and Wenger, E. (1991). *Situated Learning: Legitimate Peripheral Participation*. Cambridge: Cambridge University Press.

Licklider, J. C., and Taylor, R. W. (1968). The Computer as a Communication Device. *Science and Technology*, 76(2), 1–3.

Mehrabian, A. (1977). *Nonverbal Communication*. Piscataway, NJ: Aldine Transaction Publishers.

Neisser, U. (1967/2014). *Cognitive Psychology*. New York: Psychology Press.

Norman, D. A. (1988). *The Psychology of Everyday Things*. New York: Basic Books.

Norman, D. A. (1999). Affordance, Conventions, and Design. *Interactions*, 6(3), 38–43.

Preece, J. (2000). *Online Communities: Designing Usability and Supporting Socialbilty*. New York: John Wiley & Sons.

Preece, J. (2001). Sociability and Usability in Online Communities: Determining and Measuring Success. *Behaviour & Information Technology*, 20(5), 347–356.

Renninger, K. A., and Shumar, W. (2002). Community Building with and for Teachers at the Math Forum. In K. Renninger and W. Shumar (eds). *Building Virtual Communities: Learning and Change in Cyberspace*, Cambridge: Cambridge University Press, 60–95.

Renninger, K. A., Shumar, W., Barab, S., Kling, R., and Gray, J. (2004). The Centrality of Culture and Community to Participant Learning at and with the Math Forum. In K. Renninger and W. Shumar (eds). *Building Virtual Communities: Learning and Change in Cyberspace*. Cambridge: Cambridge University Press. 60–95.

Rheingold, H. (1993). *The Virtual Community: Homesteading on the Electronic Frontier*. Cambridge, MA: MIT Press.

 (1996). A Slice of My Life in My Virtual Community. In P. Ludlow and M. Goodman (eds.) *High Noon on the Electronic Frontier: Conceptual Issues in Cyberspace*. Cambridge, MA: MIT Press. 413–436.

Richardson, J. C., and Swan, K. (2003). Examining Social Presence in Online Courses in Relation to Students' Perceived Learning and Satisfaction. *Journal of Asynchronous Learning Networks*, 7, 68–84.

Rogoff, B. (1994). Developing Understanding of the Idea of Communities of Learners. *Mind, Culture, and Activity*, 1(4), 209–229.

Rourke, L., Anderson, T., Garrison, D. R., and Archer, W. (2007). Assessing Social Presence in Asynchronous Text-Based Computer Conferencing. *International Journal of E-Learning & Distance Education*, 14(2), 50–71.

Rourke, L., and Kanuka, H. (2009). Learning in Communities of Inquiry: A Review of the Literature. *International Journal of E-Learning & Distance Education*, 23(1), 19–48.

Rovai, A. P. (2002). Building Sense of Community at a Distance. *International Review of Research in Open and Distance Learning*, 3(1), 1–16.

Rovai, A. P., and Jordan, H. (2004). Blended Learning and Sense of Community: A Comparative Analysis with Traditional and Fully Online Graduate Courses. *International Review of Research in Open and Distance Learning*, 5(2), 1–13.

Salmon, G. (2004). *E-moderating: The Key to Teaching and Learning Online*. New York: Routledge.

Salmon, G., Nie, M., and Edirisingha, P. (2010). Developing a Five-Stage Model of Learning in Second Life. *Educational Research*, 52(2), 169–182.

Short, J., Williams, E., and Christie, B. (1976). *The Social Psychology of Telecommunications*. Hoboken, NJ: John Wiley and Sons.

Tu, C. H., and McIsaac, M. (2002). The Relationship of Social Presence and Interaction in Online Classes. *American Journal of Distance Education*, 16(3), 131–150.

Vygotsky, L. S. (1978). *Mind in Society*. Cambridge, MA: Harvard University Press.

Vygotsky, L. S., Rieber, R. W., and Carton, A. S. (1987). *The Collected Works of LS Vygotsky. Vol. 1, Problems of General Psychology Including the Volume Thinking and Speech*. New York: Plenum Press.

Walther, J. B. (1996). Computer-Mediated Communication Impersonal, Interpersonal, and Hyperpersonal Interaction. *Communication Research*, 23(1), 3–43.

Weiser, M., Gold, R., and Brown, J. S. (1999). The Origins of Ubiquitous Computing Research at PARC in the Late 1980s. *IBM Systems Journal*, 38(4), 693–696.

6 The relationship between space and place in internet-infused education

The relationship between the new information/knowledge–building spaces created through the Internet and traditional, place-based learning environments may be one of the most understudied topics in Internet-infused education. It is a relationship with important implications for the topics of each of the chapters that follow this one: hybrid/blended learning environments – especially the idea of augmented reality; open educational resources – especially the relationships between universal learning objects and local use; massive open online courses/scaled online learning environments – especially their meaning and impact in bringing large, distributed populations of learners into a single, online learning environment; and the development of open educational infrastructures. How we deal with the evolving relationship of this emerging cyberspace/place-based dynamic may be one of the defining issues for education and perhaps community and society in the twenty-first century. This chapter will necessarily be more abstract and speculative than the other chapters because so little research or even theorizing on this relationship in educational contexts has taken place.

An obvious question is if the relationship between augmentative/community space created and maintained through Internet activity and traditional educational places is so important, why has so little research/theorizing been done on the idea? One reason might be that it is extremely difficult to conceptualize let alone study the relationship between Internet spaces and the places occupied by Internet users in any systematic way. The actual concept of individuals creating integrated space/place systems by criss-crossing easily recognizable boundaries (e.g., Qwerty keyboard, LCD screen) between the two has a history that predates the web and popularization of the Internet. The science fiction writer William Gibson was one of the earliest to define the coming information age relationship between everyday place and virtual space. He coined the term *cyberspace* in his 1984 novel *Neuromancer*, describing it as a "consensual hallucination" where individuals are able to leave their physical, mundane, restricted (by geography, time, cultural rule systems) lives and engage in new types of online activities with trajectories that expand out beyond our imaginations – a virtual world reachable through electronic technologies, creating new tensions in human existence as place and cyberspace challenge each other in veracity and importance. Gibson's ideas foreshadowed the difficult transactional relationships that needed to be explored together and apart – an idea that does not fit easily into many views in philosophy, psychology, and/or education.

Space and place in a virtual community: the WELL

Two important early examples stand out of the relationship between the new spaces of thinking and community created by the Internet and the continued role of place in our lives – and how difficult it is to disentangle them, especially in educational initiatives. The first goes back to an early conception of the *virtual community*, a term suggested by Howard Rheingold (1993) (like Ted Nelson, Rheingold is something of a poet laureate of the early "*nethead*" culture). One of Rheingold's most important experiences – one that informed his early view of viable Internet-based communities – was as a member of the Whole Earth 'Lectronic Link community, known as the WELL. As reviewed earlier in this book, the WELL was originally a dial-up bulletin board system (using a Unix-to-Unix copy program/conference system that later expanded to include possibilities offered by the invention of the Web). The WELL (Hafner 1997) was based in nascent computer conferencing technology with members of the larger community coming together creating targeted, topic-driven swarm intelligence discussion forums; members came together around different interests, some extremely important and some trivial, but all transient (there was no coherent site project/narrative and only minimal governance).

It was not the technology that made the WELL important (in many ways the conferencing system was rudimentary and the original programmers had little concern for user-friendly applications) – but the way(s) in which it was used and the ways those uses evolved over time. When the physician, technologist, and entrepreneur Larry Brilliant first approached Stuart Brand – the founder of the *Whole Earth Catalog*-with his Unix-based computer conferencing technology it was with the idea of using the Whole Earth community as a test population for exploring the viability of online communication using computer conferencing technology (as suggested by Licklider and Taylor 1968). The *Whole Earth Catalog* was an eclectic, counterculture magazine that focused primarily on reviews of tools in the broadest possible sense – not only information-based tools (books and maps) but also tools individuals could use to experiment with their own vision of the world (the *Whole Earth Catalog* was an early proponent of the Do-It-Yourself movement). The reviews were continuously changing based on reader feedback, always reaching out to connect to new ideas. Steven Jobs would later suggest that the *Whole Earth Catalog* was a pre-Web version of Google – a search engine in hard copy. The catalog also had strong connections to the development of cybernetics as a field of inquiry, publishing works of early pioneers such as Norbert Wiener and Gregory Bateson. Brand published his own pamphlet on the subject of cybernetics. The community that supported the development and publication of the catalog (or just enjoyed the intellectual atmosphere) was interconnected (especially locally in northern California), adventurous, and looking to experiment with new tools, including ones that created a new virtual activity space few had previously experienced (Turner 2010).

Steward Brand initially thought it was important to give the discussion forum a definite location, a sense of place to complement the newly developing spaces of information flows (Hafner 1997). Circumstances created an initial abstract sense of place for the community – with most continuing members of the WELL already in the San Francisco area and having connections offline. For instance, some members had ties to the Palo Alto Research Center. People from other parts of the country could dial in to the Bulletin Board System, but they were a minority and never really seemed to become central to the community (Rheingold 1993). This abstract sense of community was not really enough for Brand; he believed a human-corporal aspect to the discussion was needed for any type of meaningful online community to flourish.

The early days of the WELL, which had a number of fits and starts, did not really fit Brand's vision, for the most part based on online communications, primarily moderator-run conferences on different subjects. The WELL did not gain momentum until its members started holding "Office Parties" where the administrators would invite members of the different conferences to a place-based get together at the Whole Earth San

Francisco offices. The place-based lives of users began to merge with and influence online personalities (which were often very different in identity presentation) and vice versa. The bringing of everyday place into the bulletin board/conferencing system seemed to increase both commitment and conflict on the WELL.

Rheingold (1993) describes two important interrelated aspects of the WELL community that highlight the implications of space-place relationships in the development of virtual communities. The first is the importance of individuals' being able to meet and know each other in traditional community places – especially the types of (culturally developed) formal functions that naturally bring members of a community together. Rheingold, for instance, recalls going to weddings of WELL members locally. He believes those who did not engage in local-place-based activities with other members of the WELL (e.g., if they lived too far away) were less likely to develop strong ties into the online community. The second aspect is problem solving that continuously crossed the boundary between place-based activity and space-based activity – much as Gibson suggested in his initial descriptions of cyberspace. In an important example of this type of space-place–integrated problem solving, recounted by multiple members of the WELL, an active member of the community had made a life-changing decision to go traveling for a long period (most WELL members knew her only from her participation in conferences). She signed off from the community and disappeared from their shared cyberspace. It was later found that the former "WELL-Being" had become a Buddhist nun, traveling to India where she became sick with a liver ailment and lay dying more than half a world away. One of the traveler's friends from the WELL found out about her condition and brought the problem to the online community. As Rheingold recounts, there was an immediate short period of intense activity in which members attempted to figure out what the sick traveler needed and how to get it to her. Different members of the community were able to combine online and offline resources in ways not previously considered to get the WELL member a desperately needed medical instrument. Facing an urgent problem the WELL members consulted online and then went into their place-based world to find new information – which they then brought back online in a shared problem-solving context (much as Engelbart and Licklider envisioned), engaging in probably one of the earliest and most prototypical examples of computer-supported collaborative learning. The members of the WELL were able to transform swarm intelligence (the ability to quickly form a community around a problem) into collective agency (becoming a directed, problem-solving community).

Reading the accounts of Rheingold and others on initiated activity it is apparent that the bulletin board/conference system was at its strongest and most meaningful when there were compelling, interactive relationships between the online space that the community members created through their computer conferencing and the traditional place-based activities that were part of the fabric of their everyday, and not so everyday, lives. The spaces of the Internet gave the members of the WELL more of an impact in the world, while the things that happened in the world gave definition and meaning to their online lives.

Space and place in the open source movement: the goal-driven community

A second example of the relationship between space and place is the Linux community – the first of the Open Source programming communities (Raymond 1999). The online Linux community started offline when the Unix operating system shared by most of the computer-using community became proprietary, limiting the abilities of individual users to modify or even use it. Richard Stallman's GNU (standing for "GNU Not Unix" – what might be called a layer acronym) project began distributing (a not very well developed) operating system kernel that could be used in place of the Unix system, offering the nascent program to anybody who wanted to use and/or work on it (originally through traditional, place-based mail systems) – the beginnings of what would become the Free Software Movement and the Free Software Foundation. Linus Torvalds's online development of the GNU/Linux system (he started based on an early copy of GNU operating system kernel he received in the mail) was a reaction not only by him but by many of the users/hackers who responded to his request for comments to the problems that had emerged through the place-based activities of Unix's owners. Some engaged in the knowledge building of operating system development because for economic reasons they needed an affordable operating system. Some engaged for political reasons – they believed that proprietary software is antithetical to the anarchy-driven, do-it-yourself nature of the evolving Internet. Some were just hackers (the term *hacker* is misunderstood; it basically refers to people who enjoy "hacking" things open to see how it works).

As the Linux community grew in cyberspace, the place-based proprietary software community (e.g. Microsoft) also began to change in response, becoming even more protective of their source code and restricting its distribution as much as possible (Glassman 2013). Attempts were made to use the growing tension between Open Source program development and the place-based needs of programmers and software companies to create new models for the programming community. For instance, Larry McVoy, a programmer at Sun Microsystems, wrote a paper suggesting that the company should move away from development of proprietary computer programs, make all source code open, and then redefine the company in terms of support and packaging of software. Sun did not take McVoy's advice, but his ideas suggest dramatic ways in which online space and traditional place can, sometimes does, and almost certainly will impact each other as the Internet makes greater penetration into everyday activities. The ideas underlying McVoy's (1993) early position paper on integrating space-based and place-based activities may have important implications for the use of Open Educational Resources and scalable education initiatives as part of an interconnected educational infrastructure.

There is a darker side to space-place relationships as outlined here in the discussion of Manuel Castells's ideas of growing tension between the spaces of information flows and the spaces of place. There are possibilities for those who control the flow of information in online spaces to dominate or even completely negate the role of traditional place, drawing users away from the stabilizing effect of their everyday sociocultural activities. Risks can also be found in traditional places attempting to negate the potential impact of the new information universe (either by delegitimizing it or completely shutting it down). The larger point is that the relationship between cyberspace and traditional place has been at the heart of the role (s) that the Internet is playing in life in general and education in particular.

Space, place, and a new type of human thinking

The idea that the body is not a container for the mind, that human thinking is distributed across a larger ecology that the individual reassembles at the point of need (one of the bases of Baran's ideas on distributed information and packet-switching technology), is not a new one – it has a long history in philosophy, psychology, and education (Cole and Engeström 1993). But the idea that a separate space exists – one that transcends physical boundaries, where minds can meet, engage, and interact with each other – is primarily a concept of the twentieth century. Various possible (integrated) reasons for this can be identified – the development of evolutionary theory, the rise of the philosophy of mind and psychology as fields of study specifically focusing on the human mind as the critical force in human actions, the dominance of the machine during the Industrial Revolution forcing us to reexplore the role(s) of humans in the world from the standpoint of production, and two world wars forcing us to reexplore the role(s) of humans from the standpoint of moral (and immoral) action.

One of the first theorists to raise the prospect of a separate space dedicated to collective human thinking that could transcend physical limitations imposed by place was the paleontologist/geologist/philosopher Pierre Teilhard de Chardin (Glassman 2013). A Jesuit priest working on a series of archeological digs in the early part of the twentieth century, Teilhard suggested that the world was moving through three phases or spheres. The initial sphere is the geosphere, the geological/physical makeup of the earth. The second sphere is the biosphere, the materials that populate the earth – the fauna and flora, the animals including humans. The third sphere is the noosphere, where the most powerful forces on earth in the service of goal-directed action, human minds, can come together into an integrated whole – a voluntary psychic unity (Teilhard was clear that this unity had to be voluntary, which was prophetic considering the role that agency plays in Internet use). A good deal of controversy surrounds Teilhard's ideas (as well as some of his actions) – but his work has had a large impact on evolutionary theory (McCulloch 1996) – the idea that the human mind is naturally looking for new, expansive modes of communication and would naturally develop spaces for unified activities (such as problem solving).

The helmsperson's task

Two more modern (and more readily accepted) concepts exploring the dynamic relationships between space and place have emerged over the last few decades: cyberspace and cyborgs. Both are based on the concept of cybernetics, which has had a relatively short but highly influential impact on various fields including incarnations of computer sciences, cognitive sciences, and social sciences. The prefix *cyber-* is often associated with computers, but the concepts of cybernetics while readily embraced by Vannevar Bush and John von Neumann (von Neumann was actually part of the Macy conferences/discussion groups[1] where the idea of cybernetics originated) developed separately from computer technology.

The word *cybernetics* is taken from the Greek word *kybernetes* meaning steersperson or governor; cybernetics is based on the idea that successful adaptations are navigational readjustments to a changing ecologies. Understanding the feedback loops emanating from a changing ecological system leads to an understanding of exactly how and why some organisms adapt to changes – and some don't. The field of cybernetics (Wiener 1948) emerged at almost exactly the same time as the earliest computers and Bush's more advanced vision of the Memex machine (it is hard to believe that the Second World War was not a tipping point for multiple understandings and experimentation of the human condition). It is based on an idea with a long history – that action and change can be and often are self-corrected through complex feedback loops – continuous streams of information where organisms exist in interactive/transactive communication systems, responding to input from other nodes in the interconnected system and in turn producing new output that will eventually cause/force readjustment in the nodes within the system so that there is a constant readjustment. The most important aspect of these feedback loops is that they can lead to self-correcting (adaptive) behaviors, bringing the organism back to a point of stability or, in biological terms, homeostasis. It is at its core based on (an interpretation of) Darwin's principle of natural selection.

Cybernetics advances the idea that by studying systems it is possible for humans to engineer feedback loops as a system of interconnected circuits that continuously lead back to adoption of self-correcting

---

[1] The Macy conferences were a series of conferences where scientists/researchers could come together to discuss and debate work in progress. It was probably more a reflection of the collective research groups emerging out of World War II than modern day conferences.
A large portion of the Macy conferences were given over to the development of the field of cybernetics.

actions by a target organism/node. The manipulation is not based on a model of direct causation but on negative, system constraints (Bateson 1967): Feedback is adjusted to restrain the range of response in activity so that the organism's choices are limited to predetermined and/or progressive action trajectories. The individual(s) manipulating the feedback loops in the systems are able to navigate the perceived choices of organisms.

The idea that a human-engineered system of restraining feedback loops was capable of explaining human activity was challenged by some of the original attendees of the Macy conferences (as human hubris or worse), in particular the smaller group of social scientists (including the cultural anthropologists Gregory Bateson and Margaret Mead and the social psychologist Kurt Lewin). If the helmsperson is steering an organism by adjusting to possible changes and controlling the feedback loops within the observed system, who or what is controlling the helmsperson? The frustration led to a second, breakaway idea looking to understand the relationships between cybernetic systems and human actions, and in particular the role and functioning of the human mind in the feedback system – that came to be known as second-order cybernetics, or the cybernetics of cybernetics (von Foerster 2003). In addition to being (or having the potential to be) helmspeople or governors of local systems, humans must also be recognized as adaptive organisms within a much larger system that they cannot control or even know (Bateson 1972 refers to it as the supreme cybernetic system or the Mind). The human mind reacts to feedback loops established by the larger, unknowable system in the same way any organism would react within a more controlled, human-created system.

Second-order cybernetics assume the human mind is part of a larger circuit of activity that extends beyond the body into the local or "reachable" ecology, continuously reacting to new input. Human attempts at engineering more linear, goal-oriented local first-order cybernetic systems to achieve immediate goals can work against the balance of the larger, second-order systems and the trajectory of the Mind – in Can't See the Forest for the Trees types of activities. It is these attempts at human control in attempts to attain certain goals that throws the larger, self-correcting systems off course. The only way to regain self-correcting balance is disruption to the system The Internet can make it easier for human engineers and scientists (social and otherwise) to use cyberspace to create highly controlled educational feedback systems that set students on specific learning trajectories; but these human-made determined control systems cause imbalances within the larger system. The Internet, however, when used within second-order cybernetic learning contexts, can also offer students greater access to larger self-correction mechanisms as they construct greater understanding through search/selection exploring a web of trails.

First-order and second-order cyberspace: self-regulation or cyber-cowboys?

It is believed that author William Gibson was the first to use the word cyberspace – to represent a vast, feedback-oriented data space. Gibson's definition of cyberspace in his novel *Neuromancer* (1984) is overtly tied to cybernetics and offers a worthwhile description of a separate space of human activity:

> Cyberspace. A consensual hallucination experienced daily by billions of legitimate operators, by children being taught mathematical concepts ... A graphic representation of data abstracted from the banks of every computer in the human system. Unthinkable complexity. Lines of light ranged in the nonspace of the mind, clusters, and constellations of data. Like city lights receding. (ellipses in original)

Interestingly Gibson ties this idea of cyberspace to "lab animals wired into test systems, helmets feeding into fire control circuits of tanks and warplanes," very close to some of the early cybernetic models taken from experiences of the original Macy conferences attendees in the Second World War. Gibson's own use of cyberspace as an uncontrolled – at least by humans – freewheeling space where "cybercowboys" are capable of disrupting autocratic, closed systems is closer to second-order cyberspace.

The term cyberspace was initially brought into discussions directly related to the Internet and the new types of feedback system it creates, or can create, during a conference on cyberpunk science fiction on the Whole Earth 'Lectronic Link. As mentioned, the Whole Earth community had a strong relationship to the emerging field of cybernetics – publishing a number of articles on both first-order and second-order cybernetics – and

there was a good deal of overlap with other Whole Earth–endorsed philosophers such as Buckminster Fuller (Turner 2010). Steward Brand also
had a close relationship with Bateson. There is probably a good chance that
Bateson at least logged into the WELL at some point. At the very least it can
be assumed that members of the WELL had a very good understanding of
the implications of the term cybernetics, and by extension cyberspace.

The meaning of cyberspace, and in general the cyber-prefix, has become
more ambiguous as it has penetrated general discourse involving the Internet. In defining cyberspace Sterling (2014) suggests that cyber-connotes
agency on the part of the user as well as a network of communication
channels and information stores that allow individuals to communicate
with each other. Space connotes the infinite expansion of things, so many
that they all can't be (and perhaps shouldn't be) grasped at once (much the
same the way Bateson describes Mind and Bush the coming information
universe). A cyberspace promotes a journey rather than a destination –
adhering to the idea of helmsperson searching for their own means of self-
correction – reflecting Bush's notion that the information universe is
self-correcting, the blind alleys that will lead explorers to search for a new
trajectory of ideas, a new web of trails. Space also connotes free movement,
the ability to use agency to travel anywhere. Perhaps most important, it
connotes distance, direction, and dimension – all defined in a given network
by the (potentially infinite number of) links that the user travels in the
search for new ideas with the spaces of the Internet being primarily transit
stations and routes – an idea that becomes important in the later discussion
of net neutrality.

Second-order cybernetic online space (shortened to cyberspace)
creates a new type of transactional ecology where the user continuously
self-corrects based on newly discovered input, creating new output that
helps in bringing the system into balance – an ecology that is expandable, navigable networks with different definitions of distance (qualities
and numbers of links needed to reach a destination), direction (non-
linear), and dimension. It is also a space that is open to development of
virtual communities and Open Source collaborative projects. Rheingold
(1993) refers to it as a social Petri dish.

It is important and possibly critical that educators be aware of the
difference between first- and second-order cybernetic online spaces in
the development of Internet-infused education initiatives. First-order
cyberspace represents closed networked systems where the reactions and

development of the user can be managed (or thought to be managed) by human engineers through a combination of design and intervention. For instance, some of the intelligent tutoring/scaffolding systems used by researchers discussed in this book (Azevedo et al. 2005; Narciss et al. 2007) tap into, or attempt to tap into, first-order cyberspace for educative purposes. An assumption holds that feedback systems within the students' accessed cyberspace can be managed to increase users' abilities to self-correct within the learning process, whether in the development of content knowledge or desirable characteristics for learning such as self-regulation. Second-order cyberspace represents more open, nonlinear relationships to information encountered in the new electronic space. The student reacts to the feedback encountered within second-order cyberspace, creating new feedback loops through intuitive leaps between ideas. Approaches that focus on search/selection and user agency in developing relational under-standing such as the *Knowledge Forum* may be more dependent on this second-order cyberspace. Both first- and second-order cyberspace repre-sent approaches based on the idea that human thinking is subject to processes of natural selection; those ideas that work or show value in the current situation are maintained while others fall into extinction.

Cybernetic organisms and ubiquitous computing

Cyberspace and cyborg both descend from the concept of cybernetics. Cyberspace suggests the idea of a helmsperson navigating a vast new information/activity space in search of new answers and possibilities. Bateson has an interesting take on how navigation is the development of restraints based on feedback (discussing his ideas in an interview with Stuart Brand, 1976). Cyborg suggests a new integrated space organism relationship where newly developed feedback loops can act as governors, directing the actions of organisms in specific trajectories. Some irony can be seen in the use of the two terms: cyberspace originated in cyberpunk science fiction but is often used in serious scientific discourse. Cyborg, the governance of human organisms through the creation of new computer-generated transactive spaces, originated in scientific laboratories but is now used in popular culture to describe action heroes (who even more ironically are often not actual cyborgs).

The term cyborg seems more indebted to first-order cybernetics focusing on development of closed, feedback systems where new, computer-generated computer systems provide designed feedback loops that restrain the actions of targeted organisms. The human mind is able to use predictable feedback loops to off-load tasks of everyday activities – with the carefully planned predictability erasing the boundaries between place-determined feedback and computer space–generated feedback loops. The term cyborg stands for cybernetic (controlled) organisms and was introduced by Manfred Clynes (Clynes and Kline 1995). Clynes was an accomplished musician as well as autodidactic in computer sciences, physiology and neurology, gaining knowledge to support himself and his family (it is interesting that both the terms cyberspace and cyborg originally came from members of the artistic community). The term was based on research done in space exploration (sending animals into space) and was originally meant to describe the relationship between those organisms and machine-generated feedback loops that could be adjusted to create restraints on possible actions in a given situation (or more particularly the organism becomes integrated into human-designed, machine-enhanced feedback loops that foster predictable adaptive self-corrections). The organism in cyborgs quickly came to refer to humans. The machines (usually computers) set up a new space for human activity that extends far beyond the traditional "bag of skin" (Clark 2004).

The notion of a cyborg resonates with Licklider's early conception of (hu)man-computer symbiosis. The human and the machine become part of a single system in which both work together seamlessly to accomplish tasks through transactive feedback loops. Human and machine live, work, and act together in this cocreated space. The difference is that while Licklider suggests this space as promoting exploration in the service of new ideas, cyborg is more concerned with the ability of humans to distribute responsibility for maintaining a comfortable balance (homeostatic state) in a challenging ecology. One example of this is the concept of ubiquitous computing that emerged at the Palo Alto Research Center (Weiser et al. 1999). The ubiquitous computing researchers were looking for an uninterrupted flow of information feedback loops between humans and computer-connected artifacts where the connections/links were completely integrated everyday activities, blurring the boundaries between human-generated activity and computer-generated activity. Interconnected, transparent tools meld to form a cohesive feedback system (e.g., spaces in a parking lot communicate with your car as to when they are open, while both are interconnected with your coffee maker to start a fresh pot as you pull into the space). Ubiquitous computing allows us to concentrate on human-to-human relationships without having to worry about human-to-computer interaction issues – or at least that was its original intentions. The user stops thinking about the computer as a separate object self-correcting or manipulating their activity (depending on the user's perspective) and instead recognizes what the interconnected network offers as affordances in completing an activity (see the discussion on affordances in Chapter 5).

Weiser and his colleagues offer a simple but powerful description of how ubiquitous computing can work in enhancing human activity without humans realizing computers have been integrated into their feedback systems. The Palo Alto Research Center workers developed an interconnected system where whenever anybody made a fresh cup of coffee they pushed a reset button by the coffeemaker. The button activated a messaging system across the local computer network (intranet) that a new pot of coffee was available. People who were working on computers gravitated toward the coffee area, often winding up engaging in spontaneous discussions about what they were working on at the moment as they communally sipped their fresh coffee. From a cybernetic perspective the individual making the coffee used the computer system to start a feedback loop creating new, self-correcting restraints on the activity of people logged into the system if they were feeling tired, or thirsty, or lonely (they should go to the coffee pot if they were feeling this way) – creating new interactions about ideas. The system was created by engineers outside of and manipulating the system, treating human thinking as another artifact in the feedback loop. If two individuals suddenly came up with a new line of inquiry based on these coffee pot discussions they probably didn't realize it was because of computer-generated feedback engineered by the person who connected the reset button to the intranet. It is hard to say whether Engelbart would be impressed or aghast at this use of interconnected networking.

The new ecologies for acting, thinking, and learning created by cyberspace and cyborgs have the potential of negating and/or reorienting (some of) the part place plays in our lives forcing us to reexamine our social, emotional, and cognitive relationships, but it does not replace them. Place plays an extraordinarily important role in our lives, offering identity, familiarity, a sense of belonging, and natural boundaries to our thinking and actions, to name a few. But place also has the potential to negate some early actions and beliefs concerning the Internet, especially if those who are heavily invested in placed-based activities feel threatened or overwhelmed by new technologies. The impact that the Internet is capable of having on human relationships in traditional forms of place (neighborhoods, local organizations, schools) is going to be one of the most important topics in understanding its role. The dialectical tensions between traditional forms of place and the new spaces created by the Internet – the ways in which they negate each other forcing us to reexamine assumptions about belief systems concerning the ways we think, learn, and act as we extend our minds out into new first-and/or second-order cybernetic space – will have implications for the ways in which we conceptualize the Internet in human activity.

Andy Clark (2004) discusses some of the worries that human relation-ships to computing, especially in the context of the Internet, may become so translucent (cyborgs do not even realize the impact new technologies are having on their feedback loops) that they lose contact with recogniz-able boundaries between self and machines. Humans may not realize the qualities they lose by giving up a part of and/or reinventing themselves within the contexts of the expanding feedback loops offered by new computer-enhanced spaces. The great fear is that humans eventually become parasites to the computer networks that restrain their activities, unable to live without them (leading to dark – sometime only half – humor about our coming robot masters.) The field of tangible computing (Dourish 2004) focuses on the need to continuously bring users back to the recognition of very real boundaries between human and computer. A dialectical relationship between space and place takes this one step further, suggesting not only that we need to maintain the concept of a boundary between the places of everyday activity and the spaces of our Internet activity, but we must recognize the ways in which they are in continuous tension, a tension that can lead to what has been termed creative destruction. Nowhere is this dialectical tension more important than in our approaches to education. It makes little sense to ignore the role that the Internet is having on our society and its growing import-ance in almost all aspects of everyday lives. But it is also dangerous to lose sight of the fact that the Internet is an augmentation of our minds, not a replacement of our cultural-historical selves.

The space of flows and its relationship to place

The sociologist/urban designer Manuel Castells is one of the first and one of the most eloquent to discuss the importance of the dialectic between the places of everyday activities and the flows of information that move through the new spaces of the Internet. Castells differentiates between a "space of flows" and a "space of places." The ARPANET was originally conceived as a time-sharing device where information could flow easily between individual nodes without any need for contiguity in space or time. The expansion of the Internet and the addition of the Web into what Castell refers to as the global network (Castells 2011) has exponentially increased the flow of both social practices and information as it moves easily and efficiently between interconnected nodes anytime, anywhere.

In comparison the spaces of places are not only dependent but in many ways defined by physical and historical contiguity – sometimes jealously guarding the sanctity of their limited, bounded networks. Place is able to use historically defined knowledge and practices to act as a centripetal force on the thinking and activities of its inhabitants. The space of flows is capable of acting as a counterweight centrifugal force pulling on participants to expand their thinking in new, unanticipated ways in the exploration for new ideas and/or solutions (Glassman and Burbridge 2014). One of the difficulties that human societies are currently facing is that the Internet has emerged so quickly that the spaces of place have been caught off guard with little understanding of the powerful, countervailing forces of the Internet, whether as an augmentation of place-based thinking or an enhancement of activity. To put this in an educational context, the traditional elementary classroom in China, the college classroom in the United States, and the madrassa in Saudi Arabia are all representative in some way of place-based practices and belief systems (some overt and some covert) built up over generations. And all are challenged by the new, Internet-based spaces of information flow and asked to adjust their practices in a matter of a few years.

As Castells suggests, spaces of flows have their own dangers. Online information can be (and often is) controlled by large, powerful organizations. These organizations can be committed to extending the reach and influence of their information networks. Large, existing organizations (social, political, economic) may (and some already do) attempt to use their wide-ranging networks to manipulate distance (the types and amount of links available to users in search of information) and direction (influencing the choices individuals make in their searches for information – for example, by buying dedicated space or manipulating algorithms). Organizations can (and often do) attempt to use their networking capabilities to create specific command and control feedback loops, restraining behavior of users (e.g., monitoring online work behavior through terminals). There is as much motivation toward utilitarian uses of the Internet for information providers as there is for consumers; organizations might and often do provide links, information, and feedback loops based on what they can gain from them. At the same time excluding or even restricting populations from cybernetic space and/or cybernetic organism interactions can lead to increased marginalization (Castells 2001) – an idea illustrated by the library study conducted by Neuman and Celano (2012) where children with less access to computer portals and bandwidth in their lives (based on economic circumstances) had a more difficult time navigating an increasingly important online universe. There is then a second, perhaps more ominous, dialectic between organizations that are increasingly looking to control the distribution of norms and values through dominant hubs in the space of flows, with these organizations looking to usurp and/or eclipse information gained in place-based activities, and the dangers of further marginalization if individuals are limited in their chances for vital online experiences (e.g., does introducing handheld computers and their applications sponsored by large private or even public interests enhance the possibilities of marginalized populations to flourish or destroy their local culture?). Part of education in the twenty-first century is being aware of the ways in which the positive and the negative effects of importing and looking to integrate new technologies into communities will have on the everyday lives of its members.

At a more macrolevel an important part of education in the twenty-first century is teaching students how to traverse the information minefield that the Internet can be. In some ways it is an addendum to the concept of tangible computing. Using the Internet in the search for new information, for extending ideas, for engaging in shared thinking has occurred so quickly and so easily that the processes have become transparent – for many a natural part of thinking-based engagement with the world. How many times have you heard (or thought to yourself), "What does that mean? I'll just Google that" without even realizing that using a search engine is not the same as thinking an issue through. In some ways Internet penetration has already made us intellectual cyborgs. Although tangible computing suggests easily recognizable boundaries that remind users of the separation between students' humanity and the ways machines augment that humanity, an Internet-based corollary demands intellectual fail safes that remind students that information and discoveries they make through their Internet explorations need to make sense in their place-based everyday activities – they are the beginning of understanding through experimentation (the Pragmatic definition of knowing), not the end point. Discoveries need to have meaning and be empirically sustainable in the offline universe. Formal education may be the only place where these abstract, intellectual boundaries can be highlighted and discussed as a critical element of Internet activity so that the user stops and recognizes that the augmentation of thinking, this ability to search for/select solutions to problems, to collaborate across time and space, is provided by a machine. It is productive to use the flow of information the Internet offers, but also important at least every once in a while for individuals to step back and realize that (except in a metaphorical sense) they are not the Internet. There is no obvious way to make Internet activity "tangible," creating yet another challenge for Internet-infused education.

At the same time it is critical to make sure that all individuals, including those in marginal communities, have good access to the Internet (both devices and broadband) *and* the types of skills that allow them to use it to make new connections, join collaborative online communities, and bring ideas back to their local offline social groups in a productive manner. And to have this access without being swallowed up by its providers. Perhaps yet one more digital divide is the divide in education between those for whom the boundaries of the Internet must be made more tangible and those for whom computing needs to be more ubiquitous.

The space-place relationship in a classroom

The relationship between the space of places and the space of flows presents (sometimes very) different issues for hybrid classes and purely online classes, for Open Educational Resources and massive open online courses, for blog-centered curricula and the attempts to integrate augmented reality. It is a complex puzzle that has so far received scant attention in education. The following example of the way the space-place relationship played out in a hybrid classroom at a large, Midwestern university (Glassman and Burbridge 2014) might help illustrate some of the issues that come into play when the Internet begins assuming a growing and sometimes uncontrollable role(s) in teaching/learning processes. The class discussed here used a blogcentric curriculum in which students were required to make one class topic–relevant post, one comment to another student's post, and one link to a new information source each week.

The initial space of place in the anecdote was actually away from the classroom and anything to do with traditional teaching and learning. One evening near the middle of the semester the course instructor was sitting with his high school age daughter at the dinner table. The daughter asked the instructor without provocation why the United States does not go into the jungles of Uganda to hunt down the military outlaw Kony (the head of a rebel force there who infamously recruited child soldiers). The instructor/father stumbled around the question (not really even knowing who Kony is – something the daughter assumed he did) without offering an answer. A little later the instructor wondered about the suddenness of the question – his daughter had never been much interested in Ugandan military situations or the topic of child soldiers. He attributes the question to another place: There must have been a discussion in one of his daughter's classes. That night when the instructor logged on to check his class blog he founds two new posts about the same topic – Kony and child soldiers. Following the link from one of the posts the instructor found a video that had recently gone viral examining the plight of child soldiers in Uganda and the role Kony played in their recruitment/kidnapping. The video was produced by the Invisible Children Foundation, a well-known charity dedicated to helping child soldiers escape their militaristic, brutal existence.

When the class met the next day the instructor got caught up in a long discussion with his class on the video and the global reaction to child soldiers. The class in Child Development had already moved on from the unit in moral development but the Kony video pushed the instructor and students into reconsidering many of the issues discussed in a different light. For the rest of the week posts went up on Kony and Invisible

Children, many of them with links to other videos or articles – some directly on child soldiers, others on forcing children into horrific adult activities (e.g., sex trafficking). Many students in the class were extending their thinking out into cyberspace, finding new information and bringing it back to blog discussion, and through the blog discussion into the traditional, place-bound classroom discussions, changing the boundaries of place (not only the physical boundaries but also cultural-historical boundaries as the students used new information they found to take ownership of both the online and the in-class interactions). The teacher temporarily abandoned the syllabus and the assigned reading. At this point cyberspace was acting as a force in negating the traditional structure of the classroom. The students' links and posts were challenging the textbook-based explorations of a central subject in the curriculum pushing the teacher to rethink not only his syllabus but his approach to the subject (really not that different from Larry McVoy's ideas on changing the traditional structure of Sun – except in this case the teacher decided to let the space-place relationship evolve).

During the next week as the discussions on child soldiers and the plight of children forced into military combat continued, a long, intricate, eloquent post concerning child soldiers in Uganda and the Invisible Children Foundation appeared on the blog. The poster explained how he had spent time on the ground in Uganda working with issues such as child soldiers for more than a decade. He reported that Kony had fled Uganda and was no longer of much concern to the Ugandan people; few child soldiers were left, and the major task currently facing the Ugandan people was acclimating those who had been forced into military service as children back into mainstream society. He believed this was where the people of Uganda wanted resources to go. Some expressions of shock and dismay were seen among other members of the blog community, some of whom had participated in fund-raising events for the Invisible Children Foundation a few years earlier. But students soon also started posting links to articles and other resources that supported the poster's position: The viral video was primarily a fundraiser for a well-known charitable foundation that was losing its reason for being. The next class revolved around a discussion that was not originally on the syllabus – the impact of war trauma on children and the ways in which it follows them into adulthood. The instructor scoured the Internet to find relevant readings for his class. A few nights later when the instructor was having dinner with his daughter again he asked her about her current thinking on the Kony issue – without discussing any of the things that occurred with his college class. She replied that she now believed she misjudged the issue and that the situation in Uganda was complex and not really in need of military solutions. He asked her how she came to this conclusion. The daughter shrugged and said, "Somebody sent me some links."

The second part of the anecdote suggests ways in which place can negate powerful flows on information in cyberspace. The Invisible Children's Foundation was a dominant hub both offline and online. The video from the foundation had almost every advantage – it was being promoted by a very well-known organization, one that had been sanctioned by local schools and the media. It was an organization that many believed had important, authoritative knowledge about the specific situation of child soldiers. The organization had a large in-place network that allowed it to spread information quickly, dominating the consciousness of many users. All of these helped Invisible Children material move to the top of retrieved links when typing "child soldier" into a search engine. In the early days of the video posting on YouTube the information went more or less unchallenged. But what happened in the class is probably a microcosm of what was occurring across the Internet. Those with actual place-based knowledge were able to offer an alternative discourse that challenged the flow of information – even from a powerful organization (suggesting that the space of flows moves in multiple directions when it comes to power relationships).

The (specific, place-based classroom) students' information/experience on the Internet became more diverse – at least partially because a member of the community with place-based information with strong ties to everyday activities was able to redefine knowledge of the issue. The Invisible Children's video was not posted as hypertext either by the originating source or by those who first brought the links to the community (or to the instructor's daughter), but the natural momentum of a space-place dialectic pushed it in that direction. Information developed in a place-based context – the video – was posted within the space of flows where it impacted the trajectory of the place-based classroom. Discussions and subsequent searches emerging out of the place-based class then changed the meaning of the space-based media pushing students to develop new trails of thinking on the subject. Internet posts and new links redefined the meaning of the video in the particular classroom and across the Internet. These new meanings then looped back into the place-based classroom, changing the discussion and the syllabus a second time.

Net neutrality and its impact on space-place relationships

The term *net neutrality* is somewhat opaque but critical for education, especially when considering the space-place dialectic and issues of education. The term net neutrality was coined in 2003 by Tim Wu and is based on the principle that no Internet carrier should be able to offer preferential treatment to information moving through the internetworked system. It is a bit odd that that the argument as it has developed over the last decade focuses on keeping the Internet in the form it naturally evolved over decades rather than how some interests are attempting to change it; part of the reason for this is that net neutrality is couched in legal concepts such as *common carrier* (certain essential carriers of products/information should be regulated so that all customers are treated the same). But from an information/knowledge perspective it might be more precise to label the issue attempts at "Internet control."

To understand the depth of the issue, and why it is important to frame it within the context of the Internet itself, it is helpful to have some understanding of the related Internet history (separate from much of the augmentation/community technological frame history discussed in this book). Leonard Kleinrock, one of the pioneers of the Internet (he was one of the early proponents of packet-switching technology), led a committee attempting to outline a move from NSFNet to a more expansive internetworking system (at the time there were competing systems; Abbate 2000): *Toward a National Research Network*. The report was looking to establish "an operational network that is stable and predictable, offers high quality performance, and does not require advanced knowledge of networking" as well as "widespread access, user friendly service orientation, quality and performance" (p. 2). The committee included a recommendation in their report that was to have an ongoing impact on the way the Internet is understood in the United States. It argued that the development of the proposed networked communication system should not take away funds and energy from other research projects (at the time internetworking was envisioned as one among many for research) – the proposed internetworking initiatives should forge public-private partnerships as quickly as possible and turn management (for gateways and local network systems – not the global system) over to those who understood networking issues. Most of the other early countries kept internetworking management in the public realm (Abbate 2000). However, reading through the report it is clear that the private companies were meant only to be managers of the new internetworking systems – meant to be stage managers, not directors of the systems. The challenge to net neutrality is an attempt on the part of private companies to break out of this stage-managing role (in the current debates in the United States it is based on money, but really once the precedent is established it could be for any reason).

A basic way of describing net neutrality in the context of this chapter is that all users have the same capabilities in the space of flows. If you think of the Internet as a series of tributaries into larger flows of information, each tributary starts from the same point with the same slope (leading to similar force and speed) and the same boundaries (leading to similar amounts of information entering into the network system with similar force). Some tributaries are better known and/or better coordinated so they initially have more adjoining sources (sometimes many more) flowing into their central information source (hubs). Other flows of information must find their way based on clarity and the ability to find their own adjoining tributaries through quality of the information and/or emotional appeal rather than raw power and coordination. There is little doubt that the more famous, well-coordinated tributaries can create central meeting points (information/activity hubs) that eclipse the impact of the small tributaries, making even their neutral starting points meaningless. But the fact that all individual information flows are treated the same in transit (e.g., same slope) gives each information tributary a fighting chance to offer alternative information and create different knowledge sources that can act as (sometimes unwanted) instigators of hypermedia – a chance for independent users to develop a web of trails as they define and redefine their thinking on a subject. Challenges to net neutrality would give the managers of the system the ability to put up sluice gates on some of the tributaries based on their own utilitarian needs. To push the stage manager metaphor a bit it would be like the stage manager of a production of *Romeo and Juliet* could decide when to send on Mercutio, when to bring the curtain down on the first act, when to allow the Friar to enter based on utilitarian needs (e.g., the actor playing Mercutio spurns the advances of the stage manager, the Friar lets it be known he has deep pockets).

Abbate (2000) in her excellent history of the technical development of the Internet suggests that what is most predictable about it is its unpredictability (as this book suggests, putting the Internet in a social/educational context perhaps makes its evolution somewhat more predictable). But Abbate also points to two enduring legacies of the Internet – one is packet switching (and its relationship to distributed information systems) and the other is "the establishment of a unique tradition of decentralized, user-directed development" (p. 218). It is in part the focus on user-directed activity that has helped, at least to some degree, to maintain a balance between the users' sense of place and the new information spaces created by other users. This focus on direct relationship between users is referred to as dumb pipes (Anderson and Wolff 2010), where the network acts as an uninterested transit system with either no or only some global/unintended mediating impact on the information itself (the slope of the ground that holds the tributaries).

Challenges to net neutrality puts both of these legacies in danger. The carriers would be able to engage in deep packet analysis so they could differentiate between origination points of each information packet, giving preference to some information packets over others in the transmission process; this seems a contradiction to Baran's ideas on distributed information systems. More important is that the point of deep packet analysis becomes a sluice gate on the information flow. The carrier insinuates itself as a mediating force completely separate from users. This is often presented as a business and/or legal issue, but it goes much deeper, directly challenging the structure of the Internet (to the point where it is questionable whether it can even be called the Internet anymore), allowing what were supposed to be uninterested carriers to redefine themselves as gatekeepers. To push the theater metaphor a bit, the stage manager allows the Friar to eclipse Mercutio's death scene by paying a hefty sum. As Kurt Lewin (1947) suggests in his seminal article on gatekeeping, these decisions can have an enormous impact on the (equivalent of an) end user without their even realizing it. The ability of carriers to make preferential choices in transit can completely, separate from any sense of place and/or user-directed activity, change the power relationships between space and place across a number of activities, including educational activities, situating power not in information producers or information consumers but in the carriers of the information. It is an idea to keep in mind when reading the chapters on Open Educational Resources and massive and scalable education.

The changing nature of place and space in the information age

One of the reasons Vannevar Bush envisioned a new information universe was because available information was already dramatically increasing, opening up new possibilities for discovery and creative thinking. Information was no longer controlled by place-based conventions and rule systems – or at least we could no longer allow it to be. The development of an information universe may be as much a reaction to as a function of the quickening of technological development in the twentieth century. New technologies that might challenge human existence could emerge in a matter of years if not months. Problems emerge more quickly, are faster moving, demanding meaningful responses that sometimes create even greater problems. Climate change, nuclear/environmental disasters, growing income inequalities – the problems are more interconnected so the solutions must be more interconnected. Populations remain insular at their peril.

The role of place and the histories it carries with it become more complicated as electronically derived interconnections break down traditional boundaries, at least the ways humans recognize and understand them. However, this does not mean it is possible to simply jettison or negate the consequential role(s) that place plays in life. Place-based activities currently and will continue to far outweigh cyberspace. Our need to stay in touch with our own humanity still far outweighs any advantage gained from cybernetic-organism relationships.

References

Abbate, J. (2000). *Inventing the Internet*. Cambridge, MA: MIT Press.
Anderson, C., and Wolff, M. (2010). The Web Is Dead. Long Live the Internet. *Wired*, 18.

Azevedo, R., Cromley, J. G., Winters, F. I., Moos, D. C., and Greene, J. A. (2005). Adaptive Human Scaffolding Facilitates Adolescents' Self-regulated Learning with Hypermedia. *Instructional Science*, 33(5–6), 381–412.

Bateson, G. (1967). Cybernetic Explanation. *American Behavioral Scientist*, 10(8), 29–29.

(1972). *Steps to an Ecology of Mind: Collected Essays in Anthropology, Psychiatry, Evolution, and Epistemology.* Chicago: University of Chicago Press.

Brand, S. (1976). For God's Sake, Margaret: Conversation with Gregory Bateson and Margaret Mead. *CoEvolution Quarterly*, 10, 32–44.

Castells, M. (2001). *The Internet Galaxy: Reflections on the Internet, Business, and Society.* New York: Oxford University Press.

(2011). *The Rise of the Network Society: The Information Age: Economy, Society, and Culture* (Vol. 1). New York: John Wiley & Sons.

Clark, A. (2004). *Natural-Born Cyborgs: Minds, Technologies, and the Future of Human Intelligence.* New York: Oxford University Press.

Clynes, M. E., and Kline, N. S. (1995). Cyborgs and Space. In D. Haraway and C. Hables-Gray (eds.) *The Cyborg Handbook.* New York: Routledge, 29–34.

Cole, M., and Engeström, Y. (1993). A Cultural Historic Approach to Distributed Cognition. In (G. Salomon, ed.) *Distributed cognitions: Psychological and educational considerations*, New York: Cambridge University Press, 1–46.

Dourish, P. (2004). *Where the Action Is: The Foundations of Embodied Interaction.* Cambridge, MA: MIT Press.

Gibson, W. (1984). *Neuromancer.* New York: Ace Books.

Glassman, M. (2013). Open Source Theory. 01. *Theory & Psychology*, 23, 675–692.

Glassman, M., and Burbidge, J. (2014). The Dialectical Relationship between Place and Space in Education: How the Internet Is Changing Our Perceptions of Teaching and Learning. *Educational Theory*, 64(1), 15–32.

Hafner, K. (1997). The Epic Saga of the WELL. *Wired*, 5 (5).

Lewin, K. (1947). Frontiers in Group Dynamics II. Channels of Group Life; Social Planning and Action Research. *Human Relations*, 1(2), 143–153.

Licklider, J. C., and Taylor, R. W. (1968). The Computer as a Communication Device. *Science and Technology*, 76(2), 1–3.

McCulloch, W. (1996). *Teilhard de Chardin and the Piltdown Hoax.* Woodbridge, CT: American Teilhard Association for the Future of Man.

McVoy, L. (1993). The Sourceware Operating System Proposal. *Bitmover. com.* www.landley.net/history/mirror/unix/srcos.html.

Narciss, S., Proske, A., and Koerndle, H. (2007). Promoting Self-regulated Learning in Web-Based Learning Environments. *Computers in Human Behavior*, 23(3), 1126–1144.

Neuman, S. B., and Celano, D. (2012). *Giving Our Children a Fighting Chance: Poverty, Literacy, and the Development of Information Capital.* Teachers College Press.

Raymond, E. (1999). The Cathedral and the Bazaar. *Knowledge, Technology & Policy*, 12(3), 23–49.

Rheingold, H. (1993). *The Virtual Community: Homesteading on the Electronic Frontier.* Cambridge, MA: MIT Press.

Sterling, B. (2014). *The Hacker Crackdown, Law and Disorder on the Electronic Frontier.* Bookpubber.

Turner, F. (2010). *From Counterculture to Cyberculture: Stewart Brand, the Whole Earth Network, and the Rise of Digital Utopianism.* Chicago: University of Chicago Press.

Von Foerster, H. (2003). Cybernetics of Cybernetics. In *Understanding Understanding: Essays on Cybernetics and Cognition.* Springer: New York.

Weiser, M., Gold, R., and Brown, J. S. (1999). The Origins of Ubiquitous Computing Research at PARC in the Late 1980s. *IBM Systems Journal*, 38(4), 693–696.

Wiener, N. (1948). *Cybernetics.* Paris: Hermann.

Wu, T. (2003). Network Neutrality, Broadband Discrimination. *Journal on Telecommunications & High Technology Law*, 2, 141.

7 Open educational resources: how open is open?

The difficulty in discussing Open Educational Resources (OER) is the same bifurcation of technological frames (this book argues) that plagues many Internet-based initiatives: Whether you are looking at the Internet as an advanced tool for communication or as a means for new types of cooperation/collaboration goes a long way toward defining practices and outcomes. In few places are the differences more consequential while at the same time less overtly recognized than with OER. The OER movement (and it is often referred to as a movement by its proponents) has multiple definitions, multiples forebears, multiple lines of contributing research and activity, and multiple trajectories. One of the commonly raised issues in discussions of OER is that too many competing platforms/repositories are creating competition for the human and material capital necessary for sustainability. This is complicated by many self- and other identified OER platforms having different perspectives on the meaning of open, the meaning of resources, and the best models for sharing them. At the same time many of the OER platforms/repositories are more advanced in grappling with the complex questions inherent in a technology-based approach to teaching and learning than most other Internet-infused initiatives. Part of the reason for this is that a few highly committed organizations are pushing OER concepts forward with little interest in monetizing the concept: the William and Flora Hewlett Foundation, UNESCO (United National Education, Scientific and Cultural Organization), and OECD (Organisation for Economic Co-operation and Development) to name a few.

The OER concept is complex and at times confusing, because it combines (very different) initiatives of *OpenCourseware* (OCW) (free, easily accessible course syllabi and support material), freely available, *granular learning materials* that can be appropriated by educators in a variety of circumstances and reassembled to meet local needs, and to a lesser (but growing) extent user collaboration in the creation, use, reuse, and remixing of learning materials in everyday education. Different branches of OER have (often multiple) theoretical and pragmatic roots in Open Education, Distance Learning, the Free Software/Open Source movement, cognitive psychology/science, object-oriented programming, and cultural historical approaches to education. Many OER platforms for OER have been developed around the world, with most in North America. One of the most pressing and discussed issues in the OER movement is both sustainability of repositories/platforms and the willingness of participants to contribute to and become engaged with repositories/platforms at an advanced level. Sustainability is an especially salient issue because few apparent economic advantages are seen in developing and maintaining OER platforms.

This chapter will start with the convergent history of the OER movement as it moved from distributed ideas (geographically, academically, culturally) into a single, though broadly defined, educational concept. Next the chapter will explore some of the issues involved in promoting an OER ethic among educators and educational institutions and organizations. As with so many new ideas (especially, it often seems, those involving the Internet) the OER movement started very strong with a great deal of energy and innovation, but as difficult problems have emerged, the pace of development has slowed. Advocates, researchers, and local educators struggle with challenging issues at the local, institutional, and governmental level – including issues of quality (who determines the value and appropriateness of a particular resource and why?) and sustainability (who pays and why?). The second part of the chapter will present an exploration/explication of some of the more well-known OER repositories/platforms. The last section will be a discussion of how educational psychology might play a constructive role in helping OER take the next steps in becoming part of an interconnected, worldwide, educational infrastructure. One thing this chapter will not do is offer a certain definition of OER.

Atkins and colleagues (2007) refer to Amartya's Sen's work in discussing OER as expanding people's substantive freedoms by removing their unfreedoms, including "Inadequate education and access to knowledge" (p. 1). When Sen speaks of this idea it is often from the more positive perspective, referring to resources that increase individuals' capabilities for flourishing – to recognize new possibilities in their lives

(Sen 1999). One of the things that becomes apparent reading the different definitions of OER is that it may be better to consider it as a process that individuals and communities engage in to increase (as much as possible) access to educational materials, helping to create greater capabilities for flourishing within unique contexts – using the promise of the Internet to extend possibilities and opportunities, including (perhaps) changing conceptions of what education means.

A history of open educational resources

Generally two reported starting points are identified for the OER movement (and therein lies one of the difficulties in establishing a cohesive definition). The most commonly referred to starting point is the development of OCW at MIT. Interestingly the OER movement did not start out about either openness or educational resources. MIT, looking to integrate the Internet into their larger educational infrastructure, hired a consultant team to help them develop possibilities for taking advantage of fast-moving technologies – as many universities were attempting to do at the time (Abelson 2008). Many recommendations were made by the consultant team, including virtual, lifelong education classes for MIT alumni along with a for-profit Knowledge Update program. At the last minute Dick Yue, a dean at MIT, inserted into the report the idea of faculty putting their course materials online so that anybody could access them. Despite having no prior analysis or research as to efficacy and/or worth, this idea of making course materials retrievable Web-based resources spurred the most interest of any of the recommendations presented to the newly formed educational technology council. The idea quickly gained momentum within the university, eclipsing other recommendations. The initiative of putting coursework online took the umbrella name OCW.

OCW was revolutionary in that while other universities were trying to understand how the Internet could fit their business model, MIT went the other direction and started putting some of their most valued assets, their faculty-developed curricula, online in accessible formats. Even though MIT faculty embraced this new concept of putting academic product online as open resources, the university had an erratic relationship with the ambiguous concept of "Open." Richard Stallman, who founded the

Free Software Foundation, worked in MIT's Artificial Intelligence Lab for almost a decade, but one of the things that impelled him to become a free software advocate was being denied the source code to a program he helped develop. (There is no evidence of any relationship between Stallman and OCW.)

The OCW idea almost immediately gained a great deal of publicity. The initial OCW went online in the spring of 2001. By the summer of 2002 UNESCO organized a major conference to explore the possibilities of OCWs as global educational resources. One of the goals of the short conference was to develop an appropriate shared name and a definition. The name the conference attendees settled on was Open Educational Resources (OER; Open Courseware was considered but not adopted, which turned out to be a prescient decision as the concept has developed). The conference was also able to develop a mutual definition of OER: open access to resources through ICTs that could be used for noncommercial purposes – though in contrast to the name this definition did not really have a lasting impact for reasons that may become obvious through this chapter.

That same year (2002) the William and Flora Hewlett Foundation introduced a new component into their strategic plan for *Using Information Technology to Increase Access to High-Quality Educational Content*: increasing access to high-quality educational materials on a global scale (Atkins et al. 2007). It is difficult to know if the Hewlett initiative was in response to or in concert with the UNESCO conference, but the Foundation also adopted the term OER. In any case the OER movement had begun in earnest – initially tied to access of course materials from educational sponsors (e.g., well-known universities).

Learning objects – creating curriculum at a distance

A second stream of ideas contributed to the concept of OER – at the time less celebrated – on the other side of the country from MIT. One of the originating forces of this stream was David Wiley, who had been doing research with the idea of learning objects and had also been heavily influenced by the free/open source software movement – in particular Stallman's GNU operating system kernel and Torvalds's Linux operating system. Linux in particular was having a major impact on ideas of how online communities could develop and freely distribute resources to whoever requested them without any prior stipulations. Wiley was looking to establish the same type of open development and use protocols for educational content (Caswell et al. 2008). The difficulty was getting educators to buy into the same social/development ethic as was emerging through online Open Source software communities such as Linux and Apache (Glassman 2013). No social precursors existed for this type of behavior among educators in the way that the Free Software movement was a precursor to Open Source software communities. Wiley established the first license for open educational content in 1999 (opencontent.org) in an effort to balance the individualist orientation of many educators with the more cooperative principles of the Open Source communities. The issue of open licensing and ORE will be discussed at length later in the chapter.

Along with open licensing Wiley brought a second idea into what would become central to the OER movement – an openness to the sharing of learning objects. Learning objects build off a concept that revolutionized and democratized software development – object-oriented programming (object-oriented programming had a major impact across a number of disciplines including psychology, cognitive sciences; and education; see Glassman 2013). Initially computer programs were logical structures that needed to be built from beginning to end – with each program created as a whole, standalone enterprise. This was necessarily limiting (by time and level of expertise of individual programmers) for both the speed with which programs could be developed and especially who could be involved in the programming process. Object-oriented programming created a series of "black box" modules of programming code that could be fit together relatively quickly and easily. The emphasis changed to creative abilities to put different pieces of a puzzle together in building a problem-solving program (Downes 2001 has an intricate and interesting discussion of this idea and its relationship to education).

Learning objects take the same approach as object-oriented programming to development of (contextualized) educational curricula. Rather than developing a specific educational course from beginning to end – which not only takes a good deal of time but is often geared to specific teaching contexts and instructor expertise – it might be better to establish a general repository of learning objects that teachers could tap into, fitting different objects together to develop specific targeted courses and/or continuous learning experiences. As with object-oriented programming, a targeted educational experience is as much putting together the puzzle as creating a product (where there is a dynamic relationship between the producer of the general learning object and the generator of the specific course). Modularity is a key aspect of design – so that the learning objects can be used as self-contained building blocks for different purposes (Friesen 2009).

Learning objects also have important relationships with distance education (not to be confused with e-learning). The concept of open education, which long predates the Internet (Broudy and Palmer 1965), and distance education have been showing higher levels of convergence in the Internet age. Open education, while having many definitions, usually focuses on processes rather than specific outcomes of learning (Giaconia and Hedges 1982) as well as the importance of relevance to specific learning contexts. Distance learning (which also predates the Internet; Butcher et al. 2011) emphasizes the importance in recognizing the learner's sense of place in the educational process. By engaging a learner at a distance you are necessarily forcing them into a dialectic between their local assumptions, understandings, and experiences and the educational materials that have been designed at both a material and psychic distance. The ability of learners to navigate this dialectic is critical to the success of the educational relationship. The malleability of learning objects for developing educational experiences makes them an interesting and potentially important vehicle for open/distance education (Lane and McAndrew 2010; Downes 2001). The Internet offers possibilities for both teachers and students to search for and explore learning objects that meet the needs of their local environments. The idea of creating online repositories for learning objects as modules for specific educational contexts has become an important counterpoint to OCW – one that is often more demanding of the traditional social practices of educators and institutions.

Important differences can be found between OCW and freely available learning objects when considering sustainability. Hollands and Tirthali (2014) in a cost-benefit analysis of massive open online courses (which share issues with OER) mention expansion of "brand" as an important benefit for development of online open education initiatives: "For many higher education institutions building and protecting brand serves to attract and retain students, faculty members, and partnership opportunities with other institutions, funders and alumni networks" (p. 67). Sharing OCW as complete courses that can be applied in different educational contexts can potentially enhance brand across continents. It would be more difficult to establish and/or control brand through granular learning objects that can easily be reused and remixed.

A second conference and a merging of tributaries

The OER movement took another important step forward at a second conference on OER in 2005 held by UNESCO; but it was also a step into the complexities and multiple identities of Internet-infused educational initiatives. The 2005 UNESCO forum was much more extensive than the 2002 version, encompassing a series of discussions between stakeholders and potential stakeholders (with the definitions of both greatly expanded) over a six-week period. Emerging during this second conference were realizations of a number of natural tensions; tension between a desire to distribute rich learning materials that might require complex and/or expensive technologies and skills and the need for wide distribution dependent on free and open access to all materials; tensions between social and economic practices of academic institutions and the open approaches to educational activities needed to make OER initiatives meaningful to a varied population; tension between the ethical push to make OER widely and easily accessible to all populations and the drive of academic institutions to monetize their assets; and tension in the differences of what quality means for different populations in different circumstances (an international university as opposed to a local classroom).

Perhaps the most influential session/discussion came with the third and last meetings of the forum, where participation went truly global including participants who had experience with OCW such as Mohammed-Nabil Sabry, Director of the Centre for Research, Development and International Cooperation, Université Française d'Egypte; Peter Bateman, Manager of Instructional Technology and Design, African Virtual University; and Pedro Aranzadi, Director of Projects at Universia. Coincidentally (or perhaps not so coincidentally) the second week of this third session focused on the idea of learning objects.

An important theme of this final session was that if the OER movement was to become truly transformational it would need to move from a provider-user model to one that employs collaborative local communities in the creation, use, and reuse of globally available educational materials. OER could be made more relevant if the entire, interconnected education community was capable of engaging in activities leading to the development of localized courseware and other learning material that might be easily adopted to the immediate learning ecologies – creating an atmosphere of volunteerism and collaboration among all users. The idea of moving away from a provider-user model was especially important because, at least at the time of the conference, a vast majority of OER originated in the English-speaking world, potentially reflecting culturally biased learning theories. The session participants also pointed out the importance of recognizing that OER is as much a cultural (historical) movement as it is an educational movement. Not only do those developing OER, and especially repositories, need to be aware of cultural differences but also of opportunities for intercultural understanding by observing, adopting, and reusing locally remixed, adopted resources.

For instance, a faculty member at a university in the United States develops a learning object with certain objectives in mind. A teacher in a small classroom in West Africa adopts the learning object for her classroom but experiments with it so that it is more relevant for the local ecology of her students. The classroom teacher reposts the object, the experiment, and the outcomes. The original faculty member recognizes not only an expanded use of the learning object but also its cultural limitations/possibilities. The sharing of learning objects, or at the very least promoting the concept of granularity in OER (breaking down resources into their smallest, most manageable components), makes OER more amenable to intercultural development.

Issues in OER

A number of issues confront the OER movement, some more immediate and some more long term. In 2007, individuals involved with development of OER were (virtually) brought together to try and identify many of the most important concerns (D'Antoni 2008). Issues identified included awareness raising and promotion of OER along with community building and (global) networking; new approaches to and definitions for intellectual property and the ownership of product including abilities to remix and re-create resources for public use (and the ways in which these new approaches might wreak havoc on traditional educational social practices of the industrialized world in general and academia in particular); sustainability of OER initiatives; the dynamic relationships between production of resources and the use of resources including, but not limited to, access and skills in Internet technologies; and the question of quality assurance (and how quality is perceived differently in different contexts). Solutions to some of the early, seemingly intractable problems are already being implemented, whereas solutions to more difficult baseline problems, including the two seen as most critical in this particular survey, seem years away.

Intellectual property and creative commons

Protection of intellectual property initially seemed the Achilles heel of Open Source-type Internet initiatives. The issues of ownership are extremely complex in terms of profitable assets (at the institutional level) and career development (at the individual level). It quickly became apparent that licensing of open educational materials needed a scalpel approach more than a sledgehammer (which was often enough for Free Libre Open Source Software such as the Free Software Foundation and the Apache Licensing Foundation). David Wiley established the first license for open educational content in 1999 based at least partially on the Open Source movement as mentioned earlier. In 2001 the Creative Commons (creative commons.org) – a much more intricate approach to open online content – was established through the Center for the Public Domain to create intellectual property. With Creative Commons licenses authors/developers of materials could maintain some level of control over their work product while making it available for use in the public domain. Individuals can obtain four general types of licenses for their work (through the Creative Commons website):

Attribution or share and share alike license: Where any person, group, or organization (noncommercial or commercial) can freely use licensed material, including adapting it to new forms and/or initiatives as long as they attribute the work back to the original author/developer.

Attribution nonderivative license: Where any person, group, or organization (noncommercial or commercial) can use licensed material but cannot (publicly) adapt it to new forms or initiatives.

Attribution noncommercial license: Where any person, group, or organization can freely use licensed material, including adapting it to new forms and/or initiatives, as long as they attribute the work back to the original author/developer and as long as the uses are for noncommercial purposes.

Selected license: Where any person, group, or organization (noncommercial or commercial) can use licensed material but cannot (publicly) adapt it to new forms or initiatives, as long as they attribute the work back to the original author/developer and as long as the uses are for noncommercial purposes.

The Creative Commons licenses solve a number of problems – especially in academic contexts – by tying works back to their points of origination, giving authors control and recognition while allowing them to openly share their material. It also fits into the initial intent of Bush's web of trails approach to information and Nelson's ideas of hypertext forming a shared database. There is a difficulty with Creative Commons licenses for the OER movement: The repositories where authors deposit their work are for the most part institutional/organizational while in many cases it is the individual author/developer who must apply for a specific creative commons license. This is especially true of repositories focused on more modular/granular resources. A difficulty also exists specifically with the share and share alike license: There is an assumption that the new adapted work will be put under the same type of license (so that the material can keep evolving without limitations) but subsequent developers might not follow through in adopting the same license. This can lead to what Eric Raymond (the person who coined the term Open Source with colleagues) refers to as forking (1999), where original material can move off in two completely different directions, losing any type of relationship to each other or common history. In spite of any difficulties Creative Commons may be the most important OER innovation to date.

How do you sustain an open resource site?

The question of sustainability of OER has turned out to be a more difficult problem than intellectual property – especially in an environment where education, especially higher education, is being pushed more toward self-sustaining economic models (see, e.g., Hollands and Trithali 2014). Of course, it is important to separate how much of the discussion about sustainability of OER is ideological in nature – whether educational resources should be treated as a value asset or a common good (the two are not necessarily exclusive). Early pioneers within the augmentation/community technological frame such as Bush, Engelbart, and Nelson seemed little concerned with issues of sustainability. This might be because they were naïve and/or idealistic about the cooperative development of knowledge and innovation, but it also might be partially attributable to the shared idea that interest and potential creativity drives development of shared resources (at least the learning objects type). Downes (2007) makes more of a utilitarian argument (of course), one that seems closer to the Open Source ethos: Individuals cooperate in knowledge development communities because they believe these communities will offer them something of value in their individual lives – perhaps make their own teaching a more enjoyable enterprise. Downes suggests that noneconomic views of sustainability should not be taken lightly.

This does not mean that no costs will be incurred in the development of OER sites. At the most basic level costs will be needed for cataloging information and maintenance of a platform with user-friendly search functions. Systematic checks are needed for quality assurance at both the institutional and local levels. The more distributed producers and users of materials, the more dynamic the relationship between the two, the more important are on-site individuals (at both the institutional and local levels) who have a broad understanding of the subject matter and abilities in translating (both language and cultural) courseware and/or learning objects (Butcher et al. 2011). The development of OER needs to be integrated into an ongoing educational system, held together not only by the shared interests/motivations of the participants, but also by skills in searching for, organizing, and differentiating information so it fits the everyday needs of educational contexts.

Most discussions of OER sustainability deal with education as it is now – where some dedicated stream of support is needed for any new initiative. Beshears (2005) notes that course development at Open University of the United Kingdom can cost up to three million dollars – others put development of Open Courseware closer to $25,000 (Johansen and Wiley 2011). Whatever the costs, some dependable stream of revenue needs to be dedicated to the development and sharing of educational resources – especially considering the needs for continuous expansion and readjustment. Downes (2007) suggests eight possible models for funding OER through a separate stream of revenue (most articles discussing sustainability of OER refer to at least a few of these models):

An Endowment model – where a separate charitable organization (e.g., the Hewlett Foundation) or institution provides funding through a separate mechanism.

A Membership model – where a consortium of organizations/institutions pays dues, a subscription, or an entry-based fee to participate in repositories.

A Donations model – where the repositories are dependent on large and small donations from the greater community. This is used by a number of new amalgamation sites on the web that run annual or semiannual fundraising campaigns.

The Conversions model (also referred to as the segmentation model) – this is one of the most interesting because it mirrors primary business models for Open Source Software. In this model individuals who develop and/or nurture Open Source repositories are then hired by local educational environments to manage their information relationships with the repositories.

The Contributions Pay model – this is more open access than Open Source, where authors are paid one-time fees to allow universal access to their materials. This model has been adopted by many journals.

The Sponsorship model – this is where organizations/institutions looking to reach specific audiences sell advertising space that can be displayed with the repository/search engine site and/or the material. This method is used by numerous free blogs and websites.

The Institutional model – this is where a (usually academic) institution supports an open repository for their own internal reasons (e.g., build their brand).

The Government model – this is where there is direct government (e.g., Institute of Educational Studies) or international (e.g., UNESCO, OECD) funding for OER initiatives.

Partnerships and Exchanges – this is where organizations/institutions develop overt partnerships for the exchange of information (although it can be argued that this does not really provide a dedicated revenue stream and does not really fall within the broader idea of OER; it is also possible that this model could limit global access to information).

At this point, for the OER movement to develop, sustain, and grow educational resources (how long can a system dependent on advertisements maintain independence?), it probably needs to be based on an integrated, interest-based approach to education (which would require a rethinking of current approaches to and ideologies of educational access across all grade levels) or a conversion/segmentation sustainability model where those who help create and sustain the system globally are also hired to manage it locally.

Turning OER into a truly global initiative-cyberinfrastructure

A danger of OER (and many other initiatives that look to extend the reach of information and knowledge building) is that it might increase rather than ameliorate educational divides. Those without resources fall even further behind, with the gap between the haves and the have-nots increasing rather than decreasing. Two general reasons can be given for this happening, one technical and one cultural, both extremely difficult to deal with (although the cultural difficulties can be the more insidious). The technical problems are relatively obvious but often ignored, related to what has been referred to as the digital divide – or more precisely differences in available cyberinfrastructure (Atkins et al. 2007) that can support advanced online learning. (The term cyberinfrastructure might be a better descriptor of the issue than digital divide because it combines issues of Internet-ready tools and bandwidth and because it is less fatalistic, putting more emphasis on national and international initiatives for dealing with Internet access-related issues.) Differences in cyberinfrastructure lead to choices on the part of providers between providing rich materials that have the potential to engage the learner in advanced cognitive learning activities provided through sophisticated applications and more generic materials that can be easily accessed under a variety of technological circumstances. For instance, Atkins and colleagues point to online immersive educational experiences that model human immune systems or 3D visualization of protein folding. Although the learning opportunities for these types of learning objects can be extraordinary, they demand the types of tools, skills, and bandwidth that are far beyond not only nations with nascent or non-existent cyberinfrastructure, but rural communities with limited bandwidth, or even neighborhood schools only a few blocks apart physically but far apart in terms of their immediate cyberinfrastructure. The problem will become only more acute as we learn to harness the educational possibilities of virtual reality and augmented reality applications.

Ways can be found of dealing with cyberinfrastructure differentials. One is to increase access to Internet tools/portals in any way possible. Various initiatives have attempted to distribute mobile devices to rural and/or poorer populations, including mobile devices (e.g., Kim et al. 2008) and public Internet kiosks (Mitra and Rana 2001). An even larger problem on the technical side is Internet connectivity and bandwidth. Many of the less developed/rural areas of the world have no or limited Internet connectivity – and even where there is connectivity it is with limited bandwidth. Perhaps the most interesting attempt to overcome this differential is Google's Project Loon, which attempts to use high-altitude balloons to establish Internet/3G connectivity for rural areas. Although this sounds a bit like science fiction, some early successes have occurred (https://en.wikipedia.org/wiki/Project_Loon, 2015). But even if tools and connectivity are increased in educational contexts, we also face the issue of how technologically advanced learning objects would be perceived and used by populations who have little everyday access to high-bandwidth Internet connectivity. As the Neuman and Celanano (2012) library study discussed in Chapter 4 suggests, similar access to cyberinfrastructrue in a single venue does not necessarily lead to similar development of Internet literacy/intelligence and/or learning outcomes. Those who have access to bandwidth as part of their everyday activities maintain an advantage.

A second approach to cyberinfrastructure differentials can occur along with increasing Internet connectivity (which in the best of circumstances could take years). Conscious development of courseware and learning objects that can be used independently of Internet connections. As Butcher and colleagues (2011) point out, although the rise of the OER movement owes a great deal to the Internet's connectivity and distributive capabilities, it is not necessarily dependent on continuous Internet connectivity. It is possible to develop OER that can be stored on servers and then used in local connectivity scenarios (e.g., earlier versions of the

Knowledge Forum) or even printed as hard copies and distributed by hand. For instance, the African Virtual University (AVU is a pan-African, intergovernmental organization attempting to increase access to higher education materials and training through the Internet across the African continent) has developed local server storage as "mirror sites." Through collaborative efforts they have been able to develop an OER portal (OER.AVU.org) where members of the AVU consortium can use to develop and access material (demanding only low levels of connectivity) in multiple languages that can be remixed to suit different learning contexts.

Turning OER into a truly global movement-culture

An issue that might be even more complex than technological capabilities in the development of wide-ranging OER are cultural differences in teaching and learning, especially expectations and belief systems of what knowledge means and how it is important in everyday life. In a groundbreaking study of the meanings and practices of literacy Scribner and Cole (1981) found that the most broadly appropriated reading and writing skills among the Vai people of Liberia are much more tied to everyday needs and practices than to formal school learning. Individuals learn to read and write the unique Vai language not to reach some cognitive ideal of achieving new levels of thinking, but for concrete practices such as business communications and funeral arrangements. Many societies, especially those that live close to the land, do not separate knowledge from practice in ways education systems in Western, industrialized countries often do (Fals-Borda 1985). In these situations OCW can be problematic. Learning objects might be more successfully implemented in local education initiatives if they can be easily be integrated with meaningful local, everyday activities.

The cultural differences inherent to widely distributed OER can be a problem, but they can also be a solution – a solution that might best be realized through an emphasis on collaboration, setting up platforms where educators with very different perspectives can come together and discuss the meaning of curricula and learning objects for different populations – how teachers think learners will respond to introduction of new educational materials in different educational ecologies, and how they actually do respond. This takes the emphasis off the finished product and puts it on the needs of the users (Dholakia et al. 2006), creating a less hierarchical more dynamic relationship between users and producers.

The African Virtual University, for instance, not only works to serve distributed populations across the African continent but has over an eighteen-month period been visited by more than a million users from 193 countries, "which means that through AVU, Africa is contributing to global knowledge and is therefore not only a consumer of content from the north" (OER.AVU.org). The wide distribution of the AVU portal suggests possibilities for multiple levels of translation and remixing of globally available OER – with multidirectional relationships between local, regional, and global repositories in the continuous development of resources. There are various other regional OER initiatives such as the China Open Resources for Education, the Paris Tech project, and the Japanese OCW alliance. As the OER movement develops it may look toward creating strategies for greater integration of resources at different levels. Hylén (2006) in his report for OECD/CERI offered a chart helping situate the different types of OER repositories, portals, and platforms:

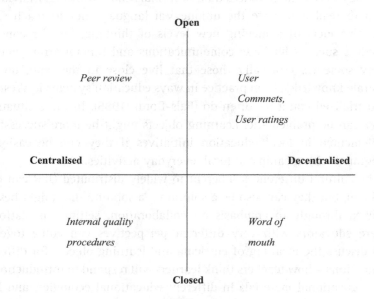

All of these types of OER have value independently but also have possibilities for contributing to each other. Broad access and sharing across levels not only increases possibilities for success but also enhances cultural understanding and the heterogeneous nature of education. It is very possible that learning objects developed in small villages in Africa could be successfully employed in parts of the United States. Or experimentation with OCW in South America could have important implications for how mathematics is taught to indigenous populations in Australia. It is also offers opportunities for bringing "nontraditional" educational resource authors who have no institutional affiliations but may have unique insights into a topic or subject – what Dholakia et al. (2006) refer to as "shut-outs" – into the discussion. For example, a private music teacher's learning objects related to music composition were one of the most accessed resources on the connexion.org site.

Educational collaboration/cultural collaboration

An important part of collaboration as a tool in the development of OER is the openness of the technology used to create the shared material. The ability of authors and potential authors to edit material is critical for broad participation in the OER movement. Dholakia and colleagues (2006) borrows from Apple's rip, mix, and burn campaign (where you rip out the most granular unit of music to meet need, mix it within a new ecology, and burn it to a CD) to describe a collaborative OER ethic: copy whatever materials you need for your specific learning experience, mix it with other granular/modular materials, and reform it into a standalone curriculum or lesson. Hilton and colleagues (2010) propose a four-part analysis for determining whether an educational resources community is truly open – ALMS: participants have Access to editing tools, participants have the Level of expertise required to reuse and remix materials, the material can be Meaningfully edited, and participants have Source file access. It is difficult to meet all these conditions for all potential participants in an OER initiative – the more distributed the community, the more difficult it is. But every attempt should be made to come as close as possible to this ideal. For instance, at the more basic level all source materials should be in XML rather than PDF format. Posting material as uneditable PDF not only makes it extremely difficult to remix and burn in any meaningful way, it is also a signal of conscious (or unconscious) division between producer and user of product, suggesting a hierarchical relationship between the two. OER platforms/communities also need to develop easily recognizable licenses for materials. There should be as little ambiguity as possible as to the author's intentions and expectations about ripping, mixing, and burning when posting materials.

Currently more complex initiatives for developing software packages increase the possibilities for collaboration, integrating the technological with the psychological in attempts to create a more collaborative ecology for OER use, reuse, and remixing – a view that moves beyond issues of ubiquity and affordability to take into account cognitive and physical differences of users (Kahle 2008). This more targeted approach to OER as a collaborative enterprise focuses on a universal design (Mace 2006) where tools are extremely flexible, "equitable in use," "simple and intuitive," and have a high tolerance for error. One example of this type of approach is the Visual Understanding Environment (VUE), which is being developed as an Open Source project at Tufts University. VUE makes no assumptions about how users might organize materials as they process them, supporting easy manipulation of the text (one of the principles of hypertext is offering tools that allow them to connect ideas in a nonlinear manner). The software overtly recognizes that users often make decisions based on issues far beyond the immediate human-computer interaction – decisions that take into account broader social and political contexts (i.e., decisions that are transactional). The emphasis is on the design of flexible and adaptive technologies so that teachers and learners are not restricted by the tools themselves (or perhaps more accurately the intentions of those who develop the tools). This gives users a greater sense of agency in developing their own knowledge trajectories through the use of the resource.

The VUE offers an overt form of online co-ownership, which includes both the ability to modify and maintain some level of attribution (but not control) through the processes of developing the resource. The software is designed to promote participation and collaboration through smaller sets of tools such as wikis and blogs. The promotion of agency and participation in particular involve very complex psychological issues (as outlined in the first part of this book), and any design without acknowledgement of this would probably have limited impact.

VUE seems one of the first initiatives to really grapple with the psychological implications of OER.

At a more macrolevel attempts are being made to develop collaborative forums as part of OER platforms – with the assumption that the ability to communicate about resources will lead to greater understanding of their meanings and uses for both authors and users and may motivate remixing and reposting of materials. Open collaborative communities are one of the least developed but perhaps more promising trajectories of the OER movement. Sites such as Connexion.org (now cnx.org or Openstax) at Rice University have established open platforms to try and create a dynamic community around their repository of learning objects – perhaps the most important next step forward for creating a true participatory, distributed community that doesn't just use resources but is engaged in developing and experimenting with them (Atkins et al. 2007; Kahle 2008).

Market research conducted by Dholakia et al. (2006) suggests a three-step process for this type of community building: (1) users perceiving OER repositories having functional value for their offline activities/ needs; (2) users perceiving the repositories as online limited networks where they are willing to make multiple visits and help other members of the community if it is not too difficult; and (3) users perceiving OER repositories as vibrant and engaged communities. We should not be surprised about this type of evolutionary scheme of community – it is central for much of the research on online student engagement. The question is how to foster this type of development of an active community through activities that support the long-term goals of OER repositories. This is the general model for development of an engaged community for the *Math Forum* (Renninger and Shuman 2002) discussed in Chapter 5. Users initially access the site as a general resource for learning math (e.g., the problem of the week). Through problem-based interactions with members of the *Math Forum* some of the users begin to recognize it as a limited network and then a smaller group of users join into a vibrant community. A second example is an ongoing discussion board that is part of Utah State University's Open Learning Support.

However, relatively few platforms seem to be promoting collaboration connected to OER repositories. To move into the next, arguably more productive phase of OER – what Atkins and colleagues refer to as an Open Participatory Learning Infrastructure – there will need to be a merging of new trajectories for "organizational practices, technical infrastructure and social norms that collectively provide for the smooth operation of high-quality open learning in distributed, distance-independent ways. All three are objects of design and engineering; the creation of a successful infrastructure will fail if anyone is ignored" (Atkins et al. 2007, p. 60). Although it is probably true that the three are interdependent, it can also be argued (from much of the research presented in this book at least) that new trajectories for organizational change and social norms cannot be developed simply through design and engineering. At their core these issues are about human-to-human interactions that are multifaceted and transactional. This may be one of the reasons why even though many in the OER movement discuss the importance of community, relatively little advance has been made in initiatives that actually lead to online community collaboration (also because it is really difficult).

Quality assurance

Important relationships can be seen between development of online communities surrounding OER and the issue of quality assurance, which is essentially "gatekeeping" (Lewin 1947). Gatekeeping is very much dependent on who controls the channels of communication and especially the purpose(s) they have in controlling them. Quality assurance is probably better thought of as a dynamic interaction between authors and users, based on the form and the goals of the available resource – at the most gross level whether the resource is OCW or learning objects, the type of license it has attached to it, and whether a collaborative exists that invites future development. For instance, OCW often involves syllabi and supporting materials for full courses with specific predetermined goals, so it might be best for QA to be done at the point of origin (by the institution sponsoring the courseware and/or the institution managing the repository). The QA is tied to the "brand" of the relevant organization/institution – if you have MIT open courseware, the user can assume the same QA as a course that is taught at MIT. This is one of the reasons "branding" has become a big issue in online education. But this also means that to maintain QA the courseware needs to have an "as is" license.

If the courseware has a broader attribution license – and/or if the resource involves learning objects – the issue of QA becomes more complex. One possibility is global QA organizations that offer a seal of approval and/or shared protocols for determining quality at the local (or perhaps regional) level. The difficulty with global organizations is they can work against OER principles such as teachers and students adopting materials to their own needs and the development of resources over time through experience and experimentation at the local level. Shared protocols would mean having well-trained/qualified curators of resources at the local level who are able to trace the development of resources both over time and in different contexts and make judgments about immediate worth in current educational circumstances. Part of this would involve the establishment of the collaborative forums suggested earlier where potential and experienced users could discuss possibilities and directions for particular resources (or at the very least access previous discussion threads). Quality assurance, sustainability, and collaboration are closely tied together.

Examples of OER sites

As mentioned at the beginning of the chapter, one of the difficulties the OER movement faces is numerous sites but limited coordination between them. This section offers a short discussion of five different sites (many more interesting and important sites can be found, some of them already mentioned in this chapter) that are partially representative of the broad OER movement: the MIT OCW site because that represents the beginning of the OER movement proper (at least from a historical perspective); the MERLOT site as representative of a learning objects approach; Curriki, which is one of the first OER sites devoted to K-12 education; the African Virtual University site because it is representative of the role(s) that regional repositories can play within a larger OER system; and Carnegie Mellon's Open Learning Initiative because it is representative of possibilities for integrating a cognitive perspective into an OER approach.

The open education consortium (oeconsortium.org)

The Open Education Consortium is a consortium of more than eighty OCW initiatives encompassing forty countries with direct links to more than thirty thousand learning modules. This site is mostly a clearinghouse/

database for OCW from member institutions and is relatively top down. The definitions of open education and OER are necessarily general (needing to encompass all of their members), and there is little in the way of discussion among participants (other than unilateral webinars and presentations) or links to discussions of different OER and how visitors might use them. A visitor to this site should probably have prior knowledge of OER/OCW and have some idea about what they are looking for in order for the site to be meaningful. The Open Education Consortium also has links to all of its member sites.

MIT opencourseware (ocw.mit.edu)

The MIT OCW site is devoted primarily to MIT-developed course syllabi and supporting materials. The amount of materials published for a particular course is determined by the individual course authors, but there is usually a syllabus. The site has a series of drop-down menus that make it extremely easy to navigate (e.g., find a course on a particular topic). The courses are usually presented as finished products with specific purposes. If the course is posted under a share and share alike license, users are free to abstract out pieces of the courses and remix them as they see fit, but there is no application for discussion of attempts at this type of abstraction/reuse or reposting of remixed materials. Little attention is paid to the idea of interactive learning objects. In other words authors on the site generally show no interest in granularity as an important aspect of sharing their work product, or building their content with future use in mind (Wiley 2007). Instead authors post their work in traditional formats where form can often dictate substance. The site is clear that most of the materials have share and share alike Creative Commons licenses – but it is difficult when accessing a particular course to determine which license an individual course is under. This is an important problem for OER in general – the sites/repositories are collective but the licenses are individual. Eventually there will probably be some universal system for establishing a badge or icon for licensing that will always appear in the same place when OCW or a learning object is accessed (something akin to the role ICANN plays for the Internet). Perhaps the most important part of the MIT OCW site, and the reason why most individuals looking to use or even just understand the OER movement should visit the site at least once, is their "fair use" page (ocw. mit.edu/help/faq-fair-use) and their frequently asked questions section in general. Especially in societies with strong ethics of individual ownership it can be intimidating and even frightening to use OER. The MIT OCW page provides some of the most concise and straightforward responses to questions about use.

Merlot – multimedia education resource for learning and online teaching (merlot.org)

Merlot is considered both a learning objects repository and a "referatory" (Lehman 2007) – meaning they don't house a lot of data but make the data available through links. Merlot has links to full courses and open textbooks, but it also offers links to granular learning objects. As opposed to many of the institutional OCW repositories, Merlot allows for learning materials from a highly diverse population of product developers. Quality assurance is done through a site-based, online peer review system. Teachers and students who use materials can offer comments and ratings based on their experiences. Users can request that resources be sorted by user ratings (or other search categories such as relevance). Many of the objects are smaller and (at least in some cases) designed to act as modules in different (and different types of) educational experiences. The Merlot search engine can be much more specific than OCW search engines, using a key word/category system (i.e., you can type in words that might relate to information sought along with specific attributes such as the language and the target learners). When you select a link the search engine offers an information page for that learning object with comments, peer reviews, and ratings (but again it is difficult to determine the type of license the material is under).

Merlot has also established Merlotx, which is a portal specifically for students. There students can find materials that might help them in specific, contextualized learning and to share the materials that they have found useful with other students (or theoretically instructors). The Merlot site is more interactive than most dedicated OCW sites, but participation is tied to commentary on the value of specific learning objects.

Curriki (curriki.org)

Curriki is an OER repository started in 2006 primarily geared toward K-12 educators – so much so that the site has recently instituted standards-aligned tagging tied to Common Core. In spite of the concentration on Common Core (which some might consider questionable) the site strives to be international with translations to Japanese and Finnish (individual learning objects are in a number of languages). Curriki is different from various other OER repositories because it sets up specific templates for contributions that must be followed as well as listed choices for tags (e.g., audience with kindergarten as a possibility). There is a peer review, but not all entries are reviewed: An internal system is used for nominating entered resources for open review. The resources can be edited, but only if the user is logged in to the Curriki site and if the original author has overtly given permission for editing. Permissions seem to be mostly internal with no (obvious) mention of Creative Commons or other types of international open licensing systems. It is difficult to know if it is acceptable to repost materials (especially remixed materials) as open resources on other sites.

Many of the resources on Curriki are granular, at the level of units, lesson plans, or particular multimedia presentations. The directed tagging and recommendation systems and the easy comments section are designed to make it easier for users to understand the learning object as a module in putting together a larger educational experience. There are also groups (both closed and open) where users with shared interests/ needs are able to create virtual discussion communities. Curriki is unique not only because of its emphasis on K-12 education – it also has a more "corporate" rather than academic orientation (much of its leadership is from Sun Microsystems). It is among the most directed and controlled OER repositories, which makes it easier for individuals to search for and understand learning objects but this can also limit the abilities of users to transcend traditional boundaries in knowledge development. The choice to adopt a narrow and in some ways political tagging system like Common Core standards may confuse or even alienate some potential users. It is possible to see a site such as Curriki as having (even slightly) different goals than MIT OCW or Merlot. Although many of the academic-oriented sites are based on the processes of sharing knowledge, the Curriki site is in many ways about creating a specific place to find specific, site-developed educational resources. It would be interesting to see a K-12 site using a more Merlot-like referatory model.

African virtual university (avu.org)

In some ways African Virtual University has been as important to the trajectory of the OER movement as MIT OCW. While MIT OCW led to the first UNESCO conference on the subject, it was African Virtual University (along with a few others – see earlier) that outlined the potentials and problems with OER as a global movement, helping to define it going forward. AVU is in some ways a hybrid site, being part of the Open Education consortium but also committed to localized remixing by and for different contexts. One of AVU's most interesting initiatives is capacity development – the branching out of development and use of OER across Africa-based institutions through the AVU Capacity Enhancement Program.

Carnegie mellon open learning initiative – http://oli.cmu.edu

The Carnegie Mellon Open Learning Initiative is an OER initiative that might be identified as an OCW-plus program with similarities to massive open online courses (which emerged later). The Open Learning Initiative is different from most other OER (it is not really a repository or a referatory) in that it attempts to incorporate particular educational strategies from the learning sciences into their courseware, creating a "complete enactment of instruction" of the educational process (Thille 2008, p. 167). The Open Learning Initiative is looking to develop not only open resources, but also open (best) practices for appropriating those particular resources. Each course is developed as a standalone unit based on collaboration between content experts, learning scientists, software engineers, and experts in human-computer interactions. The development teams create learning approaches that are more tied to the context of instruction than to the individual instructor.

The emphasis in the Open Learning Initiative moves away from development of granular learning objects and toward not only directed content, but also the ways in which that content would best be presented/taught over the course of instruction. For instance, in an open chemistry course based on research into how students actually learn in college-level chemistry courses, the Open Learning Initiative uses virtual reality scenarios to create an applied, problem-based learning context (e.g., arsenic contamination of a water supply). This approach can help in using resources to create active, dynamic learning contexts, but it can also be technologically and/or culturally limiting (best practices in one locale may not work at all in another). The Open Learning Initiative looks to overcome cultural limitations by developing partnerships with international universities, but the emphasis is still on Open Learning Initiative courses as they are developed at Carnegie Mellon (and then adjusted to the local ecologies). Opportunities are available for extending Open Learning Initiative courses (though not necessarily remixing them), but those seem expensive and/or labor intensive.

Educational psychology and OER

The OER movement has followed the pattern of many initiatives over the last few decades looking to merge information technology and education. Realizations are seen of new possibilities in using the extraordinary advances in access to and distribution of information for education-based activities along with new types of human connectivity that dwarfs anything that has come before. There are early success stories such as MIT's OCW that suggest possibilities for new frontiers in education that were not considered even a decade earlier followed by a euphoria about how this might solve some of the most difficult problems, including issues such as equity and the reach of knowledge to underserved and often educationally marginalized populations. As researchers and innovators come to understand more about not only what the Internet gives humans as a new tool in education, but what it demands of humans in terms of engagement and commitment, including dramatic changes to (traditional) place-based practices, the pace of innovation slows, sometimes to a crawl, and the euphoria begins to dissipate, sometimes replaced by a cynicism of lost promise. The pace seems to have slowed for Open Education Resources – not because those working in the movement do not know where to go, or what trajectories might push the OER movement forward: There is some agreement on this, including making sites more collaborative, breaking down distinctions between producers and consumers, making the development of learning objects more dynamic, and perhaps most important and most difficult, changing the social practices of educational institutions to make them more amenable to the principles of OER. The pace has slowed because researchers/practitioners/innovators have trouble figuring out how to effectively challenge these problems.

One area where educational psychology can have an impact on the OER movement is in developing strategies for moving OER sites to evolve from product-based platforms that users access primarily for material support, to limited, cooperative networks where users look to support and be supported in use and development of educational materials, to vibrant and engaged collaborative communities where the development of materials is dynamic and multidirectional – an educational process for the educators themselves. Sites such as Merlot have worked hard to support movement from simple repositories to limited networks by establishing forums that promote commentary and peer review, but it is the move to engaged, collaborative communities – an important aspect of contextualizing resources – that may present the greatest challenges: the types of dynamic virtual teaching/learning communities where educators at a major Western university can learn important lessons from a small, regional educational institution on the plains of Africa. These issues are specifically relevant to OER, but they are also generally important to Internet-infused education. As early research suggests, establishing these types of online collaborations will require new types of social space whether through design and/or strategic use of facilitators/moderators – social spaces where *all* members of the community can develop new manifold relational understandings not only of subject matter but also of what it means to teach these ideas/subjects in local contexts: an ongoing community discussion about what resources mean in different contexts in different periods with different audiences – a true breaking down of boundaries.

Development of the types of online social spaces leading to collaboration, or even cooperation, does not usually happen spontaneously without some obvious shared motivation; they must be cultivated. There need to be dynamic social support systems that help authors, teachers, and curators navigate increasingly large and complex corpus of materials. Referring back to the analysis by Kreijns et al. (2013) of social space, the repositories need to develop the types of constraints (affordances) that lead to substantive interactions about materials. This can occur through comment sections, but those are often generic and can even be alienating. OER repositories might be one of the greatest beneficiaries of something akin to group awareness tools that put authors, teachers, and curators into contact with individuals/groups exploring or having an interest in some of the same learning ecologies and/or use of materials.

Emerging social spaces can create forums where individuals from different regions, with different teaching experiences, dealing with different learner populations would feel safe and welcome making suggestions on choices, relationships, links, and implementation of different resources – bringing their own remixed learning objects and curricula culled through their active experimentation into discussions – discussions that can be archived as participants collaborate on developing educational histories for courseware, textbooks, and learning objects. The ongoing discussion can also offer an organic system of quality assurance – tied more to experimentation than abstract, expert knowledge. The development of these types of online communities, very similar to the goals of computer-supported collaborative learning and Community of Inquiry initiatives, is a difficult task that needs to delve deeply into online behaviors and motivations of potential users to engage in online inquiry and collaboration.

This suggests a different definition of sustainability of OER – tied less to material resources than the ability to create vibrant, problem-solving communities that will gain rather than lose momentum. At the heart of OER and sustainability is their abilities to complement and when necessary change pre-Internet, preexisting place-based education social practices, both K-12 and higher education. There is a tendency for institutions, and those who act within the structures of institutions, to hold on to what is already known and comfortable. OER can directly challenge traditional concepts of ownership, the role of teachers in learning processes – and really the definition of teaching itself – classroom relationships, and the sharing of information, to name a few.

References

Abelson, H. (2008). The Creation of OpenCourseWare at MIT. *Journal of Science Education and Technology*, 17(2), 164–174.

Atkins, D. E., Brown, J. S., and Hammond, A. L. (2007). *A Review of the Open Educational Resources (OER) Movement: Achievements, Challenges, and New Opportunities.* A Report to the William and Flora Hewlett Foundation. www.hewlett.org/uploads/files/ReviewoftheOERMovement.pdf.

Beshears, F. (2005). The Economic Case for Creative Commons Textbooks. Utah: 2005 Open Education Conference. https://oerknowledgecloud.org/content/case-creative-commons-textbooks.

Broudy, H. S., and Palmer, J. R. (1965). *Exemplars of Teaching Method.* New York: Rand McNally.

Butcher, N., Kanwar, A., and Uvalić-Trumbić, S. (2011). *A Basic Guide to Open Educational Resources (OER).* CITY: Commonwealth of Learning/UNESCO.

Caswell, T., Henson, S., Jensen, M., and Wiley, D. (2008). Open Content and Open Educational Resources: Enabling Universal Education. *International Review of Research in Open and Distance Learning,* 9(1).

D'Antoni, S., and International Institute for Educational Planning. (2008). *Open Educational Resources: The Way Forward: Deliberations of an International Community of Interest.* CITY: IIEP.

Dholakia, U., King, J., and Baraniuk, R. (2006). What Makes an Open Education Program Sustainable? The Case of Connexions. www.oecd.org/document/32/0,2340,en_2649_33723_36224352_1_1_1_1,00.html.

Downes, S. (2001). Learning Objects: Resources for Distance Education Worldwide. *International Review of Research in Open and Distance Learning,* 2(1).

(2007). Models for Sustainable Open Educational Resources. NRC Publications Record/Notice d'Archives des publications de CNRC: http://nparc.cisti-icist.nrc-cnrc.gc.ca/npsi/ctrl?action=rtdoc&tan=5764249&lang=en.

Fals Borda, O. (1985). Knowledge and People's Power: Lessons with Peasants in Nicaragua, Mexico and Colombia. Report to the World Employment Program. New Delhi: Indian Social Institute.

Friesen, N. (2009). Open Educational Resources: New Possibilities for Change and Sustainability. *International Review of Research in Open and Distance Learning,* 10(5).

Giacona, R., and Hedges, L. (1982). Identifying Features of Effective Open Education. *Review of Educational Research,* 52, 579–602.

Glassman, M. (2013). Open Source Theory. 01. *Theory & Psychology,* 25, 675–692.

Hilton, J., III, Wiley, D., Stein, J., and Johnson, A. (2010). The Four 'R's of Openness and ALMS Analysis: Frameworks for Open Educational Resources. *Open Learning,* 25(1), 37–44.

Hollands, F., and Tirthali, D. (2014). MOOCs: Expectations and Reality. Center for Cost-Benefit Studies of Education, Teachers College, Columbia University. www.academicpartnerships.com/sites/default/files/MOOCs_Expectations_and_Reality.pdf.

Hylén, J. (2006). Open Educational Resources: Opportunities and Challenges. Proceedings of Open Education, Utah State University, Logan, Utah, 27–29

September, http://cosl.usu.edu/ conferences/opened2006/docs/opened2006-proceedings.pdf.

Johansen, J., and Wiley, D. (2011). A Sustainable Model for OpenCourseWare Development. *Educational Technology Research and Development*, 59(3), 369–382.

Kahle, D. (2008). Designing Open Educational Technology. In T. Iiyoshi and V. Kuman (eds.) *Opening Up Education: The Collective Advancement of Education through Open Technology, Open Content, and Open Knowledge*, 27–45. Cambridge, MA: MIT Press.

Kim, P., Miranda, T., and Olaciregui, C. (2008). Pocket School: Exploring Mobile Technology as a Sustainable Literacy Education Option for Underserved Indigenous Children in Latin America. *International Journal of Educational Development*, 28(4), 435–445.

Kreijns, K., Kirschner, P. A., and Vermeulen, M. (2013). Social Aspects of CSCL Environments: A Research Framework. *Educational Psychologist*, 48(4), 229–242.

Lane, A., and McAndrew, P. (2010). Are Open Educational Resources Systematic or Systemic Change Agents for Teaching Practice? *British Journal of Educational Technology*, 41(6), 952–962.

Lehman, R. (2007). Learning Object Repositories. *New Directions for Adult and Continuing Education*, 2007(113), 57–66.

Lewin, K. (1947). Frontiers in Group Dynamics. II. Channels of Group Life; Social Planning and Action Research. *Human Relations*, 1(2), 143–153.

Mace, R. (2006). About Universal Design. www.design.ncsu.edu/cud/.

Mitra, S., and Rana, V. (2001). Children and the Internet: Experiments with Minimally Invasive Education in India. *British Journal of Educational Technology*, 32(2), 221–232.

Neuman, S. B., and Celano, D. (2012). *Giving Our Children a Fighting Chance: Poverty, Literacy, and the Development of Information Capital*. New York: Teachers College Press.

Raymond, E. (1999). The Cathedral and the Bazaar. *Knowledge, Technology & Policy*, 12(3), 23–49.

Renninger, K. A., and Shumar, W. (eds.). (2002). *Building Virtual Communities: Learning and Change in Cyberspace*. Cambridge: Cambridge University Press.

Scribner, S., and Cole, M. (1981). *The Psychology of Literacy* (Vol. 198, No. 1). Cambridge, MA: Harvard University Press.

Sen, A. (1999). *Development as Freedom*. New York: Oxford University Press.

Thille, C. (2008). Building Open Learning as a Community-Based Research Activity. In T. Iiyoshi and V. Kuman (eds.) *Opening Up Education: The Collective Advancement of Education through Open Technology, Open Content, and Open Knowledge*, 165–180. Cambridge, MA: MIT Press.

Wiley, D. A. (2007). The Learning Objects Literature. In *Handbook of Research on Educational Communications and Technology*, 345–353.

8 Tools for a blended classroom

The hybrid classroom, also known as the blended classroom (the two terms are often used interchangeably), combines, or attempts to combine, the immediate, synchronous interactions of placed-based education with the online asynchronous, transactional relationships made possible through Internet applications. The basic assumption is that traditional place-based learning and the information flows of cyberspace can generate feedback loops that complement and/or enhance each other in teaching/learning processes. Place-based educational practices can serve as structured, centripetal forces on student thinking while the second-order cyberspace attempts to open students up to new information sources, experiences, and approaches to problem solving – the web of trails. But sometimes it is (first-order), teacher-generated or-sponsored cyberspace that creates structured learning feedback loops, giving time for more active, experiential educational practices in the classroom (e.g., the flipped classroom). And sometimes the Internet is used primarily to reinforce the structure of the classroom (e.g., the way many instructors use course management systems). The difficulties in understanding the face-to-face/online distinction can be compounded by different uses of technologies. The distinction is based primarily on differences in nonverbal cues, but in the current Internet-infused education ecology applications involving video conferencing and podcasting help ameliorate these differences, while digital storytelling can accentuate the use of nonverbal cues in ways direct classroom communications cannot or do not.

It might be better at this point not to think of the traditional classroom and the hybrid/blended classroom as two completely separate learning environments but as being on a continuum of physical, logical, and conventional constraints. The traditional classroom generally involves more physical, logical, and conventional constraints to the learning processes. Physically classrooms are highly constrained by time and space considerations. Logically they are constrained because only so much can be accomplished within a restricted place-based learning

ecology: A teacher cannot ask a student in the middle of a discussion to
have a conversation with a relative or friend or to experience something
that might take hours and then return to add their newly gained
knowledge to the class. Attempts at establishing nonhierarchical relationships can devolve into chaos – a cacophony of voices competing to
be heard within a limited time frame. There are conventional constraints, whether turn taking, deference to the teacher, or even the
way the student needs to dress. The use of the Internet as part of the
class experience offers instructors the opportunity to move toward less
and/or different types of constraints.

Choice of applications in the development of hybrid/blended classrooms can be the most consequential decision a teacher makes and can
go a long way in determining the trajectory and success of a specific
course or learning objectives – in large part because all applications are
not created equal: Different applications have different types of constraints. It makes sense to tie choice of application to the instructors'
educational goals, their perspectives of efficacious teaching/learning
practices, and their comfort levels with different Internet activities/behav-
iors. Internet applications often do not have the same physical constraints
as place-based classrooms – but differences in access to bandwidth and/or
advanced portals can lead to pernicious physical constraints (e.g., some
students can complete assignments only at school or on library computers). Differences in physical constraints between individual applications must also be considered – for instance, Twitter and other microblogs
limit length of messages (usually between 140 and 200 characters). Podcasts and other videos often cannot be treated as hypermedia – teaching
videos used in flipped classrooms (e.g., Khan Academy videos) are for the
most part unilateral communications of information. There are differences in logical constraints: Discussion boards are fast moving and easy to
access, but they make it difficult to establish commentary threads dedicated to the goals of specific posts, and students can become lost or
frustrated as they try to keep up with who is saying what to whom.
Differences are found in conventional constraints – students are often
reluctant to edit the work of their peers on wikis, and course management systems tend to be hierarchical and deferential to the instructor/
course originator. Teachers need to carefully consider what they are
trying to accomplish in their blended classroom and balance it with what
they are comfortable in terms of educational constraints.

This chapter explores some of the more popular applications and approaches to developing a blended classroom including course management systems, learning management systems, blogging, microblogging, wikis, virtual reality, augmented reality, digital storytelling, and the flipped classrooms. These are necessarily short explorations/discussions of the different applications/technologies, partially because of space, partially because we are just in the earliest stages of research on integrating many of these applications into the classroom, but also partially because the choice(s) or applications are very local decisions based on subject matter, course goals, teaching styles, and student populations. As a caveat it should be mentioned that all of the applications mentioned here can be used in purely online contexts, but limited research (especially of success) has been done in this area.

Course management systems and learning management systems

Course Management Systems and Learning Management Systems are often conflated, but they are two very different tools often existing in different technological frames (Watson and Watson 2007). Course Management Systems, at least as defined in the literature, are prepackaged collections of education-based applications that originate and are usually used within a communication/service technological frame. Course Management Systems are primarily developed to reach distributed sets of students while helping instructors with efficient administration of everyday tasks such as grading, testing, and paper collection. The most dominant and well known of these Course Management Systems is the proprietary Blackboard/Web CT and to a lesser extent the Open Source initiative Moodle. Learning Management Systems are designed as platforms for integrating more teaching/learning-directed applications to create a holistic educational context for students that (can be) tied to a larger educational theory, philosophy, and/or approach. Learning Management Systems tend to be more theoretically coherent, starting with a basic idea of how teachers/instructors can use Internet technologies to influence and/or support specific learning trajectories and then offering targeted tools and related teaching strategies to pursue these goals.

Course Management Systems are often eclectic, different applications put together piecemeal over time (e.g., paper drop box, blogs, discussions boards, grade books) and therefore have limited internal logic that users can appropriate for their specific teaching projects. Learning Management Systems involve a single designed application (e.g., intelligent tutoring systems) or a set of consciously interconnected applications – with strong theoretical and practical rationales underpinning what should be a cohesive approach that makes (evolving) sense to teachers and students, but there is little concern for making the overall course more efficient or making the technology user-friendly for teachers or students. For instance, the *Knowledge Forum* (Scardamalia 2004), one of the most well-known and researched Learning Management Systems, has various interrelated applications and functions involving creation of, search for, reaction to, and archiving of public notes that (might possibly) lead students toward stretch-hypertext or possibly even grand hypertext. But to be successful users (instructors at least) must be well steeped in the theory behind the integrated system. No separate applications are available for keeping a gradebook or collecting individual assignments. Other Learning Management Systems might include applications leading to development of an evolving, online social space (Kreijns et al. 2013) including group awareness tools and some of the aforementioned omniscient Internet tutoring systems (Woolf 2010).

Overlaps are also seen between Learning Management Systems and Open Educational Resources. For instance, Carnegie Mellon's Open Learning Initiative is basically an open, highly directed Learning Management System. The Khan Academy also can be defined as a Learning Management System but one that can be integrated into different Internet-infused pedagogical approaches. The difference between these Open Educational Resource systems and the more controlled systems like *Knowledge Forum* at this point seems to be available means of support.

Course management systems[1]: opt-in/opt-out

One of the difficulties in the use of Course Management Systems is that they offer teachers various different applications all together with little

---

[1] The acronym CMS is sometimes used for course management system, but it is often used for content management system. Content management systems have (at least currently) little to do

direction on how to integrate them into a class. The applications can be so different as to fall into separate technological frames: gradebooks and student contact applications that falls into the communication/service frames alongside blogs and wikis that reflect an augmentation/community technological frame. Course Management Systems can be very consumer oriented; for instance, Blackboard/Web CT developers will add in almost any application that users ask for (Lane 2009). This might initially seem beneficial, but if applications are introduced without strong support systems, these Course Management Systems applications can create a confusing hodgepodge of possibilities that the instructor is left to sort out – or more likely abandon on their own. It is the equivalent of bringing a novice cook into a kitchen with an extraordinary amount of ingredients (five different types of chocolate) and cooking technologies (convection ovens and high-speed mixers) and instructing them to bake a cake. Many might eschew extraordinary possibilities for the more familiar no matter how mundane – something that seems to happen too often with the introduction of Course Management Systems. "Even experienced instructors continue to use Blackboard/WebCT primarily for grade administration, e-mail and presenting static content" (Lane 2009).

Ways can be found to make Course Management Systems easier to navigate, less likely to cause frustration for the user. Lane (2009) offers a differentiation in the way Course Management Systems are presented to prospective instructors – Opt-out Management Systems and Opt-in Management Systems. Opt-out Management Systems such as Blackboard/Web CT provide a predetermined list of possible education applications to the instructor who must consciously decide not to use one or more in the development of their course (e.g., the instructor is left with the responsibility of turning off the wiki function). The novice cook is dropped into the kitchen with little more than a supportive wave. Lane suggests that there is something "insidious" about these types of predetermined, Opt-out course systems, that they cannot help but guide the online teaching and experimentation of the instructor – in part because (especially inexperienced) online instructors will choose the applications that are easiest to use and/or fit traditional teaching models they are

with education. They are more generally concerned with setting up programs/procedures for creating advanced websites that manage content from different sources (e.g., RSS feeds). For that reason I have tried to avoid using CMS in describing course management systems.

most comfortable with (e.g., directed discussion boards where teachers maintain firm controls on the discourse and encourage classroom-style turn taking).

In an Opt-in system the menu of options is not predetermined in a way that covertly (or overtly) guides online teaching activities – either by overwhelming instructors with choices, paralyzing them into pursuing the obvious, or pushing teachers to use as many options as possible, leading to diffusion of effort and almost certain failure and frustration. Instead Opt-in systems such as Moodle put the range of available course options in the hands of the instructor. In the best of circumstances instructors think about the applications they want and why they want them before building their teaching platform. Exploration of applications starts with the instructors' approach to pedagogy, goals for their students, and courses as a whole. Instructors are treated as active agents where the choice of applications is a conscious extension of the larger teaching experience. To compare it with the kitchen metaphor used to describe Opt-out Management Systems, an Opt-in system would be akin to allowing the instructors to shop for their own ingredients and cooking technologies as they plan baking their own cake. The instructors must already have some idea of what cake they want to bake and how they want to go about the process of baking it, so there is less chance of experimentation but also less chance of frustration/confusion. Potential instructors are also making an individual choice about course structure based primarily on their own perspectives and practical experience, so there is less chance of a standardized, cohesive, theory-driven approach to the teaching/learning process.

There are then three different types of Web-based educational management systems, with very different approaches to human-computer interaction, and how and why Internet-based applications should be introduced into development of Internet-infused blended courses. The Opt-out Course Management System is heavily design driven, offering sets of predetermined educational tools that if implemented will enhance student learning experience; it probably requires high levels of "just in time" support so that instructors are not overwhelmed and develop strategies for integrating applications that fit their teaching styles. The Opt-in Course Management System focuses more on the agency of the teacher/course designer – more aware but also more dependent on the experience and pedagogical perspectives of instructors and their knowledge and beliefs about the efficacy of different applications. Opt-in Course Management Systems probably require less simultaneous support but more preparation so that instructors have a good idea of the applications they would choose and why they are choosing them. Learning Management Systems focus on student response to applications in a larger theoretical context. The instructors' choice is based less on prior course experience and more on understanding and buying into the rationales behind the (integrated) applications; success is more dependent on instructors' belief in and adherence to specific theoretical frameworks and a willingness to follow through even in the face of obstacles.

Blogging in the classroom

The term *blog* is a contraction of the words *web* and *log*. Blogs originally appeared on the Internet as personalized online diaries started by individuals with deep roots in early web-based communities – often with experience in bulletin board/conference systems (the term blog was coined on a UseNet site). Posters could use fast-developing web technology (e.g., browsers such as Mosaic) along with hypertext markup language to create standalone text sites with their own universal resource locator. Many of the early weblogs were highly personalized initiatives meant to establish an individual social presence on the Web. The motivations behind these early blogs had important influences on the ways they have and continue to evolve as Internet applications, including in educational contexts.

A couple of logical constraints developed during the early periods of blog development continue to have important effects on the ways blogs are used, both in education and in general. One set of constraints is based in blog posts being almost always presented in reverse chronological order – with newer posts more accessible and later posts serving as something akin to idea archives. Well-designed, compelling posts will often include hyperlinks, sometimes to offer evidence for arguments, sometimes to set readers on a web of trails that might eventually come back as hypertext to the original blog, but also to refer the reader to relevant, earlier posts. Even the casual reader is given the opportunity to experience the evolution of the poster's or posters' thinking. After more than two decades of blogs this seems natural, but it is hard to think of any other narrative form that does this. This blog structure has some important philosophical and psychological implications – creating a new definition for, or at least a new way of experiencing what William James (1893) referred to as the "specious present." Every event, every thought that we have (that is not simple habit) exists within an extended time frame. To try and understand an activity outside of this larger span of genesis is often to misinterpret it. The blog makes it possible for the reader to understand the individual post – the immediate moment of thought – within the specious present of the poster's or posters' thinking processes. Theoretically conversations become richer, misinterpretation or misappropriation of ideas less likely.

A second important constraint related to the structure of blogs comes from the role(s) of online comment sections: Each post has its own dedicated comment section (this is not true of all blogs, and many blogs turn off their comment sections). The comment structure was originally for the blogger to make an emotional and/or social connection (which is an argument for using blogs to develop community social presence). Political blogs (where some believe blogging came into its own; Downes 2004) took this idea one step further by offering space for original posts to dedicated commenters, creating a community of bloggers focused on a particular topic. An argument can be made that educational blogging emerged out of this model (Glassman and Kang 2010).

In a review of articles reporting on attempts to integrate blogging activity into course curricula Kim (2008) found blogging to be capable of increasing student self-motivation through shared commentary. Blogs were also found to increase student agency and autonomy as a result of decentralized systems of learning relationships. Some of the research into social presence discussed in Chapter 5 (e.g., Rourke et al. 2007) suggests the importance of nonhierarchical social interactions and affect-laden posts: Dedicated comments sections offer a good forum for these types of interactions.

Yang (2009) examined the ways in which blogging could help promote critical self-reflection through commentary and the ways that posts were able to build on each other. But there may be limits to the ways and the degree to which bloggers are willing and/or able to merge their thinking with fellow bloggers. Deng and Yuen (2011) found that although blogs offer high levels of connectivity, it is usually one-to-one or one-to-many communication, suggesting that blog posts are often more about individual expression than constructing a shared knowledge base (this is not surprising considering the history of blogging). The question becomes whether bloggers' abilities to recognize the specious presence of individual thinking can be translated into community problem solving and knowledge creation. Can blogging community members use the constraints of blogs' reverse chronological structure to recognize how and why their shared ideas are developing together as they move together toward relational understanding of a topic/idea/question?

It is possible for specific topics to gain momentum on community blogs (Glassman et al. 2013). This, however, might be based more in emotionally laden, swarm intelligence–based interactions, which is different from students and teacher working to merge their perspectives together in collaborative, step-by-step problem solving that leads to collective agency intelligence. For instance, in the study conducted by Glassman and colleagues a topic that gained momentum at one point in the semester was abusive peer relationships. There was initially tremendous energy around the topic with different posters offering their own experiences and thinking, along with a high number of supportive posts (e.g., "that's really interesting," "I'm glad you shared that," building strong community). There was an early push in the community for more reliable information (guest speakers, articles), but interest in the topic died out as quickly as it emerged. Little if any collaborative merging of different perspectives to build any type of new understanding was seen.

Ellison and Wu (2008) found in an exploratory study that what students seem to enjoy most in blogging is reading other students' posts: This may be because they gain satisfaction in finding their own ideas in the specious present of the writings of others. As Bush suggested, individuals are often drawn to activities that help them find new connections to their thinking/contributions. It is the process of putting together the pieces rather than the finished product that is the most attractive aspect of human learning (Dewey 1916). Blogs, because of their reverse chronology of posts and abilities to provide embedded links in complex but focused text and to sustain an ongoing narrative on a topic, seem particularly well suited for reciprocal reading. In my own use of blogs, when the class is ending students (in the successful classes) often comment on how they will miss regularly opening up the blog and reading new posts (although to this point no student has posted or commented on a blog after grades were assigned). It is also possible that reading posts and making comments serve as an organic group aware-ness tool (e.g., Jannsen and Bodemer 2013), helping students recognize who is really engaged in the community and who is thinking like them.

The Ellison and Wu study also found, however, that students felt they did not get that much out of direct comments to their own posts and that comments were often repetitive. Part of this may be that comments can often take the form of social support with short but affirmative remarks such as "Interesting post" and "That's interesting." The comments are not really adding to the dialogue in any substantial way, but this does not mean they do not have value. If the research on social presence is valid, these comments may serve as important underpinnings for building sustainable community – at least for a short period. Teachers might become frustrated with the repetitiveness and socioemotional qualities of these types of comments. If one of the primary goals of the class is to develop critical analysis of the work of peers, blogs may not be the best online vehicle.

Blogs, because of constraints, can provoke direct, often emotion-laden communications (e.g., dedicated comments sections, unlimited/unre-stricted space for expressions of thoughts, support of peer expression). And implicit, sustainable interactions (e.g., reverse chronology of posts) can offer a natural baseline for developing the type of social space described by Kreijns et al. (2013). The difficulty is in balancing develop-ment of sociability with motivation for knowledge building through merging of thinking/perspectives of community members. Blogging is a high-maintenance, expressive activity. If students do not put up strong, interesting posts, blogs can quickly deteriorate, even if there is initially high levels of interest in the shared topic, and there is probably little the teacher can do to reverse this. Studies suggest the importance of interest in content for successful blogging – something that cannot be assumed (at least initially) in many educational contexts. Teachers can use extrinsic motivations such as grades and/or badges to at least establish regular blogging, but this may not engender the type of auton-omy on the part of students that leads to a successful learning commu-nity (Rovai and Jordan 2004). Another possibility is for the teacher to be highly flexible, allowing students to write about what they are interested in, waiting for a theme to catch fire online, and then find a way to tie it back to the course topic – but this type of interest-based writing can be more about self-expression and/or swarm intelligence than the types of reflective thinking that lead to collective agency, and it makes it difficult to predict specific course outcomes.

Microblogging/short messaging services

The term/descriptor *microblogging* is in some ways a misnomer, suggesting a shrunken version of blogs. But blogs and microblogs, based in short messaging services (SMS) technology (sometimes the two are used interchangeably), are similar only at the most superficial level: writing original text and publicly posting it. The two tools have very different origins. Blogs developed organically as a way for early web users to express themselves and develop an online identity. Twitter, the model for microblogging and the model for many applications that followed, was developed as a conscious business venture – the development of an online service that people might find useful (and the creators could make money from). Blogging and microblogging were born to two different technological frames for different purposes

The term microblogging emerged (ironically enough) as part of a comment stream on a public blog. They were first associated with *tumblelogs* – basically short text and/or links posted online as a sort of stream of consciousness (kottke.org, 2005), part of a "put your thinking out there and let the Internet sort it out" attitude. The idea of stream of consciousness remains important to many conceptions of microblogging including Twitter, which basically took individual streams of immediate thought and archived it as public information on the web, creating a sort of public background murmuring that could lurch in different trajectories based on who was posting and what was happening in their lives at the moment.

Twitter, which emerged after the term microblogging was coined, was initially based on courier dispatch systems, a digital way of knowing where other nodes (e.g., bicycle messengers) within the larger, continuously moving network system were at any given point in time (Bussgang 2011). Twitter started using SMS technology, but instead of using it for one-to-one communications posts, for it to go directly into a shared system so every person in the network could see what every other person in the network was thinking and doing at a particular time (metaphorically where they are at any given moment). It is the network rather than the individual poster that is the primary source of information for members of the community (almost the opposite of blogging). The reason Twitter is limited to 140 characters is completely functional. The service was initially based on SMS technology. After 160 characters messages into a phone need to be split (creating in essence two separate but related messages). Twitter saw posts as declarations to the network at the moment so split messages might cause confusion for no real reason. Twitter then splits off 20 characters for the user name and uses the other 140 characters for content (*L.A. Times* 2009).

Microblogs differ from their namesake blogs in a number of ways. Although blog posts usually have conscious titles with following text that is (at least expected to be) related to that title, microblogs from the beginning have been more about a continuous tumbling out of information: an idea, a link, a picture a user finds immediately interesting and posts. Recognizing this difference, and the idea that community microblogging can quickly become a shared stream of consciousness, may be critical to how it is used (or not used) in educational contexts. One analysis of Twitter use suggested that tweets were more pointless babble than anything else (Ritter et al. 2010) – but stream of consciousness considered out of context is often perceived as pointless babble. This would be especially true of a technology such as Twitter that is meant to convey important information through the network rather than through the individual. Teachers have to make decisions about how much they want to encourage or discourage students posting whatever comes to mind at the moment – whether they want to highlight a general network activity or individual communication.

The short message constraints in microblogging are usually too short to involve personal emotions or attempts to socially connect to other users – making it difficult for microblogs to offer the same types of social presence/community-building interactions as blogs – and this was not the original intent of the technology anyway. This is not to say there is no emotion in microblogging, but these are often public, aggregated emotions rather than personalized feelings. To offer an example, an individual is reacting to a highly charged socioeconomic situation involving oppression. A blogger has the opportunity to write a post about their own experiences and how it impacted their life and view of the world. A microblogger might post a link of a picture or video of a painful incident. The blogger is making a social and/or emotional connection and perhaps helping develop a community around the topic. A microblogger is trying to create, reinforce, and/or extend shared community themes by expressing an immediate position in the network.

Not very much research has been done on microblogging in education to this point. Dunlap and Lowenthal (2009) discuss the ways in which "just in time" communications offered by Twitter might be used to increase social presence (within a community of inquiry context). Students should be encouraged to Tweet immediate experiences and or thoughts from outside the class, blurring boundaries between formal and informal education or perhaps between traditional place and the information flows in online space, creating a merged network of activity. It was hypothesized that ongoing dialogue that combines class content with everyday activities of community participants would increase connectedness. The authors, however, seem to be using Twitter more as a traditional short messaging service (direct person-to-person communications) than as a web archive/network.

Ebner and colleagues (2010) suggest using microblogging to establish background conversations very much like a stream of consciousness, which is closer to Twitter's original purpose(s); students are constantly communicating their thinking or responding to the thinking of others as they move through the processes of learning. The authors tracked thousands of students' posts in a master's level course over a six-week period. They found a continuous information flow between students where they could "participate with others in their thinking" (p. 99). Ideas could be reframed, remixed, or even resuscitated (participants would drop ideas that other students would later pick up). Perhaps most interesting was the idea of creating a "murmuring" of thinking in the background of students' online activities, allowing them to visualize a continuous audience that is ready to share their thinking – or perhaps through network movement influence their thinking. Learning becomes less of an isolating experience, thought becomes more of a shared network endeavor. Of course, the students in the studied class were at the master's level, taking a course in "New Media," which suggests preexisting motivations for participating in the Twitter community. It is possible that one of the reasons people enjoy using Twitter is that by placing themselves at a specific place within the network they can have a hand in moving the entire network of users into a specific trajectory.

How much of that is lost when there are carefully defined educational goals involved?

Microblogging can be used simply to draw students into a course. Junco and colleagues (2013) found greater increases in student engagement and grades when Twitter posts were required and instructors were highly engaged in the emerging online community. They suggest that students should be required to use the application as part of the class grading structure (e.g., 20 percent of the grade based on Twitter activity) and that Twitter posts should be integrated into courses in educationally meaningful ways – which moves it away from the stream of consciousness and/or network perspective.

There may be issues in creating a critical mass or network of messages, especially since Twitter does not seem to have some of the community-building attributes of blogs or other long-form posting applications. Microblogging is much less likely to have the social and/or emotional triggers of effective blog posts – if only because of their length. It is important to remember that Twitter posts are much more about where you are in the network than who you are as a human being. Also the advantage of Twitter as an information technology, outside of quickly shifting network trajectories based on posts, is the ability to know where any other member of a network is at any given point in time. People may be interested where important personages are (a function of celebrity culture), but it is much less likely that students will have as much interest in classmates they barely know and are with for only fifteen weeks.

Wikis

Wikis are one of the most interesting and frustrating Internet applications, at least when used in educational contexts. As mentioned earlier in the book, wiki technology was initially developed by Ward Cunningham at least partially as a way to extend Bush's concept of continuously editable text. The Internet turned out to be a much more comfortable home to the concept of hypertext than Nelson's proposed Xanadu program. For educators wikis offer perhaps the purest approach to collaborative work that transcends the individual intellectual ego. Wikis have some of the most obvious potential for using Internet technologies to move students toward what Dewey (1916) referred to as reflective or scientific thinking – a social process where the development of ideas is an ongoing, stepwise problem solving, where the ends are uncertain and steeped in ambiguity and the most important part of the activity is the shared intellectual journey.

Wikis represents not only Bush's vision of an annotated web of trails as an easily accessible application, but the experimental and theoretical musings of Engelbart and Nelson as well. And wikis offer the extra benefit to educators of allowing any participant (including the instructor(s)) to observe and/or track all individual writing and editing. The teacher can determine knowledge levels, processing of new information, and writing capabilities at any point in document creation – and even have an archived finished document that can be retrieved for grading, discussion, and/or tutoring purposes. Wikis represent the great promise of the Internet as a collaborative, knowledge-building tool. It seems like the perfect educational tool, except for one flaw – it almost never seems to work as envisioned. The use of wikis in education is reminiscent of the fable of the fox and the grapes. A hungry fox comes across an incredibly attractive bunch of grapes hanging from a branch just out of reach. The fox jumps for the grapes again and again but keeps missing. Finally the fox gives up, certain that the grapes must be sour anyway.

One of the reasons wikis remain just out of reach as an educational tool is that, as opposed to many of the other applications discussed in this chapter, students don't seem to enjoy them much (Ma and Yuen 2008), don't want to use the technology (Glassman et al. 2011), and don't engage with the technology (Cole 2009). Various reasons have been given as to why it is so difficult to get students to engage in wiki-based activities, many of them echoing Karrasavvidis (2010), who found through interviews with students compelled to use wiki technology to achieve a course grade that they had problems "because they lacked the requisite knowledge, attitudes, skills and strategies" (p. 227). Karrasivvidis concludes that the differences between educational uses of wikis and traditional educational practices should be taken seriously.

Wiki use as part of a preset curriculum can easily become almost forced collaboration. But the type of grand hypertext that wikis are attempting to create only really works when individuals relinquish ownership over knowledge creation (Nelson 1974); this includes, and may be especially relevant to, teachers. Much of our education systems (and our society in general) promotes individual knowledge and information as a protected commodity. The idea of copying or building upon the work of others is often portrayed as an actionable crime (e.g., plagiarism). Editing an individual's work is seen as a personalized, negative evaluation (the dreaded red pen) and outside the bounds of collegial behavior. Students can see changing another person's text, or having their own work changed, as an overt form of aggression. Reluctance to change the work of others is an issue that runs the gamut of our education systems, found to be an important difficulty in getting students to engage with wiki technology at the grade school level (Désilets et al. 2005; Grant 2006) as well as with older/university students (Forte and Bruckman 2010; Glassman et al. 2011; Grant 2006). A second related issue is that most students don't have the same type of experience with wiki technology in their everyday lives that they might have with many other Web-based applications (e.g., blogs, YouTube). Little in everyday use of the Internet resembles successful wiki activity. Karrasivvidis suggests a scaffolding of knowledge, but the success of wikis in the classroom may be dependent on what Rittella and Hakkarainen (2012) refer to as instrumental genesis, where both teachers and students recognize its value as a tool in achieving goals by using it to create conceptual and especially epistemic artifacts. Wikis are the perfect platform for instrumental genesis – if you can get anybody to use them.

This is not to say there have been no successes using wikis in educational contexts. Su and Beaumont (2010) were able to have some success in using wikis with PhD students. They used a model where advanced students posted literature reviews for their dissertation and other students in the class offered comments. However, ownership of initially posted information was never really challenged by the structure of online interaction. A grand or even stretch hypertext environment where participants work together to re-create information and expressions of knowledge in a dynamic space of flows was never really promoted.

Wikis on the surface are highly attractive applications for education – so attractive that they have been incorporated into a number of Course Management Systems and are discussed as one of the great innovations of the Internet (Glassman and Kang 2011). This type of advanced hypertext – text that is able to go through continuous change – is the physical manifestation of one of the most radical, challenging concepts of the information age. In spite of this, or perhaps because of this, wikis are rarely adopted into courses even though instructors have access to them

(Lane 2009). Wikis feed in to our visions of what collaborative learning should look like, and this perhaps is the technology's fatal flaw – they cannot help but be disappointing, the grapes just out of reach. If Ritella and Hakkarainen are correct, perhaps we will develop a new understanding of wikis as instruments through our use of them – but a lot of work probably needs to done both in approach to information and in expectations of collaborative effort before we see meaningful progress.

Learning in virtual reality and augmented reality

A blurry line divides virtual reality and augmented reality – sometimes referred to together as part of the mixed reality spectrum. (Yuen et al. 2011 offer a history in which augmented reality emerged directly out of virtual reality. At a very general level this is probably true – engineers and gamers were reading the same people and often times were the same people.) But where the two can come together, at least in educational contexts, is in the development of new types of (collaborative) multiuser educational initiatives. The major difference between virtual reality and augmented reality is that virtual reality looks to serve as a (usually) more controlled replacement learning ecology whereas augmented reality looks to enhance place-based learning ecologies (this distinction is an extension of a general differentiation outlined by Feiner 2002). Historically virtual reality seems to have closer ties to online gaming and the types of multi-player communities developed through multiuser dungeons – augmented reality emerged more directly out of engineering needs. At a more abstract level virtual reality looks to leverage abilities to redesign and remix learning ecologies, offering students more interesting, urgent controlled problem-solving situations than is possible in a place-based learning environment. Augmented reality can have a different purpose, preparing students for new types of everyday engagement created by ubiquitous computing and the disappearing of obvious boundaries between human-computer interactions and human-human interactions. Augmented reality compared to virtual reality can be more complex at a technological level, a psychological level, and a philosophical level.

Virtual reality education applications often involve development of a (sometimes three-dimensional) online world that is completely independent of the offline world, where users can explore unique landscapes, problem solve, and develop online social relationships. A number of active stakeholders are found in virtual reality–based education initiatives including (possibly) program authors/originators (e.g., Linden Labs, owners of Second Life) , those directing individual learning experiences based on theoretical/practical considerations (e.g., Gilly Salmon's five-step process for integrating the Internet into educational contexts), instructors who appropriate the learning ecology to meet their general educational goals (e.g., college professors, online instructors looking to develop specific problem-solving abilities in students), users who act as guides to or initiators of virtual experiences (e.g., those who have experience with or quickly become advanced in using their avatars), and of course the student users who are moving through the learning ecology as some or all of the other stakeholders mentioned attempt to recruit them into problem-solving scenarios. Some of these roles can overlap. Users are able to develop avatars, online projections of themselves or some alternative version of the self, that are able to navigate these environments and engage with other avatars, theoretically with increasing ease as they acclimate to the virtual environment.

There are two types of augmented reality – or actually two devices that can be used to create augmented reality learning environments – and the difference has important implications for how it is used in education, including relationships between stakeholders mentioned above. (1) Devices can reflect a three-dimensional image of a computer program. This was actually the first manifestation of augmented reality, providing manageable models that engineers can use in trying to fix engines (the term *augmented reality* was coined at a Boeing engineering plant) or surgeons can use in trying to determine the next steps in a procedure. (2) Video-mixing technologies can be used to overlay or merge cyberspace-generated information with placed-based objects/subjects (initially using special, sensitive computer equipment involving helmets and backpacks, but more recently using handheld computer technology or even cyberspace glasses). The former technology is used to create three-dimensional models that can aid in complex, activity-based learning. The overlay/merge technology is used to re-create controlled learning in interesting ways that engender collaborative problem solving – different from virtual reality because no tangible boundary exists between movement through everyday reality and entry into augmented reality – and can involve moving back and forth over a disappearing boundary between spaces of information flow and place-based activities. The lack of tangible boundaries can be considered a positive because it teaches students how to engage in a world increasingly dominated by ubiquitous computing, but it can also be a negative for almost the same reason – students might lose contact with tangible boundaries between their concrete everyday lives and possibilities provided by computer technology.

Virtual reality – gaming education

James Gee (2003) was one of the first to realize the educational potential of video games, suggesting that many games can mirror optimal learning experiences. Games naturally push users to make new connections, often ones that they had not realized even a moment before, while engaged in activities driven by interests in ongoing tasks – whether it be raiding a village of trolls or stealing a car to get to a funeral. Information arrives on a "just in time" basis as the user navigates through complex sets of interactions that draw them deeper into constantly evolving problem sets. The games can be especially valuable for education because of the way they keep presenting common problems until the user has mastered a set of tools that allows them to move to the next activity (perhaps closer to Vygotsky's original vision of zone of proximal development than many intelligence tutor/scaffolding programs, also close to a second-order cyberspace version of Salman Khan's ideas on mastery education).

To this point gaming has been understudied (and perhaps underused) in educational contexts (Young et al. 2012). One of the difficulties is the primacy of individual actions when playing games. Different individuals play different games in different ways at different times. In a modified review of the research on gaming and education for K-12 students Hew and Chueng (2010) did find some evidence for benefits of video games in language learning, history, and physical education but found few initial benefits for learning STEM subjects. It is important to point out that gaming is more based in a process-driven approach to education while the researchers were reviewing concrete outcomes of integrating gaming into the curriculum. One of the questions gaming brings to the forefront is now that we have the technology where students can easily engage in reflective, step-by-step thinking processes and teachers have the abilities to observe and reobserve and potentially manipulate their students' activities at will – increasing the difficulty of getting to a funeral on time so that the student has to engage in more complex calculation – do we (can we) eschew the testing of artificial outcomes that are at best imperfect measures of thinking?

Kurt Squire (2006) suggests three ways in which educators might conceptualize using gaming integrated into teaching/learning activities. The first is "games as participation in ideological worlds." Prepackaged games such as *Grand Theft Auto* stimulate offer free-flowing discovery and connection as players work their way through street-based problem sets, but also place the user in a known ecology that guides their actions through series of conventional constraints (e.g., one version of the game takes place in Los Angeles in the 1990s where many players living in the United States may have preconceived notions of what is supposed to happen). A game like *Civilization III* is based on a particular, materialistic view of the rise and fall of civilizations (ibid.). Conventional constraints are often the most powerful (Norman 1999), helping to create easily recognizable conflicts. But they also restrict the connections that the user is able to make, reinforcing biases and closing off possibilities for expanded learning situations.

Squire's second way of conceptualizing gaming in education is more performance based: bringing a group of users together to engage in focused problem solving. The gaming-based problem-solving scenarios are a little different from the virtual communities that emerged through bulletin board/conference systems (Rheingold 1993) or the Open Source development communities (Glassman 2013; Tuomi 2001) in that they use virtual worlds as overt jumping off points in the development of what Kreijns et al. (2013) refer to as (dynamic) social spaces. Learners/players create online avatars capable of navigating virtual ecologies as opposed to simply contributing to them. Players can use these avatars to project either their own personalities and motives or an alternative identity into the virtual world. Depending on the interconnectedness of the programs creating the virtual ecologies, continuously developing avatars can create their own online histories stretching across any number of virtual scenarios. Avatars can take on a number of (virtual) human capabilities including socializing with one another, developing the same type of sociability often found in multiplayer online games such as *Warcraft* or *Call of Duty,* but in the service of a focused, educational agenda (e.g., instead of attacking a village of trolls, the online community attacks a sudden virus outbreak or tainted water supply).

The most well known of these virtual worlds is the program Second Life – by far the most frequently used multiuser environment for formal teaching and learning initiatives (Warburton 2009). The originators of Second Life are careful to differentiate their virtual ecologies from those created for gaming – there is no (scripted) conflict and most of the constraints on users are logical, not conventional. The Second Life virtual world experience relies much more on the development of social presence through avatars than on motivations inherent in strong narrative story lines that naturally evolve into conflict. Because there are no organic narrative conflicts and/or compelling problems in the program itself instructors can face many of the same issues as instructors looking to create high levels of sociability in text-based communities. Avatars can socialize and engage each other as projections of individual students, adding another dimension to the development of online sociability, but Second Life and similar online ecologies do not in and of themselves create reasons for users to work together, or even alone, to solve problems. The advantage of these open virtual reality platforms is that instructors have the opportunity to create compelling scenarios – but this can be as difficult in the virtual world as the real world. What if nobody cares about tainted water in some unfamiliar village? (Gaming has a complex culture and literature behind it that makes it relatively easy to create absorbing virtual worlds that draw users in. Instructors creating problem-solving dilemmas in Second Life are often starting from scratch.)

Squire's third conceptualization is "games as designed experience." This is at a basic level an opt-in learning management system for virtual worlds – where both instructors and students can choose from a series of options to create a virtual experience that fits both the needs of the course and the personalities of the students. One example Squire offers is the game *Supercharged* where users can lead a virtual group of classmates through various physics thought experiments – following the gaming concept of mastering skills to move between levels. Another example is the use by Salmon et al. (2010) of her five-stage model for online learning in a Second Life virtual ecology – where users gradually increase the breadth, depth, and frequency of their online interactions. Salmon and colleagues developed artifacts within the Second Life ecology that they hoped would spark initial interactions and allow avatars to find new paths to advanced sociability. The researchers basically used learners' abilities to move through communities and engage not only other avatars but also created artifacts to scaffold sociability in a given community. For instance, in one case avatars were teleported (within the larger Second Life ecology) to new, very different environments where they interacted with each other, and then teleported back to discuss the impact the alternative scenario had on them.

Augmented reality

Augmented reality is an interesting inversion of Bush's original vision of how the Memex machine might change human thinking. While Bush's augmentation theme focused on extending the mind as a thinking organ out into a larger information universe, augmented reality involves enhancing the feedback loop from the world back to users so they are capable of engaging in richer, more relevant, more focused experiences, allowing teachers to create "teaching moments" rather than simply waiting for them to naturally emerge (Dede 2009). As Clark (2004) suggests, instead of traversing cyberspace, users become cyber-organisms – or cyborgs. Augmented reality creates different types of feedback loops with important artifacts in ways that effect their meaning and value in everyday activities, pushing students to recognize new problem sets and possibilities.

Augmented reality is meant to provide an immersive environment, but one in which the students themselves are active agents in the learning process, physically moving through a blended universe (Dunleavy et al. 2009; Klopfer and Sheldon 2010) – experiencing new perceived affordances and abilities that put not only their thinking but their actions as well on new trajectories. As mentioned there are two branches of augmented reality – the creation of three-dimensional models that offer users unique perspectives for understanding their actions, and the overlay of virtual information on everyday objects: For the sake of brevity the former will be referred to as enhancing augmented reality and the former as extending augmented reality.

In education, enhancing augmented reality has focused on difficult to conceptualize systems (because of the level of abstraction necessary for teaching) such as solar systems. For instance, for younger students who are learning about specific cosmological phenomena it (potentially) helps to develop miniaturized, three-dimensional artifacts that students can explore and manipulate as if they were part of their everyday worlds.

One example is creating a table-sized virtual solar system (Liu et al. 2007). The solar system moves from being an abstraction to something that exists as information in a shared universe. A second example of enhancing augmented reality, closer to the early uses of augmented reality at Boeing, is the *Virtual Solar System Project* (Barab et al. 2000), which developed a curriculum where students worked together to build three-dimensional models of solar systems (the authors refer to the technology as virtual reality, but from a practical and theoretical level it seems closer to augmented reality). Students become active agents in the construction of their own knowledge, participating together in the building of cosmological systems. In general the Internet does not seem to have played an important role in enhancing augmented reality to this point.

Extending augmented reality has a closer relationship to the concept of ubiquitous computing and the idea that there is no fine line between human-Internet interactions and human-human transactions: The role of computers is so pervasive that the computer program/extension of possibilities fades into the background of the larger activity. In educational explorations of extending augmented reality instructors develop virtual artifacts and histories that overlay the real artifacts and histories of a specific, place-based ecology creating new meanings, interactions, and problems for users. Dunleavy and colleagues (2009), for example, report on students' experiences with the augmented reality narrative/game *Alien Contact*. The narrative involves aliens coming to earth and their interactions with humans after they arrive. This narrative is overlaid on artifacts that students would naturally come into contact with as part of natural exploration of a prescribed place. In the game *Environmental Detectives* (Klopfer and Squire 2008) students receive a call from a university president about a dangerous toxin in groundwater while work is being done on campus. Students are asked to discover the cause and develop solutions. Students use handheld devices networked to a central server to gain new information about the (new) meanings of the artifacts as they move through their real world environment in a shared (potentially collaborative) context. The students share not only the augmented reality, but also potentially questions and approaches to and perspectives on the unique problems it presents. The creation of a unique social/ecological/problem-based contexts that only members of the immediate learning community share creates possibilities for an organic social space. In the game *Hunting the Snark* (Scaife et al. 2005) small groups of children hunt for a mythical creature that exists in both the physical and the digital world. Interactions in the physical world can trigger interactions in the digital world, helping children learn how to move easily between the two, navigating increasingly porous boundaries.

The educational possibilities of augmented reality seem endless, but so do the philosophical and ethical implications. At this point extending augmented reality seems primarily concerned with using handheld devices to increase motivation in focused problem solving, creating artifacts and/or narratives that will grab students' interests in the same way that a naturally occurring phenomenon might lead to a teaching moment. Games such as *Alien Contact* and *Environmental Detectives* also have great potential for creating high levels of sociability (based on artificial circumstances) leading to collaboration. Developers of augmented reality programs have opportunities for creating new blended realities that only members of the targeted class share. But at what point does creating a collaborative learning experience cross over into almost Orwellian social and/or emotional manipulation (Roschelle and Pea 2002)? To what extent can augmented reality impact place-based relationships that continue long after the targeted programming fades? Social psychology offers both possibilities and warnings. *Environmental Detectives* can easily be turned into a *Robbers Cave* (Sherif 1961) experience where groups of students are able to develop extraordinary collaborative relationships; *Alien Contact* seems just as capable of re-creating relationships based on fear and mistrust found in the Stanford Prison experiment (Zimbardo et al. 2000) with a few simple twists to the narrative. Extended augmented reality has the potential to create (taking a phrase from the history of the Internet) the mother of all Learning Management Systems.

Online video and the flipped classroom

If augmented reality represents the cutting edge of Internet-infused education, online video can be seen as its baseline. It mostly involves traditional video technology disseminated through the Internet. Some of the more popular uses of online video such as lecture capture and podcasts tend to fall within the communication/service technological frame.

Their main attribute is students' accessibility to information transmission – the ability to retrieve a lecture or explanation at will and to replay it as necessary. A good deal of evidence shows that students use and appreciate these videos as learning supports. But the videos are not really meant to augment the users' thinking and/or knowledge building, or really even experiences, in exploring the information universe. In general they also have little impact on the development of community (perhaps other than providing limited teacher immediacy, depending on production values). Many uses of online videos are for the most part hierarchical, unilateral communications of information.

Some uses of online video, however, can potentially lead to development of community and possibly even limited augmentation of thinking. Two examples are digital storytelling and short videos where students can control the pace and form of their learning (such as those offered by the Khan Academy).

Digital storytelling

Digital storytelling is not really a new or even an Internet-based phenomenon. It has been around since the advent of accessible video equipment in the 1980s and was championed by the Center for Digital Storytelling (storycenter.org). As originally developed, digital storytelling is a form of narrative filmmaking, often used for documentaries and/or historical exegesis (it was developed in workshops at the American Film Institute) that combines personalized narrative exposition, still images, and usually some type of background music. Some of the best known examples are documentary series made by Ken Burns such as *The Civil War* and *Baseball.*

The evolution of easily accessible advanced filmmaking tools along with the ability to disseminate short films through the web with minimal difficulties have allowed teachers and students to create their own, short storytelling films (Robin 2008). The personal and emotional nature of the finished product can serve two simultaneous educational purposes. First, it can motivate students to explore and publicly share experiences that are important to them (whether their own stories or some meaningful historical event). Relatedly, it can foster connections between members of a learning community, increasing opportunities for advanced sociability. This can be accomplished using many of the elements from the original storytelling workshops and projects – including maintaining a personalized point of view, keeping the attention of an anticipated audience with dramatic questions and emotional content, and using the narrator's voice as a tool.

Difficulties exist with digital storytelling that should not be taken lightly. It is difficult to develop effective videos. Originally digital story-telling was done by seasoned filmmakers in intensive workshops. It is essentially an art form used for educational purposes – really not that different than asking students to express themselves through drawing or story writing. While some students may show a natural affinity for the art form, even at a young age, other students can struggle. Also, digital storytelling is dependent to some extent on emotional content. How much control does the teacher, or should the teacher, exert over the storyteller? Should the teacher actually jettison the community-building aspect of storytelling and focus instead on the individual process of putting together a narrative, creating a "story comes first" attitude (Ohler 2013) that promotes individual (multimodal) literacy and self-reflection? Or should the teacher focus on building social space through the videos?

The flipped classroom

The flipped classroom or inverted learning is where teachers switch transmission of critical information to outside the classroom activities, freeing up time for different, often more experiential, activities in place-based educational contexts. There are two general approaches to the flipped/inverted classroom: one where teachers use YouTube (or other online distribution) videos to dispense baseline knowledge to students, which can then be used in collaborative, place-based learning contexts (Sams and Bergman 2013); and one where teachers use omniscient, intelligent tutors to scaffold critical understanding outside of class so students can engage in more process-based learning activities in class (Strayer 2012). The former is by far the more common.

There are also two types of video-based flipped classrooms – those that use Open Educational Resources for out-of-class learning content and those where teachers make their own videos for their classes. The Khan Academy videos are the most well known of the open resources available to teachers looking to flip their classroom (although they were not developed for that purpose). The YouTube videos are five- to ten-minute

self-contained lessons. The videos have unique rather than high production values, which are as much the result of serendipity (e.g., Salman
Khan, the originator of the videos, initially had little money for producing
the videos; Khan 2012) as educational theory. Perhaps their most important educational attribute (at least from a Deweyan perspective) is that the
lessons focus on a step-by-step processes of finding the solution rather
than the solution itself. If the student does not understand something, they
go back and view all the steps over again – moving on based on understanding the process rather than getting the right answer. Khan offers an
interesting example from how he came up with this method – asking his
niece to scream out the moment she understood the lesson no matter
where he was in his explanation.

Jonathan Bergmann and Aaron Sams (2012) have also developed a
model for the flipped classroom – one that is more localized, focusing on
using teacher-made videos for more direct transfer of critical information,
opening up and maximizing the place-based classroom to do educational
activities that are possible (or at least much easier) only in face-to-face
situations (e.g., constructivist, experiential learning). Students learn the
fundamentals, for instance, of chemical interactions at home and then
conduct chemical experiments in the classroom: The video becomes the
blackboard and the classroom becomes the laboratory. Teacher self-
development of videos gives the individual instructor control over content
and presentation and (might) help foster more direct relationships with
students. Strayer (2012) makes an important point about the need for an
alignment between out-of-class Web-based learning of central concepts
and in-class activities: If there are important differences between the ways
the video or tutor teach a concept and the way the in class instructor
understands that topic, it can cause difficulties and frustrations on the
part of both students and teachers. The idea of having teachers themselves
develop the videos ameliorates this problem, but it puts a larger burden on
the teacher (at least initially) and can accentuate differences in quality of
local resources between learning contexts: Schools and/or teachers that
have resources for advanced equipment, video consultants (most teachers
have little experience making effective videos), and other supports have a
distinct advantage – as do their students.

Very little empirical research has been done on the flipped/inverted
classroom to date in spite of its growing popularity, and much of it reports
on very different methods of and approaches to flipping. Strayer using the

intelligent tutor approach found increased tendencies for cooperation in a flipped classroom as opposed to a traditionally administered classroom. Ruddick (2012) found that when students watched videos at home and solved problems in class they had higher final exam grades and showed greater interest in the subject matter. Mason and colleagues (2013) found the inverted classroom allowed instructors to cover more material (although this might not really be a goal of a flipped/inverted classroom), with students doing as well or better on quizzes.

On the whole the jury on, if not the definition of, flipped or inverted classrooms is still out. Some recent studies have found some positive effects, while others have found no particular impact (Davies et al. 2013; Jaster 2013). For the most part the benefits of the flipped classroom are still mostly a matter of faith (and a belief in the efficacy of active, experienced-based in-class learning).

Social network sites

Very little exploration has been done into the use of social network sites such as Facebook in education. Individuals on Facebook tend to be highly engaged in their circle of communities, suggesting that integrating the phenomenon – if not the communities themselves – might increase motivation (Ziegler 2007).

A couple of reasons may be suggested as to why so few attempts have been made to bring social network sites into formal education. One is its pervasiveness not only among students but also among educators. People not only think of it as but know it as primarily a social tool and may be reluctant to view it otherwise. A second compelling reason is offered by Neil Selwyn (2009) in what might be considered a "render unto Caesar what is Caesar's" argument. In analyzing the Facebook walls[2] of more than six hundred students he found that most of the posts about education were either informational or more about complaining about or questioning the authority structures of the college/university – a space "guided by disengagement, disorganization, and mild disgruntlement" (p. 172) – and that perhaps it was worthwhile to

---

[2] The Facebook Wall was replaced by the Timeline profile in 2011. The News Feed also now more directly provides many of the Wall's functions.

allow social network sites to maintain that role. There is perhaps little reason to appropriate social network sites for traditional educational purposes, stealing the cyberspace where participants could participate as the antistudent.

What is hybrid in the hybrid classroom?

A hybrid or blended classroom is first and foremost a social construction. It is not so much about technology as how instructors integrate technology into their educational processes. In other words it is not really about human-computer interactions, or human-Internet interactions, or even human-Internet transactions – it is still at its core about human-human transactions. The choice of applications is a decision point for instructors, and for that reason it should be left primarily to instructors. Some instructors already have some idea of the types of educational approaches and goals they are looking to pursue. Other instructors need support. But nobody should use applications simply for the sake of integrating technology into the classroom because "that is the future." This is one of the troubles with the introduction of Course Management Systems. Instructors are pushed to use technologies they don't really understand or do not align with their teaching or even their general thinking about education. They become frustrated or jaded or both and revert to using the most mundane applications – gradebooks and drop boxes. This is not to say these applications are in any way bad to use, but they barely scratch the surface of educational technologies.

References

Barab, S. A., Hay, K. E., Squire, K., Barnett, M., Schmidt, R., Karrigan, K., and Johnson, C. (2000). Virtual Solar System Project: Learning through a Technology-Rich, Inquiry-Based, Participatory Learning Environment. *Journal of Science Education and Technology*, 9(1), 7–25.

Bergmann, J., and Sams, A. (2012). Flipping the Classroom. *Tech & Learning*, 32(10), 42–43.

Bussgang, J. (2011). *Mastering the VC Game.* New York: Portfolio.

Clark, A. (2004). *Natural-Born Cyborgs: Minds, Technologies, and the Future of Human Intelligence.* Oxford: Oxford University Press.

Cole, M. (2009). Using Wiki Technology to Support Student Engagement: Lessons from the Trenches. *Computers & Education*, 52(1), 141–146.

Davies, R. S., Dean, D. L., and Ball, N. (2013). Flipping the Classroom and Instructional Technology Integration in a College-Level Information Systems Spreadsheet Course. *Educational Technology Research and Development*, 61(4), 563–580.

Dede, C. (2009). Immersive Interfaces for Engagement and Learning. *Science*, 323, 66–69.

Deng, L., and Yuen, A. H. (2011). Towards a Framework for Educational Affordances of Blogs. *Computers & Education*, 56(2), 441–451.

Désilets, A., Paquet, S., and Vinson, N. (2005). Are Wikis Usable? NRC Publications Record/Notice d'Archives des publications de CNRC. http://nparc.cisti-icist.nrc-cnrc.gc.ca/npsi/ctrl?action=rtdoc&tan=8913757&lang=en.

Dewey, J. (1916). *Democracy and Education*. New York: Macmillan & Co.

Downes, S. (2004). Educational Blogging. *Educause Review*, 39, 14–27.

Dunlap, J. C., and Lowenthal, P. R. (2009). Tweeting the Night Away: Using Twitter to Enhance Social Presence. *Journal of Information Systems Education*, 20, 129–135.

Dunleavy, M., Dede, C., and Mitchell, R. (2009). Affordances and Limitations of Immersive Participatory Augmented Reality Simulations for Teaching and Learning. *Journal of Science Education and Technology*, 18(1), 7–22.

Ebner, M., Lienhardt, C., Rohs, M., and Meyer, I. (2010). Microblogs in Higher Education—A Chance to Facilitate Informal and Process-Oriented Learning? *Computers & Education*, 55(1), 92–100.

Ellison, N., and Wu, Y. (2008). Blogging in the Classroom: A Preliminary Exploration of Student Attitudes and Impact on Comprehension. *Journal of Educational Multimedia and Hypermedia*, 17(1), 99–122.

Feiner, S. (2002) Augmented Reality: A New Way of Seeing. *Scientific American*, April, 50–55.

Forte, A., and Bruckman, A. (2009). Writing, Citing, and Participatory Media: Wikis as Learning Environments in the High School Classroom. *International Journal of Learning and Media*, 1, 23–44.

Gee, J. P. (2003). *What Video Games Have to Teach Us about Learning*. New York: Palgrave.

Glassman, M. (2013). Open Source Theory. 01. *Theory & Psychology*, 23, 675–692.

Glassman, M., Bartholomew, M., and Hur, E. (2013). The Importance of the Second Loop in Educational Technology: An Action Science Study of Introducing Blogging in a Course Curriculum. *Action Research*, 11, 337–353.

Glassman, M., Bartholomew, M., and Jones, T. (2011). Migrations of the Mind: The Emergence of Open Source Education. *Educational Technology*, 51(4), 26–31.

Glassman, M., and Kang, M. J. (2010). Pragmatism, Connectionism and the Internet: A Mind's Perfect Storm. *Computers in Human Behavior*, 26(6), 1412–1418.

(2011). The Logic of Wikis: The Possibilities of the Web 2.0 Classroom. *International Journal of Computer-Supported Collaborative Learning*, 6(1), 93–112.

Grant, L. (2006). Using Wikis in Schools: A Case Study. *Future Lab*. www.nfer.ac.uk/publications/FUTL98/FUTL98.pdf

Hew, K. F., and Cheung, W. S. (2010). Use of Three-Dimensional (3-D) Immersive Virtual Worlds in K-12 and Higher Education Settings: A Review of the Research. *British Journal of Educational Technology*, 41(1), 33–55.

James, W. (1893). *The Principles of Psychology*. New York: Henry Holt.

Janssen, J., and Bodemer, D. (2013). Coordinated Computer-Supported Collaborative Learning: Awareness and Awareness Tools. *Educational Psychologist*, 48(1), 40–55.

Jaster, R. W. (2013). *Inverting the Classroom in College Algebra: An Examination of Student Perceptions and Engagement and Their Effects on Grade Outcomes* (Doctoral dissertation, Texas State University–San Marcos).

Junco, R., Elavsky, C. M., and Heiberger, G. (2013). Putting Twitter to the Test: Assessing Outcomes for Student Collaboration, Engagement and Success. *British Journal of Educational Technology*, 44(2), 273–287.

Karasavvidis, I. (2010). Wiki Uses in Higher Education: Exploring Barriers to Successful Implementation. *Interactive Learning Environments*, 18(3), 219–231.

Khan, S. (2012). *The One World Schoolhouse: Education Reimagined*. New York: Hachette Digital.

Kim, H. N. (2008). The Phenomenon of Blogs and Theoretical Model of Blog Use in Educational Contexts. *Computers & Education*, 51(3), 1342–1352.

Klopfer, E., and Sheldon, J. (2010). Augmenting Your Own Reality: Student Authoring of Science-Based Augmented Reality Games. *New Directions for Youth Development*, 2010(128), 85–94.

Klopfer, E., and Squire, K. (2008). Environmental Detectives–The Development of an Augmented Reality Platform for Environmental Simulations. *Educational Technology Research and Development*, 56(2), 203–228.

Kottke.org (2005). Tumblelogs. www.kottke.org/05/10/tumblelogs

Kreijns, K., Kirschner, P. A., and Vermeulen, M. (2013). Social Aspects of CSCL Environments: A Research Framework. *Educational Psychologist*, 48(4), 229–242.

L. A. Times. (2009). Twitter Creator Jack Dorsey Illuminates the Site's Founding Document. Part I. http://latimesblogs.latimes.com/technology/2009/02/twitter-creator.html.

Lane, L. M. (2009). Insidious Pedagogy: How Course Management Systems Affect Teaching. *First Monday*, 14(10).

Liu, W., Cheok, A. D., Mei-Ling, C. L., and Theng, Y. L. (2007, September). Mixed Reality Classroom: Learning from Entertainment. In *Proceedings of the 2nd International Conference on Digital Interactive Media in Entertainment and Arts* (pp. 65–72). New York: ACM.

Ma, W. W. K., and Yuen, A. H. K. (2008). A Qualitative Analysis on collaborative Learning Experience of Student Journalists Using Wiki. In J. Fong, R. Kwan, and F. Wang (eds.) *Hybrid Learning and Education* (pp. 103–114). Berlin: Springer.

Mason, G. S., Shuman, T. R., and Cook, K. E. (2013). Comparing the Effectiveness of an Inverted Classroom to a Traditional Classroom in an Upper-Division Engineering Course. *Education, IEEE Transactions on*, 56(4), 430–435.

Nelson, T. H. (1974). *Dream Machine.* Chicago: Hugo's Book Service.

Norman, D. A. (1999). Affordance, Conventions, and Design. *interactions*, 6(3), 38–43.

Ohler, J. (2013). *Digital Storytelling in the Classroom: New Media Pathways to Literacy, Learning, and Creativity.* Thousand Oaks, CA: Corwin Press.

Rheingold, H. (1993). *The Virtual Community: Homesteading on the Electronic Frontier.* Cambridge, MA: MIT Press.

Ritella, G., and Hakkarainen, K. (2012). Instrumental Genesis in Technology-Mediated Learning: From Double Stimulation to Expansive Knowledge Practices. *International Journal of Computer-Supported Collaborative Learning*, 7(2), 239–258.

Ritter, A., Cherry, C., and Dolan, B. (2010). Unsupervised Modeling of Twitter Conversations. NRC Publications Record/Notice d'Archives des publications de CNRC. http://nparc.cisti-icist.nrc-cnrc.gc.ca/npsi/ctrl?action=rtdoc&tan=16885300&lang=en.

Robin, B. R. (2008). Digital Storytelling: A Powerful Technology Tool for the 21st Century Classroom. *Theory into Practice*, 47(3), 220–228.

Roschelle, J., and Pea, R. (2002). A Walk on the WILD Side: How Wireless Handhelds May Change Computer-Supported Collaborative Learning. *International Journal of Cognition and Technology*, 1(1), 145–168.

Rourke, L., Anderson, T., Garrison, D. R., and Archer, W. (2007). Assessing Social Presence in Asynchronous Text-Based Computer Conferencing. *International Journal of E-Learning & Distance Education*, 14(2), 50–71.

Rovai, A. P., and Jordan, H. (2004). Blended Learning and Sense of Community: A Comparative Analysis with Traditional and Fully Online Graduate Courses. *International Review of Research in Open and Distributed Learning*, 5(2).

Ruddick, K. W. (2012). *Improving Chemical Education from High School to College Using a More Hands-On Approach.* (PhD thesis, University of Memphis).

Salmon, G., Nie, M., and Edirisingha, P. (2010). Developing a Five-Stage Model of Learning in Second Life. *Educational Research*, 52(2), 169–182.

Sams, A., and Bergmann, J. (2013). Flip Your Students' Learning. *Educational Leadership*, 70(6), 16–20.

Scaife, M., and Rogers, Y. (2005). External Cognition, Innovative Technologies and Effective Learning. In P. Gardenfors and P. Johansson (eds.) *Cognition, Education and Communication Technology*, 181–202. Mahwah, NJ: Lawrence Erlbaum.

Scardamalia, M. (2004). CSILE/Knowledge Forum®. In *Education and Technology: An Encyclopedia*, 183–192. Santa Barbara: ABC-CLIO.

Selwyn, N. (2009). Faceworking: Exploring Students' Education-Related Use of Facebook. *Learning, Media and Technology*, 34(2), 157–174.

Sherif, M. (1961). *The Robbers Cave Experiment: Intergroup Conflict and Cooperation.* [originally published as *Intergroup Conflict and Group Relations*]. Middletown, CT: Wesleyan University Press.

Squire, K. (2006). From Content to Context: Videogames as Designed Experience. *Educational Researcher*, 35(8), 19–29.

Strayer, J. F. (2012). How Learning in an Inverted Classroom Influences Cooperation, InnTuoovation and Task Orientation. *Learning Environments Research*, 15(2), 171–193.

Su, F., and Beaumont, C. (2010). Evaluating the Use of a Wiki for Collaborative Learning. *Innovations in Education and Teaching International*, 47(4), 417–431.

Tuomi, I. (2001). Internet, Innovation, and Open Source: Actors in the Network. *First Monday*, 6(1).

Warburton, S. (2009). Second Life in Higher Education: Assessing the Potential for and the Barriers to Deploying Virtual Worlds in Learning and Teaching. *British Journal of Educational Technology*, 40(3), 414–426.

Watson, W. R., and Watson, S. L. (2007). An Argument for Clarity: What Are Learning Management Systems, What Are They Not, and What Should They Become? *TechTrends*, 51(2), 28–34

Woletz, J. D. (2008). Digital Storytelling from Artificial Intelligence to YouTube. In Sigrid Kelsey and Kirk St Amant (eds.), *Handbook of Research on Computer Mediated Communication*. Hershey, PA: Information Science Reference. 587–601.

Woolf, B. P. (2010). *Building Intelligent Interactive Tutors: Student-Centered Strategies for Revolutionizing E-Learning*. New York: Morgan Kaufmann.

Yang, S. H. (2009). Using Blogs to Enhance Critical Reflection and Community of Practice. *Educational Technology & Society*, 12(2), 11–21.

Young, M. F., Slota, S., Cutter, A. B., Jalette, G., Mullin, G., Lai, B., and Yukhymenko, M. (2012). Our Princess Is in Another Castle: A Review of Trends in Serious Gaming for Education. *Review of Educational Research*, 82(1), 61–89.

Yuen, S., Yaoyuneyong, G., and Johnson, E. (2011). Augmented Reality: An Overview and Five Directions for AR in Education. *Journal of Educational Technology Development and Exchange*, 4(1), 119–140.

Ziegler, S. 2007. The (Mis)Education of Generation M. *Learning, Media and Technology*, 32, 1, 69–81.

Zimbardo, P. G., Maslach, C., and Haney, C. (2000). Reflections on the Stanford Prison Experiment: Genesis, Transformations, Consequences. In T. Blass (ed.) *Obedience to Authority: Current Perspectives on the Milgram Paradigm*, 193–237. Mahwah, NJ: Lawrence Erlbaum.

9 MOOCs, scalability, and other dangerous things

The idea that there is educational gold (metaphorical or material) in expansive, highly distributed online courses has been developing momentum over the last few years, primarily through the popularization of the acronym MOOC – massive open online courses. It is difficult to know exactly why a sudden fixation with this particular type of online education has emerged. But as this book argues, the idea of "massive" education (if you define "massive" as many people being involved in an asynchronous, shared educational process) is one of the earliest ideas in development of an online/cyberspace information universe – going all the way back to Bush's vision of his Memex machine. Nelson was promoting massive educational ecologies decades ago, writing,

> Now that we have all these wonderful devices, it should be the goal of society to put them in the service of truth and learning. And this is the way I propose. ... We want to go back to the roots of our civilization – the ability which we once had, for everybody who could read to be able to read everything. We must once again become a community of common access to a shared heritage. (1974, p. 45)

Licklider and Taylor had similar realizations:

> if the network idea should prove to do for education what a few have envisioned in hope, if not in concrete detailed plan, and if all minds should prove to be responsive, surely the boon to humankind would be beyond measure. (p. 40)

One of the best technologies for these types of networked, large-scale education initiatives, the Programmed Logic for Teaching Operations (Plato IV), reached its height in the 1970s, capable of having up to four thousand students in a single course through intranet technologies, using innovative applications to help keep students engaged. (It is somewhat mystifying that current attempts at developing massive online courses not only don't seem to be using much of the discoveries and/or findings that could culled from Plato IV, but rarely seem to mention the project.)

Various possible reasons can be suggested why the idea of interconnecting large populations of learners into targeted online courses is suddenly receiving so much attention from so many quarters (educators, journalists, businesspeople): (1) Some of the reasons are probably philosophical – the Internet has created new interests in the potentials for human connectivity (Siemens 2005), process-based learning (Akyol and Garrison 2014), networking of relationships and relationship networks (Kreijns et al. 2013), and webs of affiliation. These ideas aren't exactly new, but before the advent of the Internet they were often relegated to the margins of education. (2) Some of the reasons are probably related to economic or social issues (Hollands and Tirthali 2014): With more difficulties securing funding for education, developing large online courses that can be administered through Internet technologies seems extremely attractive from a cost-benefit perspective. Is it possible to educate three thousand or even thirty thousand students at just a slightly higher cost than thirty students? The possibilities (and unfortunately the illusions) of teacher immediacy through Internet connectivity creates new contexts for revisiting distance education. (3) The reasons are probably partially based on technological developments – the extraordinary evolution of multiuser dungeons, especially massive multiplayer online role-playing games, has offered interesting windows into possibilities of engaging massive, distributed populations in shared projects. Abilities for using object-oriented programming techniques in creation of multiuser platforms (MOOs) has led to proliferation of gaming platforms that meet the needs of very specific groups – an idea that gives expansive, highly distributed courses greater opportunities for success with different types of populations.

Massive online education before the web and its applications

An acronym does not an educational approach create or even an educational realization. The practice of large online courses has followed a winding path, perhaps starting with PLATO IV (Eastwood and Ballard 1975; Smith and Sherwood 1976). Like the oNLineSystem and Xanadu, Programmed Logic for Automated Teaching Operations was one of the spectacularly successful failures that define modern online activity (it still exists today but in a different guise) – and the way we approach Internet-based education. Donald Blitzer was a laboratory assistant in the physics department at the University of Illinois in 1959 when a small group of professors decided to try exploring education through distributed terminals connected to a larger, mainframe computer (a variation on the time-sharing model that led to the creation of ARPANET). Headed by Blitzer, the PLATO system went through a series of innovations until it reached its apotheosis as PLATO IV in the early seventies. PLATO IV technology included plasma screens with newly developed features for generating online pictures, drawings, and music/sound. PLATO IV also developed early prototypes for chat rooms and instant messaging (many of these applications were further developed at the Palo Alto Research Center and later transferred to Apple).

PLATO was essentially a time-sharing system designed for educational purposes. Students could sit at terminals and log in to courses on a mainframe computer. Courses could be synchronous (with three hundred or more terminals logged in at the same time to the same educational program) or asynchronous (with students in different locations using a local terminal to log in to an off-site mainframe at different times). Originally the terminals, which included advanced graphics and sound capabilities, were extremely expensive, limiting the impact of PLATO IV. The invention of microchip technology lowered the cost of terminals so it was possible for thousands of students to be online at the same time. T. H. Nelson (1974) believed PLATO IV to be the future of education and, at least from his description, thought the intranetwork to have a number of important qualities that might be highly applicable to massive online education (as mentioned, PLATO IV still exists, but the following discussion is from Nelson's 1974 perspective, so it will be discussed in the past tense).

Nelson did not want to identify PLATO IV as a computer-assisted learning environment (even though that is how many of the developers of the system referred to it) but as computer graphic education – suggesting that the difference with direct online tutoring programs was that students were not passive and/or reactive to the computer prompts, but in interactive (or even transactive) relationships with the electronic education system. The most important quality of PLATO IV from Nelson's hypertext perspective was its real-time responsiveness to the individual student's needs. The students could touch the screen of the terminal if they had questions or wanted to follow another line of instruction and get an immediate response from the centralized source. The level of individual responsiveness varied based on the author of the particular course (designers of courses in the PLATO systems were referred to as authors), almost always some level of interaction existed between user and the educator-designed course. Nelson suggested that a single student could get up to 256 responses to inquiries. PLATO IV also offered the possibilities of multimedia responses. It integrated music and voice synthesizers, creating possibilities for interactions that fit the natural, everyday activities of the students outside of traditional educational contexts. Many of these qualities were picked up by multiuser game platforms, but for some reason not by (at least most) "massive" user education initiatives.

A second important quality of PLATO IV was students enjoyed using it. Game playing (and game development) was an important part of the system. As Nelson suggests, students often knew there were always games around the next corner – anticipation that helped drive action and thinking forward. Developers of the program designed applications and authored learning programs based on what they would find interesting, what would push them to continue on. There were multiple graphics and painting applications. There was development of interesting and unique (for their time) communication features including open posted notes with chained responses, term-talk text that would appear on the screens of other members of the teaching/learning network at the time the individual was writing it (the forerunner of chat), and group notes where working groups could post and share files. One of the difficulties with expansive, highly distributed courses is the high attrition rates. This did not seem to be a problem with PLATO IV – possibly because of the responsiveness, the multimedia learning ecology, the communication features, and/or the willingness to integrate functions that students enjoyed. Online learning was envisioned as an enjoyable experience. How many lessons should modern online courses take from this early initiative/experiment into the possibilities of large-scale online education?

Massive open online courses

PLATO IV was an early experiment in making centralized computer direct learning available (synchronously or asynchronously) to large numbers of distributed students. It could not really be considered publicly available because even though content was initially free it was based in intranet technology and limited to students/locations with access to expensive PLATO IV terminals. The more recent large online courses are in many ways progeny of the Internet and its applications, along with the mass production of the computer microchip. If there is one shared quality to what are currently termed massive open online courses, it is that they are available to any person with bandwidth and some type of Internet portal (computer, tablet, or other mobile devices). There are few material restrictions for moving through the open door and into an online intellectual community, and if a potential learner has even basic connectivity resources, these barriers are easily overcome (this is not to downplay the idea of great differences, especially in bandwidth, based on both location and economic status of potential students). This, however, is where the similarities end.

The rest of this chapter will focus on three very different approaches to expansive online education – two that have already been implemented and have taken or been assigned the signifier massive open online course – and one that is prospective. The first implemented initiative attempts to use Internet connectivity to create easily accessible intellectual communities where individuals can find like-minded (in a very literal sense) users to sharpen and/or extend their cognitive skills in specific arenas of thought: These are often referred to as cMOOCs, with the c standing for connectivist.

The second type of expansive, online educational course, which was actually assigned the acronym MOOC by the media, emerged a few years later. Many individuals and working groups began developing scalable online courses around the same time (one group was at Stanford where there was already a thriving educational technology program while another group was at Harvard/MIT where the idea of Open Courseware had emerged a decade earlier). These initiatives attempt to use the Internet to scale up what are essentially traditional educational practices. These are often referred to as xMOOCs, with the x standing for exponential or expansion – for instance, HarvardX is an expansion of Harvard courses out into the larger information universe (Hollands and Tirthali 2014). These xMOOCs focus more on transfer of authoritative knowledge and skills (as opposed to exercising the minds of participants, which is a central goal of the connectivist MOOC).

The third expansive online educational initiative discussed in this chapter is prospective, based on knowledge building through a combination of intragroup collaboration and intergroup cooperation. A natural extension of computer-supported collaborative learning, it is based at least in part on Scardamalia and Bereiter's vision (2003) for the *Knowledge Forum* and Hakkarainen and Paavola's (2009) trialogical approach: creating locally developed collaborative communities interlinked within a larger, distributed multiuser (group) network that challenge practices and belief systems of place-based educational institutions and networks. All three are based on very different philosophical underpinnings and/or approaches to education.

The connectivist massive open online course

The connectivist model was the first MOOC, at least by name. These cMOOCs are part John Stuart Mill, part Vannevar Bush, part swarm intelligence, part Open Educational Resources, and perhaps part PLATO IV (or at least the multiuser games that PLATO IV helped spawn). Similar to Bush (and to Nelson and Licklider and Taylor) George Siemens (2005) suggests that the new possibilities for connection, both human to human and human to machine, made possible through the Internet create dynamic relationships between ideas in the information universe similar to the creative connectivity of the human mind. Humans use fast-paced, intuitive link structures to connect different ideas, concepts, and/or experiences to create cohesive, logical thinking that meets immediate needs. It is this continuous process of connectivity that leads to and sometimes forces the emergence of new ways of thinking. But whereas Bush saw connections offered by (potential) new technologies as an extension of the human mind (i.e., augmentation), Siemens seems to see the Internet as a replication of the mind. The Internet uses the same connectivity principles in the service of human understanding and adaptation – but the development of ideas from connection to coherence takes place completely online. Individuals connect in online learning communities where, as with both new connectionism and swarm intelligence, the sum of interconnected thinking is greater than its isolated parts. Knowledge that could not even be conceived by an individual can be developed by an interconnected community (e.g., the slum children learning as a group learning how to navigate the Internet in Mitra's *Hole in the Wall* experiment, discussed earlier).

Stephen Downes, as outlined in an earlier chapter, was doing work at the same time in the field of Open Educational Resources in particular and online education in general. Downes seemed to find his utilitarian take on individuals using the Internet to create cooperative forums for their own educational purposes (2010) as a good fit with Siemen's ideas on connectivism. The Internet offered best case scenarios for creation of cooperative communities where individuals could come together to share and extend their thinking in ways that meet their needs; at the same time community members remain autonomous, able to log on or log off at will from their personal computer portal. The Internet can be used to create multiuser platforms not just for games but for learning – even blurring the lines between the two (perhaps one of the reasons some look for parallels between MOOCs and massive multiuser online role-playing games) – a more subtle version of what PLATO IV was attempting to accomplish, but without the multimedia applications and opportunities for gaming around every intellectual corner.

Later Downes would describe his concept of open as a (swinging) open door (2014) that any learner could walk through (I add "swinging" to Downes's original conception of open to highlight the idea that the information and the user move in both directions). The open forum for intellectual exchange and idea development offer perceived affordances to "cyberspace cowboys" (William Gibson's term seems appropriate here) traveling through web searching out artifacts/tools to help them extend their thinking on a given subject. Just as important, the user must have the abilities for walking through that door, the initial knowledge of the subject that sparks the desire to develop longer-term thinking skills. A second aspect of Open is that the course as an educational resource is publicly available to any cyberspace traveler: Anybody can access the course much as anybody can access a learning object or a course syllabus in an Open Educational Resources repository.

Two other interrelated aspects of these connectivist online learning ecologies tie them back to ideas developed by Bush, Engelbart, and Nelson as well as to the types of multiuser environments developed through multiuser platforms. The courses as developed by Siemens and Downes (and as described by David Cormier, the person who actually coined the acronym MOOCs – McCauley et al. 2010) place a high value on participatory relationships and the type of hypertext-driven shared databases that Nelson (1974) describes. Participatory suggests an interconnected, nonhierarchical network of users where learners freely and openly share their work with each other. The participation is, following Downes's utilitarian framework, cooperative and not collaborative: Individuals freely share their own work and thinking within the larger connected community, but the individual users can take that work and any thinking they have developed about it with them when they decide to ride off into the cyberspace sunset (metaphorically speaking). Every participant has the same access to the database developed through the course, and they are capable of adding to or even changing that information/knowledge through their own thinking/understanding. The changes to the information, and the information itself, are not as important as the processes of their development based on interconnectivity between learning community members. The development of (topic-based) hypertext exercises each participant's mind in its own way (this explanation/description was taken from multiple presentations by Downes, which can be found at *Stephen's Web*, www.downes.ca – probably the best current resource for understanding MOOCs).

An important aspect of connectivist learning ecologies that is less mentioned is the way(s) in which they are (supposed to be) designed to promote lifelong learning. Much of the thinking on using formal education settings as a way of creating lifelong learning trajectories comes from the work of John Dewey (1916). The most important task of the democratic classroom is not any specific instructional content but to teach students how to work together, especially to listen to each other, as they form collaborative problem-solving communities; the focus is more on the development of a well-functioning problem-solving group than on specific solutions (Glassman and Kang 2011). Dewey believed these types of groups function best when members become committed to each other in the service of adapting to meaningful complications in everyday life. The connectivist MOOCs are primarily cooperative enterprises – they are not really meant to promote collaborative knowledge building (Downes wonders if it is even possible with large, interconnected learning communities). The connectivist learning ecologies proposed by Siemens and Downes, however are similar to Deweyan democratic education principles in other ways, at least in intent; one of the primary purposes of the emergent learning community is to teach students the long-term possibilities of connecting into networks of action, of working together in developing shared (hypertext) databases on a particular topic, of being able to find and recognize authentic networks where individuals are willing to cooperate with each other – no matter what the individual reasons. The Internet is always there, an ongoing part of the intellectual landscape, so that individuals are able to tap into these web based skills for the rest of their lives, whenever they are looking to exercise their minds in any direction. An individual engages in the same processes engaging an online learning community in gardening later in life as used in learning engineering earlier in life.

Together Siemens and Downes created an online class that more or less combined their ideas into a single educational enterprise (I am assuming this from reading their individual perspectives, which seem to complement each other but are not the same). They would, taking the role of course instructors, set the ecological context for a learning community to emerge through Internet-based connectivity: Users/students cooperate online with each other to enhance and extend their thinking. Siemens and Downes used the basic structure of the traditional college class in this first course, enrolling students from the local university. But they also offered the course as an open resource that any cyberspace traveller could find and join (they actually advertised the course through a newsletter on educational technology that Siemens distributed throughout the world). The class proper (based on university enrollment) was relatively small, but it was joined by thousands from around the Internet.

The birth of the MOOC acronym

Downes and Siemens were participating in an online discussion group called Ed Tech Talk where different researchers presented new ideas and approaches at the same time that they were developing their open approach to online education. David Cormier, who was hosting the site at the time, invited Siemens and Downes to present their work, which he thought had important differences with other attempts at developing online courses to that point (usually large online courses were based on direct transmission of information to formally enrolled students using Course Management Systems). Cormier, wondering how to introduce this new type of online initiative, did a Skype interview with Siemens and Downes before their Ed Tech Talk presentation and came up with the term Massive Open Online Course. For whatever reason the name stuck with members of the Ed Tech Talk community (including Downes and Siemens), who began using it as a shortcut to describe this new type of connectivist/chaos-driven/utilitarian online education. One of the more clever qualities of the MOOC acronym was its similarities to other platforms that emerged out of multiuser dungeons (the acronym closely resembles MOO, which are multiuser dungeons that use object-oriented programming techniques). At the time Cormier was doing work on multiuser virtual environments but is not sure if that had an impact on coining the acronym (personal communication, 2014). It might have alleviated some of the later and continuing confusion about both the acronym and the Siemens/Downes model for online education if Cormier had referred to the course as a multiuser open online course (MUOOC?), directly connecting it to the history of multiuser platforms.

Connectivist MOOCs in practice

A recent exhaustive survey on the literature of MOOCs (Liyanagunawardena et al. 2013) found that thirteen different online connectivist learning ecologies have been analyzed, most through case studies (there have been more studies since, but general findings are not that different). The designers of almost all of these documented MOOCs consider their courses descendants of Siemens's and Downes's "connectivist" approach/model. All of these connectivist MOOCs were deployed using general college/university-level formats/approaches to education. Information adheres strictly to a theme or topic that is determined by the provider, the course is usually segmented in some (internally) logical way, presentation of topics is linear and unalterable, and each segment is self-contained. These choices are a little odd considering that connectivist learning communities are to a certain extent dependent on (theme-based) networks emerging out of nonlinear threads connecting in cyberspace (e.g., chaos theory). It may be that the developers choose to use traditional, culturally developed educational formats as countervailing centripetal forces in the creation of an emergent learning community so they would not go too far off course. Or it may be fear that universities will not buy into the concept of emergent learning communities that completely abandons traditional classroom practices. Or it could just be that Siemens and Downes's initial MOOC was based in a traditional college course.

The largest problem for the studied online connectivist courses was the quick, often steep, dropoff in user participation. Most courses had completion rates of less than 10 percent. Developers and researchers don't have a firm understanding as to why so many individuals drop out or how to capture the reasons behind the phenomenon (Koutropoulos et al. 2012). The extremely low course completion rates may be symptomatic of larger educational issues that need to be addressed if these types of courses are going to have an impact on ways of negotiating the transfer, cocreation, and development of knowledge online.

One of the larger issues with the development of connectivist MOOCs as an educational tool is suggested by Cormier (personal communication, 2014). As mentioned, the courses are similar to and probably to some degree influenced by the multiuser platforms developed out of multiuser dungeons such as *Mirrorworld*. But these early gaming platforms/programs (and bulletin board/conference systems as well) were designed for people already initiated into the online world, who wanted to be part of the emergent community for their own utilitarian reasons and to engage with other specific types of community members (in some ways these early platforms functioned as exclusive clubs). It was much more difficult for casual users to gain access to online communities in the early days of the web. In Salmon's scheme it was extremely difficult for users to even get past the first level of access, which suited the needs of both those who created and sustained the communities and those who joined. Those who became frustrated often quickly abandoned participation, and those who were left were already committed (a phenomenon that occurred, for instance, on the WELL; Hafner 1997). To put it in educational psychology terms there was already a built-in group awareness for long-term participants.

Modern online courses are trying to reach a much broader population base, many of whom are not necessarily willing to overcome barriers such as dealing with frustrating protocols to join collaborative or even cooperative learning communities. The first level of access is made much easier by advances in user-friendly technologies, but then staying with the community to work through subsequent levels such as recognizing the benefits of cooperating with other participants becomes less likely. It may be that large, educational initiatives based on multiuser platforms need strategies closer to gaming (e.g., virtual reality platforms, some of the capabilities offered by PLATO IV), or that they need advanced group awareness tools to feel comfortable acting in the community.

A different species of large online courses – that are also called MOOCs

If you went to the Wikipedia page on MOOCs on the day this chapter was being written and scrolled down the *precursors* section you would not find any mention of Vannevar Bush, T. H. Nelson, utilitarianism (the difference between cooperation and collaboration), or even PLATO IV. You would instead find short discussions of correspondence courses, radio broadcast lectures, and closed circuit television – along with a mention of Salman Khan's model for short online presentations leading to mastery learning. There is one short paragraph on the Siemens/ Downes connectivist-inspired MOOC discussed earlier. Most of the Wikipedia page is devoted to a second type of online course that has successfully appropriated the same acronym. This second initiative using the MOOC name is not a next generation MOOC, or another genre of MOOCs, or even a speciation of MOOCs (they did not break off from the original line). It is instead a completely different species of education. The confusion is exacerbated by the fact that even though the connectivists identified their online education approach as MOOCs a full three years before – and did so for overt reasons – this second species of online education is much better known among the general population as MOOCS (something that is not necessarily true among individuals studying, developing, and/or committed to online education). I have tried to limit emotional, editorial comments in this book, but I find myself with hands raised to the heavens, asking aloud, "Why didn't they just use a different name?" It couldn't have been too difficult to come up with another clever acronym.

It is something of a mystery how these Harvard/MIT and Stanford initiatives came to be identified at MOOCs: Sebastian Thrun, the first to seriously experiment with scalable online courses at Stanford, Andrew Ng, another Stanford professor, who (along with his colleague Daphne Koller) probably pushed the model further than anybody, and Anant Agarwal, the driving force behind the HarvardX/MITX consortium of expansionary online courses, all acknowledged pioneers of this type of scalable online education, have said they did not name this educational approach MOOC, the media did (personal communication with each, 2014). The most important popularization of MOOCs as a label for their work was probably the article "The Year of the MOOC" published in the *New York Times* near the end of 2012 (Pappano 2012). The author of the article does not mention connectivist MOOCs, George Siemens, Stephen Downes, David Cormier, or the fact that the acronym had been around since 2008. The acronym was simply taken from one Internet-based educational approach and applied to another. There was not even the same type of Skype discussions with Thrun and Ng that Cormier had with Siemens and Downes.

An attempt has been made to differentiate between the two models for large, online education initiatives by putting a small c in from of those courses emerging from the connectivist perspective, and a small x (for exponential or expansion) or an AI (the first course Thrun taught using this model was in Artificial Intelligence) in front of those emerging from the early Stanford experiments of Daphne Koller, Andrew Ng, and Sebastion Thrun and the Harvard/MIT initiative. This difference is often not transparent and/or can be confusing for the casual reader. It can be hard to figure out what the small prefix means if you don't already know – another layer of obscurity for a relatively obscure acronym. The reason that recognizing the divergent qualities of the types of educational initiatives is important is because they represent qualitatively different approaches to online teaching and learning – and education in general – and how we understand the Internet in relation to education.

Siemens and Downes are part of a community of educational technologists, so critical educational concepts such as extending thinking, different types of disembodied intelligence (e.g., knowledge existing in the network rather than in or complementary to the individual), emergent collective intelligence, and the role of social engagement in the evolution of learning communities play important roles in their thinking and those that work within the connectivist model. The Stanford experiments into using the Internet to develop scalable classrooms initially took place to "flip" and then to expand computer science classes out to a larger student population. The course instructors had a strong sense of the possibilities of Internet technologies for information transfer but little actual background in education as a field of study; their thinking seems closer to early distributed communication technological frames established by the work of Paul Baran and exemplified by Leonard Kleinrock than to the more psychologically oriented augmentation/community technological frames of Internet pioneers such as Bush, Licklider, and Nelson (Bush was an engineer fascinated by human thinking, Licklider was a psychologist, Nelson is a philosopher/sociologist dedicated to applying computer technologies to education).

Baran was from a traditional engineering background and Kleinrock was a computer scientist. Both focused on the information transfer and distribution possibilities offered by the concrete networking capabilities of proposed internetworking systems (Baran developed packet-switching technology based on his concept of distributed information sources – the process that allows information to maintain integrity while being transferred quickly and efficiently across nodes of an interconnected network – while Kleinrock was the first to apply packet switching to the actual intra and internetworking activities). The most important quality of the Internet for these scientists was its technological abilities to widely distribute and share information while maintaining the integrity and sustainability of that information. The "second" species of massive online courses developed at Stanford, Harvard, and MIT falls within this same technological frame. Sebastian Thrun, Andrew Ng. and Daphne Koller, who developed large Internet-infused classes (that eventually led to the educational enterprises *Udacity* and *Coursera*), were all professors in the Computer Sciences Department at Stanford (members of Stanford's education program did play a role in the early development of these large, online classes, but it seems to have been relatively minor). The *edX* initiative of Harvard and MIT, partially based on an idea proposed by a computer scientist (Open Courseware), is also being led by computer scientists from both schools.

The different technological frames of the connectivist online courses and the more communication, distribution-oriented courses probably suffice to suggest they are qualitatively different enterprises. But it can also be argued that the two forms of large, online courses are very different at a basic philosophical level. The utilitarian underpinnings of the connectivist approach are more overt (mostly coming from Downes, who has an educational philosophy background) and has already been discussed – individuals cooperating to form a community that enables greater pleasure/happiness (broadly defined) on the part of its users. The more communication, distributive-oriented approaches tend to have more individualistic/positivist foundations. Little emphasis is placed on shared community or multiuser platforms offering participants a chance to "exercise the mind." Instead information sites are established on the principle that all individuals have a right to the most authoritative and advanced knowledge available, but once these sites are established it is the individual's responsibility to use them to their needs and abilities – including training for a vocation and/or solving everyday problems. It is similar to the difference between multiuser dungeon sites where individuals can cooperate in role-playing games to achieve pleasure and distributed, marketplace sites that individuals can access and use to find the best available version of something they might need or want (treating the student as a consumer of information). Actual knowledge development/ building occurs in some other ecology, using the authoritative information gained through Internet communications to solve problems or advance fields (again closer to the activities on NSFNet than at the Augmentation Research Center).

The media's use of the MOOC label for the networked educational ecologies emerging out of the Stanford classrooms and Harvard/MIT consortium creates difficulties for both the original connectivist MOOCs and the attempts to expand the network reach of traditional classroom education. Confusion over the acronym as a signifier has pushed the emergent utilitarian/chaos-driven/connectivist initiatives into the shadows of educational technology. Expansive, distributed online education has come to be viewed as primarily transmission of vetted, authoritative information rather than a vehicle for exercising the mind. While the connectivist MOOCs (especially as envisioned by Downes) made specific information secondary, the positivist initiatives see transfer of academically scrutinized information as their primary purpose and reason for being. Some of the connectivist MOOCs have had trouble disentangling the two philosophical underpinnings in their design, mixing traditional classroom practices and more positivist approaches to information into attempts to develop cooperative learning environments.

The appropriation of the MOOC acronym may have also had a negative effect on the development of the more individualistic/positivist online initiatives. As mentioned, the name massive open online course suggests some relationship with the benefits of multiuser platforms – for instance, in a well-received white paper on MOOCs (Hollands and Tirthali 2014) the authors wrote the term was "(d)erived from "massively multiplayer online role playing games." (This actually isn't true – at least according to Comier, personal communication, 2014 – but the mistake comes from the structure of the acronym itself.) *Coursera* (the educational technology company that emerged out of the Stanford experiments) courses as well the *edX* (the company growing out of the Harvard/MIT consortium) do not seem to have been influenced at all by ideas related to multiuser platforms and developing virtual communities in the ways that Downes and Siemens and the researchers of the Ed Tech Talk community are. This may have placed unfair expectations on what these types of positivist, Internet-based, large online courses could and should do as learning enterprises.

The rest of this chapter will refer to the more individualistic/positivist approaches to large, online courses using a more targeted (and hopefully accurate) descriptor – Scalable OnLine Learning Environments (SOLE for those who like acronyms, especially when they can double as existential metaphors). The term is taken directly from Ng's vision of these types of online courses, which "pursue(s) two major online learning activities simultaneously: (1) offering highly scalable forms of learning to large numbers of learners and (2) offering blended learning to small on-campus classes" (Hollands and Trithali 2014, p. 34). It also separates courses following the scalable classroom model from other, more local, often less thoughtful online education initiatives (e.g., courses designed to fit prepackaged Course Management Systems, placed online primarily for convenience). Most local online classes are not really designed to be scalable – at least in the way the scalable online learning ecologies developed by public/mostly private initiatives such as *Coursera* and *EdX* are meant to be.

The khan academy: impetus for scalable learning

One of the major influences on the development of scalable online learning ecologies (at least for Koller and Ng) are the teaching videos posted by the Khan Academy. Salman Khan was initially an engineering student at MIT who went on to work at a hedge fund. The story of his early development of online videos that would become the core of the Khan Academy (Khan 2012) is well known by now. At a wedding Khan met his twelve-year-old niece who was having trouble in a mathematics course. He agreed to tutor her in math over the phone. The tutoring was at first unsuccessful (and frustrating). Based on his own intuitions he changed his teaching style so that his niece became more active and actually possessive of the subject matter (where she was screaming out the answer or that she did not know something – an all or nothing response). This new teaching style was so successful Khan started tutoring his two nephews and then other young math students. There were soon too many students for him to handle through individual phone sessions so he started developing short teaching videos that he posted on YouTube. The value of the YouTube videos in helping students understand mathematical concepts quickly became apparent – leading to the birth, through time and experimentation, of the Khan Academy, essentially a catalog of teaching videos based on methods Khan discovered working with his niece and early cohorts of learners. There is one more important part of the story of the Khan Academy that took place long before Khan's original long-distance tutoring. As a student at MIT he was part of a small group that used to skip class lectures (which he refers to as passive learning), do the work on his own, and then take the tests. He became, in the parlance of edX an "optimizer."

Khan's basic philosophy (at least what can be gathered from his book) is individualistic and positivist – even more so than the scalable online learning ecologies. He believes that education has a strong element of personal responsibility. It is the individual learner who must take hold of the learning process and turn it to their advantage. The videos represent specific, authoritative knowledge individuals need to master in predetermined sequence to be successful learners in a given topic/subject. Technology provided through the Internet offers multiple outlets for teaching/knowledge sources that individuals can use where they want (any place where there is an Internet portal) and how they want (at their own pace) and when they want. Once this type of anytime, anywhere, anyhow learning is provided it is up to the individual student to use these resources to learn information that is critical to their vocational/academic/intellectual well-being (Khan's main focus is on learning for a technical vocation, but he also mentions the importance of the human-ities). Khan assumes that once students have, recognize, and are taught to use these new teaching/learning resources they will be motivated to learn – in any case it is now the students' individual responsibility (he does not really explain what will happen if the student is still not motivated to learn). General motivation to learn, or self-regulation in learning, is not really part of the mission of the Khan academy.

The development of the Khan academy is based – after individual responsibility for their own education – on two major assumptions about education (both hotly contested, but certainly part of educational research of the last century): (1) individuals learn best at their own pace and (2) education is more successful over the long term when based in mastery of the subject. Every student learns different ideas in different ways. The videos are separate from the artificial time and linear learning demands of traditional classroom practices, allowing individual students to explore specific topics and problems at their own pace and go back and reexplore confusing principles and ideas when they think they need to. It is important to master one topic before moving on to the next. Khan believes that topics build on one another and even missing a little bit of a particular topic may come back to haunt the learner later. The individual student should be able to stay with a topic until they have complete understanding of it: Students should not be responsible to any learning timetable but their own. Khan and his colleagues have developed program(s) for the different topics where students must answer ten questions in a row correctly to move on to the next lesson in the predetermined sequence. Again it is the students' responsibility to stay with the subject until mastered.

Khan does not dismiss place-based learning in his model – he thinks mastery through any time learning opens up new possibilities for experi-ential face-to-face learning – not that different from Sams and Berg-man's idea of the flipped classroom (a number of teachers have used Khan Academy videos in the development of their own flipped class-rooms, but that is more a by-product of the videos than their purpose). Even though most of his book concentrates on K-12 education, Khan is probably most explicit and eloquent in how his model would change higher education in his outline of the university-of-the-future. He sees college learning of specific topics progressing much in the same way that he went through his MIT career – without formal lectures (assuming that most students are naturally "optimizers"). The actual classrooms would be replaced with Khan Academy (style) videos where students would master essential information at their own pace and to their own needs (e.g., problems they are working on in their internship that demand specific expertise). This would free up time for internships and other types of highly experiential learning. Students would come across difficult problems, using them as jumping off points for accessing relevant videos to learn the basic information to help develop solutions – a variation on "just in time" education. Khan talks a bit about how using this new technology for education, especially individualized education, would be cheaper, but the possibilities created by the Khan Academy videos are not really presented from a cost-benefit perspective. In any case, in Khan's description of the university-of-the-future it doesn't sound cheaper at all. The focus is more on an intersection of self-paced micro-learning units, mastery learning, and experiential learning.

The structure of information input

The teaching videos posted by the Khan Academy reflect two ideas – one education based and one network based. From an education perspective (especially Open Educational Resources) the teaching videos are learning objects – that is, they are short-topic-focused teaching instruments, usually between five and ten minutes, that can be fit into almost any larger curriculum. Initially the length of the videos was constrained by YouTube presentation rules, but the Khan Academy kept the time frame based on some educational research measuring normal attention spans in learning situations (Khan 2012). Perhaps because of length limitations the videos are more direct explanations than designed lessons and can be used as addendum for any number of experiential place-based lessons. The only real requirement on the part of learners seems to be using the videos in a natural order so that students master one skill set before moving on to another.

From a more network perspective Khan made the decision to depersonalize his videos as much as possible, believing that viewers might be distracted by any face that was doing the explaining, choosing to use a generic background that resembles the traditional chalkboard as graphic interface accompanying the voiceover of the lesson. The videos are highly decontextualized, short explanations that can be easily absorbed by even a casual viewer. It is difficult to know if the Khan Academy's formula for developing short, simple digital scenarios makes online education more compelling, but this relatively early model is probably one of the factors leading to a bias against "talking heads" and in favor of highly directed (short), specific presentation of material against generic backgrounds. Andrew Ng and Daphne Koller are clear about the influence that Khan's work and the ways in which he uses Internet video technologies as teaching tools had on their own development of scalable online learning ecologies (Koller initially was working from a flipped classroom model), but Khan was not the only influence on information input. Ng, for instance, was also influenced by the less generic Do It Yourself videos at Lynda.com. The Harvard-MIT consortium have done their own research on information input and come to much the same conclusions about the efficacy of short videos. The construction and presentation of teaching videos may be one of the most important areas of research for scalable online learning environments.

What is being scaled and why?

One of the biggest questions in scalable online learning environments is exactly what the designers are attempting to scale. Is it the classroom experience? Is it specific aspects of the classroom that can serve as addendums to a larger educational experience (through flipped classrooms, experiential learning, internship experiences, project based learning, etc.)? Khan, for instance, seems to assume that there will be a place-based component to the educational equation – a context for the students to use their developing knowledge in everyday lives. Other initiatives such as *Coursera* attempt to scale up the entire educational experience so that the online learning ecology completely replaces the place-bound course (what is interesting about this is that *Coursera* is led by Koller, who originally started developing scalable online learning ecologies to flip her classroom – perhaps suggesting greater integration of place into the *Coursera* framework in the future). Research by Tsai and colleagues discussed earlier in the book (e.g., Chuang and Tsai 2005) suggests that relevance may be a key to online learning. If there is little integration of significant, place based everyday activities of students into the online teaching/learning ecology, what do you replace it with?

Even when course designers/developers incorporate place-based activities into the teaching/learning processes through discussion forums, blogs, or wikis, how do distal learning networks maintain the balance and integrity of place in the space-place relationships?

Reaching different types of learners

EdX attempts to scale up an entire classroom experience – where the primary goal is passing the course rather than mastery of knowledge systems that might support any number of local course (or other activity) goals. *EdX* (2014) recently released seventeen papers that were summarized in a single report. The courses were from *Harvardx and MITx* (Harvard and MIT being the central administrators of *edX* courses). Not all the papers reported on a specific course (papers in the *Harvardx* group reported on a computer-driven methodology for analyzing student-created text and the differences between immediately releasing all materials and staggering release of materials). The specific courses discussed in the papers for the most part had the same basic structures. Each week was introduced by videos taken directly from classroom lectures and broken down into shorter segments (the length of video segments is not reported in the papers, but in another venue, Ho et al. 2014) An *edX* administrator suggests most videos are five minutes or less because often students don't watch videos for longer than that – this in spite of the fact that most Khan Academy videos are closer to ten minutes – but this may have something to do with the videos as mini-lectures as opposed to videos as learning objects. Volitional attention to online teaching videos seems to be a complex topic that involves knowledge level, motivation, teaching context, and video design among other factors. There are short interspersed quizzes to test viewer retention of information presented in videos. There is weekly assigned homework. There are midterm and final examinations. Certification is based primarily on receiving passing grades on online examinations – with passing usually between 50 and 60 percent correct answers.

A great deal of transfer of traditional classroom tools to the online teaching environment (an exception is the five minute video) takes place in the reported courses. The quizzes, homework, and tests make up the bulk of validation for credentialing. In most of the classes only about 10 percent of the students followed the credentialing outline of the course to get a certificate. Even within that relatively small population there were two very different groups in terms of learning styles: the "completionists" who achieved the highest quiz/exam scores and viewed all or most of the weekly segments and completed assigned work, and the "optimizers" who did the least amount of work possible to still receive a course certificate – not really that different from students in traditional, place-based classes. There was a potentially important difference from place-based education among the 90 percent who did not receive certification from the courses: There was a smaller population of "explorer" students who viewed more than half the chapter segments but did not accomplish all the tasks necessary to receive a certificate, and a population of "listener" students who viewed all or most of the segments but did not participate at all in the credentialing activities.

In their overall analysis of the studied courses the lead researchers make the point that success should not be solely based on those who were to achieve a certificate but on the participation of "explorers" and "listeners" as well – these are the types of students that are often missed and/or ignored in traditional education settings. In virtual communities these populations, especially "listeners," are often defined as "lurkers." (Nonnecke and Preece 2001) Many lurkers consider their choice of participation in an online community an important part of their identity – and for meeting their own needs (the value of lurking to the community and the individual is controversial, with some communities welcoming them and others deriding them as free riders). The assumption is that the participants (can they still be called students?) are getting new information through their lurking activities. But this brings to the forefront important questions for scalable education: What are the primary purposes of the courses? What are these online courses attempting to achieve? Are they looking to re-create the classroom experience online? Are they attempting to act as carefully crafted support systems for everyday activities of users? Are they attempting to reach new types of learner populations that are not as interested in collecting credentials? Are they attempting to support or create new knowledge? Or are they attempting to educate and credential more students in critical, vetted knowledge for less money – where the initiatives are more economic in nature than educational?

In some cases the differences can involve very different approaches to online education (does the site focus on mastery, or on completing the curriculum in to obtain certification, or on transmission of information for new types of populations?). For instance *edX's* purpose of design seems almost a polar opposite to the Khan Academy videos. The Khan videos focus on continued exploration of a particular concept until the users have achieved complete mastery. The learning is self-paced, but it is meant for highly motivated students. The *edX* courses keep pushing students forward each week, looking to establish a larger, predetermined knowledge that gives students a general understanding of course topics rather than mastery of more targeted skills and/or concepts – attempting to balance reach with transmission of knowledge. A little more than half right, a general idea of the topic on quizzes and tests (rather than ten right answers in succession), is good enough.

One of the most interesting findings, at least in the context of some of the ideas explored in this book, came in a more in-depth study of the first edX-developed course, *Circuits and Electronics*, offered through MIT (Seaton et al. 2014). The course used generic, ten-minute Khan Academy–style videos, interspersed with content quizzes along with assessment schemes similar to those used in the later scalable courses discussed earlier. One of the most striking findings involved the discussion forum that was attached to the course. While only 3 percent of the students who registered for the course used the discussion forum, more than half of the students who completed the certificate (completionists and optimizers) were among those users. Because such a low percentage used the forums, the findings are not really robust, and they are correlational (it is impossible to tell if the more committed students used the forums because they were engaged with the course and/or its resources, or if student engagement in a social space precipitates greater participation as research discussed earlier in the book suggests), but it seems apparent that participation in discussion forums is among important indicators. In spite of this, little reporting on discussion forums was done in the later series of papers (though this analysis may come later). A second interesting finding from the same paper was that students who reported collaborating with somebody else offline in the topic area (17.5 percent of survey respondents) did significantly better in the course, again suggesting the importance of relevance to students and/ or space-place relationships in these types of distributed, online courses.

The correlation between social participation – and to a lesser extent collaboration and achievement (at least as defined by course facilitators) suggests the possibility that even in developing Internet-infused scalable education the Internet involves teaching/learning processes that can be very different from the place-bound classroom. The Internet should not (and perhaps cannot) escape its character as an inherently transactional medium – users feel most comfortable when there is a bidirectional or multidirectional social component to activity. It could also be that as Preece (2001) argues, learning is a social activity, and computer conferencing's most important attribute is the development of new types of online sociability that transcend traditional boundaries of time and space while maintaining complex social relationships. Breslow and colleagues (2013) cite "pedagogies of engagement" (Smith et al. 2005) as a goal of edX scalable courses – an approach that focuses on the development of cooperative (though not utilitarian) learning scenarios and small communities of learners. A number of researchers looking to develop workable scalable online learning ecologies seem to intuitively recognize the interplay between traditional classroom practices such as lecture, homework, and test-based assessments and the need to develop the course as an advanced social space, trying to develop strategies that increase, or at the very least create a baseline level of, social presence. A difficulty is that applications that might increase sociability such as nonlinear discussion forums or virtual reality platforms where students can create their own avatars are very different from the traditional, positivist-based classroom practices that guide much of the design of scalable courses.

Some examples of the use of social interaction applications (usually as add-ons) to try and build social presence in scalable online learning environments include integrating the political/town hall application *Mindmixer* into the overall structure of the course (New 2013) in an attempt to turn at least part of the learning experience into an open community where students see themselves as active, responsible citizens. Developers of scalable online learning environments have also tried to approach online sociability from a more microlevel of participation, for example, attempting to provide students with their own avatars so they can create an online presence with unique communication capabilities (Fitzgerald 2013). Some have even looked to use what might be considered a modified Open Source approach to increase ownership in the course where instructors establish a teaching/learning model using five minute videos but then look to shift at least some of the responsibility for development and production of these type of Khan Academy–style teaching videos to the students in the larger learning community (Carter 2012). All of these experiments represent nascent attempts to redefine but not to reinvent teaching learning models in scalable online learning contexts. Is it possible to integrate these new applications so they are not simply add-ons that overwhelm teachers and/or students (much as with Course Management Systems)? As both research and experience in online environments suggest, even highly advanced technologies may be the least important aspect of developing an effective Internet-based social space – it is the way(s) the human component is managed that is most critical.

Participatory, multilayered online education

As mentioned earlier in the chapter, there is room for a third, at the moment prospective, model for online education that takes advantage of the unique reach of the Internet while holding on to the ideas of community collaboration and cooperation. A model that connects collaborative groups pursuing common goals into larger, distributed shared learning networks. In this model the users in the multiuser platforms would be local collaborative groups that develop socially cohesive learning/knowledge systems, using their hypertext databases to reach out and connect with the knowledge/information systems of other, like-minded groups. A multigroup design offers the stability and relevance of small online, collaborative communities with the reach and breadth of expansive, highly distributed cooperation-based learning networks, creating scenarios where smaller, sustainable groups within the (meta)-network are capable of supporting and/or challenging each other in terms of motivation, substance, and voice in ways individual participants in a network (especially those that feel marginalized) often are not. The suggested layered, expansive, distributed learning environment – from individual to collaborative group to distributed cooperative network and back again – is based at least in part on a combination of Scardamalia's and Bereiter's ideas on how the *Knowledge Forum* might incorporate Internet connectivity into collaborative learning approaches with Hakarrainen and Paavola's ideas of a trialogical approach toward Internet-based collaboration, combined with ideas taken from participatory action research (Glassman and Erdem 2014).

Downes's argument that collaboration is difficult in large/massive groups is most likely correct – at least based on what is currently known about the development of cohesive virtual communities. Without the commitment/social capital that comes with advanced social interaction and/or shared problem solving, participants in multiuser online course platforms will decide when to enter the learning community and when to leave and, most important, when to engage based on their own needs at the moment (suggesting most casual Internet users are indeed utilitarian in deed if not in word). There is little motivation or necessity for sustainability and/or collaborative problem solving beyond immediate, swarm intelligence–based problems.

Online collaborative environments, which in the literature are often limited to approximately thirty participants, usually involve easily recognized shared or developing common goals; there is also an underlying commitment to the community as community participants go through (sometimes painful) processes of creating or appropriating (from other successful online communities) common communication and governing strategies. The history of virtual communities, multiuser dungeons, and collaborative working groups (such as Open Source software development communities) suggest two ways to accomplish this – (1) purposely creating a community based on a shared topic of interest where discussion is guided by strong leaders or moderators who are willing to let community develop organically (e.g., the Grateful Dead conference on the WELL) and/or (2) shared, nonhierarchical problem solving that has relevance in the everyday lives of the participant (e.g., the Linux community).

Layered stakeholders developing an object of study

Scardmalia and Bereiter (2003) suggest an extension of *Knowledge Forum* practices into the larger interconnected information universe in service of creating larger, more far-reaching Knowledge Building Environments (KBEs): "A local KBE gains strength by being embedded in a broader KBE ... the ideal KBE is one in which the knowledge building work of a local community not only draws upon but affords some level of participation in the larger knowledge building activities of society" (pp. 2–3). Scardamalia and Bereiter envision an expansive approach to knowledge building in which strong collaborative communities use "opportunistic linking" that crosses traditional boundaries to merge thinking with other knowledge-building communities creating a more powerful whole out of parts (if individuals can coalesce around a problem why can't communities?).

The question is how to create and sustain a distributed multigroup network where different groups don't revert to old patterns of protecting their own knowledge systems and become defensive against critiques/ challenges and/or protective of existing power relationships (as Rogers 1995 suggests they often do). As Hakkareinan and Paavola (2009) have pointed out, there is often a tendency to use new tools to reinforce old habits – a tendency that might be exacerbated as larger knowledge systems and histories collide in cyberspace. What is the equivalent of "social space" when using multigroup platforms as learning ecologies where groups can develop their own online presence, create avenues for ongoing interactions with other groups, and develop a sense of trust?

A second theme along with development of social space between interconnected online, collaborative communities is relevance in everyday lives of users – or user groups. The idea of instrumental genesis to help develop collaborative communities may have potential impact in helping knowledge-building communities develop interlinked networks to create a larger, more distributed KBE. Learning ecologies are developed around problems or relevant projects that distributed collaborative groups share or find of interest. Individuals build new knowledge through their local collaborative groups and then share their new understandings in the building of epistemic artifacts and potentially instruments that will in some way alleviate the shared problem through the group's membership in the larger, multigroup online community. It is even possible to combine this approach to expansive online learning ecologies with both Licklider and Taylor's ideas on computer conferencing and Khan's vision of the future university with individuals or groups accessing open educational resources to gain better understanding of problem-related skills and concepts in the course of problem solving so that membership in the larger network motivates individual and group learning activities.

Hakkarainen and Paavolo (2009) offer an interesting example that, while not specifically the type of expansive, participatory online learning environment discussed here, points to possibilities: the Virtual Distributed Work course spread across three universities. At the end of the course sixty students were broken into multidisciplinary, virtual teams of five or six students across the different universities. The students went out into the field (everyday work environments) and would bring back their developed information/knowledge to the group (interaction between the personal and the collective). What is interesting about this model is that the groups could also come together to form a network of working groups developing collective objects of study.

This prospective view of expansive, distributed education offers a couple of attributes that are more difficult to find in place-based or even traditional distance education. The first is greater abilities for participants to integrate education with the practices of their everyday lives. Participants get to bring their understandings and their perspectives online as they discuss implications of shared knowledge built by their local collaborative group in addressing the common problem within the larger cooperative network. One of the difficulties with distributed learning networks with predetermined dominant hubs is they force division between the producers who present information as critical knowledge and the *praxis* of users from distant communities (not only spacewise but also economically and in terms of emotional and social histories). Purveyors of information remain static because their reality of what is good and reliable information is never challenged by their own everyday experience or those with experience outside of their immediate knowledge networks. The information is presented as an already defined instrument in the lives of learners (Vio Grossi 1981 outlined attempts to transfer agriculture information in this way to South American farmers as completely unsuccessful). The greater the distance (in all its meanings) learners have from the information/knowledge originating hub, the more they must choose between separating themselves from the everyday activities of their community or becoming alienated from the educational hub/knowledge provider.

The proposed model of distributed, online education offers new spaces for potential participants to bring their local *praxis* into the larger learning network through their local collaborative groups, as part of the problem-solving process – where there is no hierarchy of knowledge because the collective problem solving and its allied processes of instrumental genesis is ongoing. The interconnected groups openly compare their own experiences, the everyday successes and failures of their lives, to the narratives and belief systems of other

groups including those convinced of the efficacy of their own knowledge systems. Understanding of the artifacts used to develop instruments becomes negotiated, and the meaning of relevant knowledge
evolves. The larger, cooperative network is held together by the utilitarian development of solutions to urgent problems.

This type of layered problem solving that moves from everyday
experiences and observation of individuals to local collective agency
groups to cooperative problem-solving networks also offers possibilities
for what the educator Paolo Freire (1970) refers to as conscientization.
Freire suggests that conscientization occurs through a dialectical process
of self-realization that occurs as individuals are confronted with the
intellectual and/or social impoverishment of their appropriated worldviews and attempt to re-create frameworks and worldviews to meet
immediate and distant needs. What is difficult is creating educational
situations where this can occur as part of an organic, nonhierarchical
process (if change agents force new realizations, it becomes nothing
more than a trade of one form of control for another). The abilities for
different groups to work together on relevant, meaningful (to their lives)
targeted problem or subject sets creates opportunities for participating
individuals and groups to create understandings of shared knowledge
separate from any single community but informed by all communities –
dynamic knowledge sources that push participants to reconsider appropriated, sanctioned perspectives and information, throwing into question
the relative truth value of current frameworks. Multiuser (group) platforms committed to developing learning contexts out of shared problems
open up avenues for individuals to build new knowledge about relevant
issues in their lives.

Education as a highly distributed process

The idea of expansive, highly distributed education initiatives caught the
imagination of educators and society in general for a short while. The
ideas that this sudden fascination engendered are currently going
through a process of critique. There is a good chance they will reemerge
even stronger as we move forward. A number of reasons may be given
for this, some of them outlined in this chapter (e.g., economics, new
models of learning), but perhaps the primary reason is that highly

distributed teaching and learning scenarios have always been part of the thinking behind the Internet – if not the material structure, the ways it has developed and humans have come to understand it in their lives. The different types of expansive highly distributed, Internet-based education discussed here have their benefits and their flaws. The original named massive open online courses (developed by Siemens and Downes) open up new possibilities for expanding thinking but offer few opportunities for the types of collaborative work leading to social change (whether this should be a goal of Internet-infused education is another question). Individuals who potentially come to and/or become involved in these MOOCs already have some interest and some experience in the subject matter – and are looking to expand this to meet their own needs at the moment. Those that know will know more, but those who don't know will have a harder time finding and engaging with these communities, and those who don't know what they don't know are left for lost.

The scalable online learning ecologies that emerged a few years later are more willing to establish basic, initial experience in an idea or topic that can serve as entry point into new ways of thinking. Their positivist orientation also offers certainty to the content and goals of these courses. But these "SOLEs" are essentially scaled-up versions of traditional educational practices. They are not trying to establish the qualitatively new types education that the original MOOCs or participatory, multilayered online education might.

Participatory, multilayered online education can't be compared to the first two. There is no way to know if these types of online, open-ended courses would work. It demands a mix of collaboration and cooperation that is not often seen on- or offline. There is a good chance that collaborative groups worry more about sustainability of their local communities than engaging with cooperative, problem-solving networks.

The models suggested here will move through their own evolutionary paths. There is a (good) chance that different models for expansive, highly distributed education will emerge. One of the reasons they have garnered so much interest is that in many ways they represent the promise of an interconnected world as Vannevar Bush first envisioned it.

References

Akyol, Z., and Garrison, D. R. (2014). The Development of a Community of Inquiry over Time in an Online Course: Understanding the Progression and Integration of Social, Cognitive and Teaching Presence. *Journal of Asynchronous Learning Networks*, 12, 3–22.

Breslow, L., Pritchard, D. E., DeBoer, J., Stump, G. S., Ho, A. D., and Seaton, D. T. (2013). Studying Learning in the Worldwide Classroom: Research into edX's First MOOC. *Research & Practice in Assessment*, 8, 13–25.

Carter, D. (2012). New Online University Seeks Many-to-Many Approach in Economics Course. *eCampusNews: Technology for today's Higer-ed learner*, October 4. www.ecampusnews.com/top-news/new-online-university-seeks-many-to-many-approach-in-economics-course/2/.

Chuang, S. C., and Tsai, C. C. (2005). Preferences toward the Constructivist Internet-Based Learning Environments among High School Students in Taiwan. *Computers in Human Behavior*, 21(2), 255–272.

Dewey, J. (1916). *Democracy and Education*. New York: McMillan & Co.

Downes, S. (2014). MOOCs4Development. Philadelphia, April 11. www.slideshare .net/Downes/2014-04-11-philadelphia.

    (2010). Connectivism and Transculturality. Talk delivered to Telefónica Foundation, Buenos Aires, Argentina. Posted on *Stephen's Web*, May 16, 2010. www.downes.ca/post/53297.

Eastwood, L. F., and Ballard, R. J. (1975). The Plato IV CAI System: Where Is It Now? Where Can It Go? *Journal of Educational Technology Systems*, 3(4), 267–283.

EdX (2014). Harvard and MIT Release Working Papers on Open Online Courses. www.edx.org/blog/harvard-mit-release-working-papers-open#.VLQnLCvF-Fx.

Fitzgerald, M. (2013). MIT See Zombies and MOOCs in Education's Future. *Informationweek*, May 5. www.informationweek.com/mobile/mobile-devices/ mit-sees-zombies-and-moocs-in-educations-future/d/d-id/1110202?.

Freire, P. (1970). Cultural Action and Conscientization. *Harvard Educational Review*, 40(3), 452–477.

Glassman, M., and Erdem, G. (2014). Participatory Action Research and Its Meanings: Vivencia, Praxis, Conscientization. *Adult Education Quarterly*, 64, 206–221.

Glassman, M., and Kang, M. J. (2011). Five Classrooms: Different Forms of "Democracies" and Their Relationship to Cultural Pluralism (s). *Educational Philosophy and Theory*, 43(4), 365–386.

Hafner, K. (1997). The Epic Saga of the WELL. *Wired, 5.05*, May.

Hakkarainen, K., and Paavola, S. (2009). Toward a Trialogical Approach to Learning. In B. Schwarz, T. Dreyfus, and R. Hershkowitz (Eds.) *Transformation of Knowledge through Classroom Interaction* (pp. 65–80). London: Routledge.

Ho, A. D., Reich, J., Nesterko, S., Seaton, D. T., Mullaney, T., Waldo, J., and Chuang, I. (2014). HarvardX and MITx: The First Year of Open Online Courses. HarvardX and MITx Working Paper No. 1.

Hollands, F. M., and Tirthali, D. (2014). MOOCs: Expectations and Reality. Full Report. Center for Benefit-Cost Studies of Education, Teachers College, Columbia University, NY. http://cbcse.org/wordpress/wp-content/uploads/2014/05/MOOCs_Expectations_and_Reality.pdf.

Khan, S. (2012). *The One World Schoolhouse: Education Reimagined.* New York: Hachette Digital.

Koutropoulos, A., Gallagher, M. S., Abajian, S., de Waard, I., Hogue, R., Keskin, N., and Rodriguez, C. O. (2012). Emotive Vocabulary in MOOCs: Context and Participant Retention. *European Journal of Open, Distance and e-Learning.* www.eurodl.org/?p=Special&sp=init2&article=507.

Kreijns, K., Kirschner, P. A., and Vermeulen, M. (2013). Social Aspects of CSCL Environments: A Research Framework. *Educational Psychologist*, 48(4), 229–242.

Licklider, J. C., and Taylor, R. W. (1968). The Computer as a Communication Device. *Science and Technology*, 76(2), 1–3.

Liyanagunawardena, T., Adams, A., and Williams, S. (2013). MOOCs: A Systematic Study of the Published Literature. *International Review of Research in Open and Distance Learning*, 14. www.irrodl.org/index.php/irrodl/article/view/1455/2531.

Nonnecke, B., and Preece, J. (2001). Why Lurkers Lurk. AMCIS Conference, Boston, June. http://snowhite.cis.uoguelph.ca/~nonnecke/research/whylurk.pdf.

McAuley, A., Stewart, B., Siemens, G., and Cormier, D. (2010). The MOOC Model for Digital Practice. www.elearnspace.org/Articles/MOOC_Final.pdf.

Mitra, S. (2003). Minimally Invasive Education: A Progress Report on the "Hole-in-the-Wall" Experiments. *British Journal of Educational Technology*, 34(3), 367–371.

Nelson, T. H. (1974). *Dream Machine.* Chicago: Hugo's Book Service.

New, J. (2013). Platforms Helps Drive Conversation among Thousands of MOOC Students. *eCampusNews: Technology for Today's Higher-ed Learner*, June 28. www.ecampusnews.com/top-news/platform-helps-drive-conversation-among-thousands-of-mooc-students/.

Pappano, L. (2012). The Year of the MOOC. *New York Times*, November 2.

Preece, J. (2001). Sociability and Usability in Online Communities: Determining and Measuring Success. *Behaviour & Information Technology*, 20(5), 347–356.

Rogers, E. M. (1995). *Diffusion of Innovations.* New York: Simon and Schuster.

Scardamalia, M., and Bereiter, C. (2003). Knowledge Building Environments: Extending the Limits of the Possible in Education and Knowledge Work. In A. DiStefano, K. E. Rudestam, and R. Silverman (eds.), *Encyclopedia of Distributed Learning.* Thousand Oaks, CA: Sage Publications.

Seaton, D. T., and Reich, J., and Nesterko, S. O., and Mullaney, T., Waldo, J., Ho, A. D., and Chuang, I. (2014). 6.002x Circuits and Electronics MITx on edX Course Report—2013 Spring. January 20. MITx Working Paper no. 8. http://ssrn.com/abstract=2382295 or http://dx.doi.org/10.2139/ssrn.2382295.

Siemens, G. (2005). Connectivism: A Learning Theory for the Digital Age. *International Journal of Instructional Technology and Distance Learning*, 2(1), 3–10.

Smith, K. A., Sheppard, S. D., Johnson, D. W., and Johnson, R. T. (2005). Pedagogies of Engagement: Classroom Based Practices. *Journal of Engineering Education*, 94(1), 87–101.

Smith, S. G, and Sherwood, B. A. (1976). Educational Uses of the PLATO Computer System. *Science*, 192(4237), 344–352.

Vio Grossi, F. (1981). Socio-Political Implications of Participatory Research. *Convergence: An International Journal of Adult Education*, 14(3), 43–51.

Open source educative processes

The original purpose of writing this book was to discuss an Internet-infused education approach I have been working on for the last decade with my students and coauthors that we originally referred to as Open Source Education: I have recently (in this chapter) retermed the approach Open Source Educative Processes. We did not start to explore this approach based on any readings in educational technology or any previous work in the field. I first became interested in practical implications of the Internet in education when Min Ju Kang (at the time a student) introduced me to the Korean social media platform *CyWorld* during an independent study on exploring cognition, leading to long conversations about merging the two. As we developed some publications we kept running into the same reference to a seminal piece on the Internet and collaborative program development: Eric Raymond's "The Cathedral and the Bazaar" (1999). We began to believe application of Raymond's discussion of the Linux development community to education and classrooms practices was, if not obvious, potentially revolutionary. The reason we began to refer to our approach as Open Source Education is because Open Source is the term Raymond and his colleagues adopted (after initial publication of "The Cathedral and the Bazaar") to describe many of the ideas expressed in his piece. The descriptor Open Source Education is already in use, but it is to this point an amorphous phrase generally referring to the teaching of Free (*Libre*) and Open Source Software principles developed by the Open Source Initiative, including Open Source licensing. One of the goals of this book is to limit ambiguity, so I have decided to rename our educational approach Open Source Educative Processes.

At the end of a presentation/video explaining the principles of Open Source Software (http://flosscc.opensource.org/spread-the-word) the presenters make two critical points, at least for Open Source Education, that are central to the ideas discussed in these chapters: (1) Open Source is a great way to teach and to learn and (2) there is a difference between the Open Source license and the Open Source movement as a whole – pointing out that the movement is not primarily about licensing (although it is a critical component) but about creating great developers through community/collaborative processes. Open Source Educative Processes is an extension of these ideas, attempting to move beyond development of code and software into the realm of formal educational contexts.

Free speech versus free beer

Many interpret the phrases Free Software (Movement) and the Open Source (Initiative) as being primarily about making materials open access, publicly available at no cost to users. This is actually not the case (and is one of the reasons that some members of the Free Software movement started using the term Open Source – to limit these types of misinterpretations; Glassman 2013). Richard Stallman (2010), the founder of the Free Software movement, suggests that copyright protection is fine for mass-produced materials – but in general software is not singularly developed and mass produced. He is sympathetic to the notion that people will not spend a lot of time, energy, and effort on projects for which there is no recompense. Stallman's argument is a person or corporation should only be able to charge for their own specific work, but should not be able to control the product after it has been sold. To put it in terms used in education and this book – it makes sense to copyright one-to-many, mass-produced communications (e.g., those produced by a printing press). Where Free enters the equation is when you have many-to-many or many-to-one communications (communities working together to create products for their own benefit that are then adopted by other communities or even individual users). But even here it is possible to charge for a product to help maintain the community. (The original Free Software program – the GNU[1] operating

---

[1] GNU is one of the odd and playful acronyms sometimes found in the Free Libre Software Open Source community. It actually stands for "GNU's Not Unix." Unix was one of the original and most popular operating systems for advanced computer and internetworking activities, but it became proprietary. Richard Stallman built an operating system kernel that became the jumping-off point for Linux and named it GNU's Not Unix. To deal with some of the ownership issues discussed in this chapter his Free Software Foundation developed the copyleft license so nobody could claim it or its descendants as proprietary software.

system kernel that Torvalds used to develop Linux – actually cost $150 to help support the start-up foundation.)

What then does Stallman mean by free? He makes an important distinction – which is also one of the most important and repeated phrases among those who ascribe to the notion of Free Libre Open Source Software: *free as in free speech and not free as in free beer.* A person who buys a program buys the code along with it. Once the transaction occurs the original owner should have no control over what the buyer does with the program/code. The buyer should be able to change the code any way they want so that it meets their specific needs at the moment without having to go back and get permission from the original author. The buyer should be able to share their newly developed, adaptive code with anybody they want to help them solve a problem or meet a need. Stallman uses the simple but illustrative example of buying a sandwich: Once you have paid for a sandwich you can re-create its makeup any way you wish to suit your needs (take off the cheese, add mustard, cut it into quarters to share with friends). To Stallman this is an issue of free speech (with code as a form of speech). It is a concept based in the political ideal of liberty: Neither the person who sells the program/code or the society in general should have authority to restrict the actions of the individual who has brought or been given the program for any reason. Of course, in order to change the program to meet individual needs a (would-be) developer has to have access to the source code. Restricting the source code then is a covert form of authoritarian control on the part of the original program developer (or more likely the corporation that owns the copyright to the program). The Free Software movement is primarily political in nature.

The Open Source movement broke off from the Free Software movement just before the turn of the millennium for various possible reasons. The Open Source group thought that Free Software – especially the word Free – was too easily misinterpreted; the chance for misinterpretation is so great that European members of the movement started to always present the word Free in conjunction with the Spanish word *Libre* (as in everyone is free to do as they wish). Stallman (2010) believes that many in the Open Software movement were either afraid of or uninterested in the political implications of Free Software. Both reasons probably have some merit. But the biggest difference between the two is that Free Software is more about freedom for the individual whereas the Open

Source movement is more about development and creating an advanced development community looking to meet the needs of the interconnected information landscape of the twenty-first century.

Stallman makes the argument that Open Source tends to be more ambiguous as a concept and a movement because there is no corollary to his straightforward *free as in free speech not free beer*. In an attempt to remedy this I suggest the following for understanding the word Open in Open Source, at least as related to education (in partial homage to Stallman): Open as in open democratic classroom, not open as in open keg party. To extend this idea – when I was in college I had a friend Jim who every weekend would go around with a big red cup looking for keg parties:

JIM: Hey is this an open keg party
PARTY PERSON: Sure is, help yourself
JIM: Excellent
PARTY PERSON: Enjoy

If it was not an open keg party Jim did not take offense. People paid their (or their parents') hard-earned money for the keg. If they were collecting money at the door to offset costs Jim happily contributed – the better the beer the more he was willing to contribute. But once Jim paid his money he would drink as he wanted (occasionally adding shots of bourbon) and fill up his cup to take with him before he left – even if he was planning to stop off someplace and give the last beer to a friend. The only time Jim would get upset at an exclusive keg party was if the party organizers had gotten college funds to defray costs. Then the keg belonged to everybody. The same is true of software or data, or really any product or media. There is no obligation to make product publicly available. People make their work available for a variety of reasons, but it is their decision, not the potential user's decision – that is, unless the product was paid for with public funds (e.g., government grants) or created by a public community. Then there is a responsibility on the part of the developers to make the product publicly accessible. A danger lurks here: When public money is involved, those providing the funding get to determine a lot about the final product. If the college gave you money for a keg it got to tell you what beer to buy and the rules by which you would have to run your keg party. In any case none of this has much to do with Open in Open Source.

Then what is Open Source? The Open Source movement has four principles (Kon and Souza 2012). In these principles I replace the word Program with the word Text (because program code is really a variation of text):

1. Text can be used for any purpose. Nobody has the right to claim ownership/authority over any text.
2. Users should study how the text works (whether it solves the problems it was meant to solve) and change it for the better if they can (access to the original problem, the original basic data sources for the text, and the author's original thinking are preconditions for this).
3. Distribute the changes made to the text to help neighbors (very broadly defined – basically anybody within the larger network concerned with the problem).
4. Give the entire community a chance to benefit from the changes (by not only distributing but by being open to changes other members of the network might make to the work).

The similarities with Ted Nelson's conception of hypermedia/text (1974) are obvious. The similarities to John Dewey's approach to democratic education (1916) are perhaps less obvious, but very real. And there are quite a few ties to actor network theory as well as the theory of L. S. Vygotsky and activity theorists (read Tuomi 2001 for an extended discussion on this).

The Open Source principles are at their core not only educational principles, but collaborative educational principles as well. One of the foundations of the Open Source movement are the three Cs – code, collaboration, and community (Sharma 2008). If as suggested you replace Code with Text these fundamentals are representative of some of the major themes of this book (especially related to Open Source/ Collective Intelligence). The collaboration is in the collaborative tools "that include version control systems, IRC, mailing lists, wikis, blogs to help developers working on building code together." The community is "Sharing ideas and developing code (text) across the Internet with developers all over the globe." The Open Source Education Initiative (part of the Open Source Initiative) goes into some depth on how to accomplish this and the idea that the processes of collaboration leading to community are just as important (or possibly even more important;

Kon and Souza 2012) as the Open Source license. The central idea of the
Open Source Initiative is not necessarily to create software/programs but
to create developers capable of working together in nonhierarchical,
nonlinear development communities. This is accomplished in two ways
(very much reminiscent of Vannevar Bush's original concept of an
interconnected web of trails and the ways it was extended by Nelson's
ideas on hypertext): putting work online so that others have a chance to
work on it in ways that meet their vision and/or needs, and working on
online projects developed by others. Teaching is not about teaching how
to code but allowing others to explore and attempt to solve problems of
ongoing coding projects: ownership is fluid and distributed (the issue of
ownership is central, one of the reasons there is so much concentration
on licensing across the definitions of Open Source).

Definitions of open and source

Open is one of the most overused, ambiguously defined terms in the Internet
universe. It is important to understand all the definitions of Open as a
characteristic of Internet-derived information/knowledge. The following
are different definitions of Open – as related to the Internet – that I have
come across in researching this book. They are not mutually exclusive, but
they are also not dependent on each other. In some cases the definition of
Open treats information/knowledge as an object (something you can make
publicly available or license), and in some cases Open is treated as a process
(a way of approaching the development of information).

   Open mind – This, it can be argued, is a seminal definition of Open
related to a continuously expanding information universe, preceding
Eric Raymond and the Open Source movement by half a century. It is
the idea that the human mind is able to open up to, and extend itself out
into, the larger information universe in developing thinking and schemes
leading to the realization of new ideas. Bush saw many similarities
between his own thinking and new connectionism – as a matter of fact,
in many ways he saw himself as a new connectionist in spirit at least.
The biggest difference is that in new connectionism the mind takes in
information and then makes connections within a closed system; with
the Memex machine, the proto-Web, users open their trail of thinking
outwards, so that it does not double back on itself. The mind stretches as
far as the furthest idea along a trail of interconnected thoughts.

Open entry – This definition of open evolved separate from the Internet. Its meaning is tied to attempts to increase access to educational experiences – the critical adjective for descriptors such as Open University or open admissions. Open in this use means no or limited barriers to any person looking to join a community (e.g., the only admissions criteria for attending a university is a high school diploma). Some of the barriers open universities try to minimize include distance from the traditional place-based activities of educational institutions, time constraints (for those who have jobs during the day), and even material constraints (defraying some of the high costs of place-based education). Open universities were among the first institutions to develop inclusive distance education practices, including using Internet technologies as a means for breaking down barriers.

Open access/Public availability – Whereas open entry denotes ability to join and be part of an active community, open access means individuals or communities make their wares open to any user requesting them – such as Opencourseware. This definition contends that any (Internet) site with publicly available information can be termed open. But even this general description has different levels. Do you have access to just the program, or do you also have access to the source code? Do you have access to the article or do you also have access to the underlying database the article is based on? Are crucial aspects of retrievable information part of what has been referred to as the dark Internet (hidden from the online sight of the potential user)? At what point is an open information source no longer considered open. For instance, can you really consider an article or report that does not have links back to its original source as truly open? In many cases those who use the term Open as an important part of their presence on the Web do not consider public availability to be synonymous with the definitions of the Open Source Initiative and/or the Open Educational Resource movement.

Open licensed – For many (a text/program) being open licensed means being under a Creative Commons, GNU copyleft, or similar license. The Open Source initiative considers an open license to be the minimum qualification for considering information/knowledge posted on the Internet as being open. Without an open license some of the other definitions of open such as open to collaboration and open to critique become more difficult if not functionally impossible. Opencourseware is not really open (at least as an Open Educational Resource) unless it has a

Creative Commons–type licensing. Open textbooks are not really open unless they have a Creative Commons–type license. Because licensing is an author decision, open is more a definition of an individual artifact (or set of artifacts) than a site (e.g., there are materials on Open Educational Resource sites that cannot be considered open).

Open to change – This is perhaps the most basic condition of learning and teaching through a dynamic information universe. It is central to Bush's concept of the role of the scientist/explorer pursuing a web of trails strategy of innovation – the ability to annotate information and leave it for the next traveler – and T. H. Nelson's ideas of grand hypertext. It also important to the principles of the Open Source Initiative and the idea that learning comes through the ability to change (and improve) existing work. A share and share alike license is necessary but many times not sufficient for considering information being open to change. Often some type of platform is needed where the changes can be posted linking back to original source and forward to new possibilities. It is important to have a community ready to engage in and support change. For instance, any wiki technology is structurally open to change, but if there is not a community looking to take advantage of these possibilities, can it really be considered open?

Open to collaboration – This definition of Open is more process oriented, and while it can be related to open entry, public availability, and Open licensing, it does not have to be – at least from an educational perspective (as opposed to product development): As a matter of fact, these other definitions of open can sometimes work against collaboration. As suggested by some of the research discussed in Chapter 5, it may be easier to develop collaborative communities when entry into the community and/or information availability is overtly or covertly controlled. Collaboration is dependent not only on availability but use of tools such as blogs, wikis, and mailing lists. The ability and willingness to use these tools might be dependent on moderators, system designers, shared problems, or some other combination of factors controlling for people drawn to the community, the purposes of the community, and the policies of the community.

Open to critique – This is similar to collaboration but also includes the abilities of members of a community to share in nonhierarchical problem solving where any member of the community is able to engage in critical analysis of shared information/knowledge and authors are open to integrating this analysis into their work. The goal is a community where participants are ready and willing to use thoughtful critiques to challenge the presuppositions and belief systems of any members of the network (including their own) without fear of repercussion.

Open range – This along with Open feedback systems is more philosophical than the other definitions of Open presented here. It relates back to William Gibson's idea of the cyberspace cowboy (with cowboy as concept rather than individual) – a cyberspace where ideas can roam freely without worry or fear of ownership. A cyberspace where individuals can pursue ideas, take chances, without worrying about the rules and norms tied to traditional place; activities that can be both positive (e.g., leading to innovation) and negative (e.g., breaking into a protected site to obtain information). The cyberspace acts as a centrifugal force pulling users further out into unexplored regions of thinking, offering in the wild experiences often unavailable in, or unknowable through, their place-based everyday activities.

Open feedback system – This relates to second-order cybernetics, the idea that the Internet should be understood as a space of continuously evolving feedback loops: Whatever feedback loops are created are themselves the result of larger, often unknown, and perhaps unknowable, feedback loops – users are always recognizing themselves as much in the system as controlling it. Internet activities can bring users to points of balance in their thinking and problem solving if they allow themselves to pursue ideas based on their intuitions and moment-to-moment understandings in a continuously evolving information ecology. The more the Internet feedback loops are controlled by humans without recognition of the impact of open feedback systems, the greater the danger of users getting stuck in closed information systems.

The definition of source

The meanings of Source are not as central to Internet discussions, and generally considered less important – but as with Open there are multiple definitions.

Source as source code or sourceware – The word *source* in the phrase Open Source is customarily expanded to source code. The source code is an underlying, easily readable set of instructions that programmers can use (e.g., compile) as executable machine (computer) functions. The source code allows a (new) programmer or programming community to quickly understand the logic behind the functions – how and why the program has developed to that point – making it possible for even users who have just come upon the program to make patches (fixes) and adaptive additions that extend it in new directions. Source code can be seen as the equivalent of the design/blueprint in any structure, or even of DNA. The difference between source code and structural designs is it is relatively easy to reverse engineer the structure back to its original logic, even when the blueprints are not readily available. This is more difficult with computer programs where the underlying source code is compiled or interpreted when it is in use in ways that are not easily disambiguated. A second problem (the one that led to the Free Software Movement) is that individuals/organizations can patent or otherwise take ownership of the source code of a program – even when it has been developed communally. It becomes illegal for a new programmer to manipulate the underlying logic of a program to adapt or make additions to it, or to share this logic with others in any way. Richard Stallman (2010) is correct when he argues that this is not true of almost any other developed or built product (e.g., when you buy a house you also buy the logic behind the basic structure to do with what you will). Open Source makes the argument that underlying logic should not (and really cannot) be restricted (because source code is a logical exercise rather than a standalone innovation it actually makes less sense to patent and/or copyright than other inventions). This idea of source as underlying logic can be expanded to include many arguments, discussions, and/or claims, especially those found on the Internet.

Source as form of available information – This definition comes from the pre-Internet conception of Open Source Intelligence (Best and Cumming 2007). Sources are the places to go for the best types of specific information, whether it be a local newspaper, a television broadcast, a report on market activity – as opposed to official reports that have been vetted by individuals or institutions with a stake in what the information means. So, for instance, if you wanted to know the economic status of a specific region, you would forego the official economic report put out by the government and instead examine sources such as the amount and the price of meat being sold in local butcher shops (among other information sources). The Internet drastically increases capabilities of almost any individual (with Internet access) to go to more direct information sources, especially by following links.

Sources of hypertext – Hyypertext, at least as envisioned by Nelson (1974), places a great deal of emphasis on sources leading to the current state of an information/document source. The evolution of the text, the role that different authors play in annotating and changing it is at least as important as the text as it exists at the moment. All information should have a transparent archive that can be accessed so that the reader and potential contributor can understand the logic behind the shared thinking – very similar to source code, except the logic is more Pragmatic than analytic (Glassman and Kang 2010) and development or the source/logic is ongoing and continuous (the users become co-creators of the source code).

Source as point of (information) origin – One of the most important qualities of the Internet is that information is tagged with its destination but also the address(es) where it originates. This is inherent to the packet switching system. This means it is extremely difficult (if not impossible) to have true anonymity and/or privacy in Internet communications. With enough time and resources any piece of information that is sent through the Internet should be able to be traced back to its original source. There have been attempts to make tracing of original sources more difficult such as Tor (or an onion router) which includes five or six dummy addresses that need to be stripped away to get to the legitimate point of origin, but in general it is probably best to assume that there is little or no true anonymity or privacy on the Internet (even Tor has been breached). This is one of the most important lessons that students (or really any person using the Internet to develop and/or disseminate information) needs to learn.

Open Source Educative Processes is a general approach rather than a specific curriculum. It is different from many Internet-infused education initiatives in that the intention is not focused on instruction in traditional subject matter (although courses can be topically organized), or to give students the opportunity to exercise their thinking in specific areas of information/knowledge, or even to develop knowledge by working together collaboratively (although collaborative learning is one of the goals). The primary purpose of Open Source Educative Processes is to work with students in developing skills that will make them successful in Open Source information ecologies – understanding the concepts of online collaboration and cooperation, online critique, the issues of open licensing, the importance of creating a web of trails for information so it can be traced back to its original author(s) and intent(s), the concept of shared ownership, the positives and negatives of fluid information systems, and of course an understanding that all information is traceable. It is an approach focused on the development of lifelong learning on the Internet, taking into account many of the different definitions of open and source, especially as they evolve in the context of Internet-infused education.

For much of human history, information has been presented through hierarchically structured transmission points – points of development and points of contact (which are usually related to each other). The bounded social system determines the information it wants its populace to appropriate and think of as acceptable knowledge. The social system appoints different gatekeepers at different points in the community participant's life to act as social interlocutors. These social interlocutors provide vetted information to neophytes or other members of the community looking for solutions to problems, or just better ways of integrating their activities into the ongoing community. Students are expected to appropriate this information and incorporate it into their everyday activities, using it to lead successful lives as members in the sponsoring communities. For the most part information is presented in organized form (organization is considered a desirable characteristic in many educational contexts). The Web changes our relationships to information dramatically; it is asymmetrical (different sites/nodes approach the same topic or idea from different perspectives – which can at times be antagonistic to each other), nonhierarchical (each user, contributor to an information/knowledge system has the same access, at least initially), and nonlinear (there is no real trajectory toward an ultimate truth, with information changing as perspectives are added and/or challenged within the knowledge-building network).

Open Source educative process are devoted to teaching through targeted Internet activities the types of skills/intelligence that allow individuals to flourish in these types of online information environments. The primary skills are the abilities to search/select trails that lead to relevant information, to organize information found on the Web into coherent narratives, and to differentiate according to the quality of the information found. The ability to organize involves abilities to engage nonlinear information sources and use those sources to develop coherent solutions. This can be difficult for students, especially coming from institutions that prioritize organization in presentation of materials/ information/knowledge, where the instructional emphasis is on making information/knowledge as digestible as possible, which treat learners as consumers of information rather than innovators who use information as a tool.

Differentiation occurs through links, or more specifically learning the importance of following links. The Web is based on (but does not always adhere to) Nelson's concept of hypertext. Central to hypertext is that information sources evolve over time and through multiple users accessing information at different times for different purposes. This means that individual users have opportunities for influencing the trajectory of information and knowledge outside the purview of independent gatekeepers. This can make information development far more chaotic, but it also means that sources should have and need to have an accessible history, and that any user can be part of the history no matter how small (even if it is by changing its search engine algorithm by clinking on the link multiple times). One of the purposes of hyperlinks is to connect an information source to its development history (an idea that many search engines have not completely caught up to). Following links can offer any user a chance to make their own judgments as to the validity/reliability of the information. Individuals are capable of finding that very believable claims are actually based on limited, misinterpreted, or even no basic research and/or theory. A number of examples exist of "accepted" knowledge that might not survive following links. The ability of individuals to differentiate information is a difficult new concept for students, but many of the most valuable members of mature online communities are those who are willing and able to follow links in newly presented material – and demand links when they are not embedded (the first level of differentiation is dismissing any contribution that does not have links).

Search/selection seems the easiest of the new activities offered by the Web but can be the most complicated (something I did not realize when I first started exploring these types of Open Source knowledge/intelligence skills). It is easy to confuse search with search engine activities; but although search engines simply require typing words into a box to access opaque algorithms that recall ordered information, the larger, more complex activities of search/selection are a process of reaching out, facing multiple decision points where those decisions will at their best simply lead to another decision point (unless it is the decision to stop the search). Search/selection needs to be understood as a process that can lead to frustration, confusion, and even challenges to in-place belief systems as easily as it can lead to discovery. Willingness to engage in a web of trails, to move from information consumer to explorer, to open thinking up to the unknown can be a fundamental change in our identities as learners, as teachers, as citizens. It is a challenge to the centripetal forces of society we depend on to bring stability and continuity to our lives.

Understanding ownership and agency in open source educative processes

On a more collective level Open Source Educative Processes are focused on the ownership of information – or more accurately the nonownership of information, the idea that information/knowledge is fluid and meant to be shared with (an interconnected network of) neighbors (whenever possible). As with the Free Software movement and the Open Source Initiative this does not mean that all information posted to the Web is an open keg party – open to anybody who stops by with a big red, plastic cup. Individuals who create products should be able to ask for recompense for their work, for whatever reason they choose, and their decisions should be respected. Individuals have a right to control their own work to a point – this is one of the reasons it is so important to not only have universal Creative Commons licenses but also specific places in the initial document where they can be easily recognized. Continued education in Open Source-type licenses – what they mean, how to find them, and when they should be used – should be an ongoing part of education, along with recognition that putting information/knowledge/product out is at the discretion of the author (as long as the work originated with them and not through an Open Source license or community knowledge development). But it is also true that once information changes hands under an Open Source license (or is a work product resulting from an Open Source license) the person who receives the information can/must use the information under the terms of that license. The information/ knowledge becomes property of the larger information universe.

Any products that are developed collaboratively, are substantively built on the original work of others, are the result of public support, or are created for purposes that have little or nothing to do with payment should be treated as having an open license – it is important for students to get opportunities in working with this type of information as soon as possible, understanding that individual ownership is not really a consideration in these types of circumstances. The line between respect for other people's work and shared ownership is a fine one – a line that we have not navigated particularly well as a society to this point (often going to one extreme or that other), but one that is essential on many levels in a world where information is fluid, easily transferred, and malleable.

Open Source Educative Processes focus on a form of user agency that overrides traditional conceptions of ownership while still regarding the evolution of ideas and the roles that authors play in it – a willingness to change, annotate, and comment on existing materials in ways that are productive and respectful (and leave any additions for the next person to engage), and a willingness to put their own work out into the information universe so that it might go through the same practices of change, annotation, and/or commentary by others. These two ideas/ activities can be antithetical not only to the ways we currently treat student work in traditional education contexts but information in general. The result is often a reluctance to treat the work of peers and especially putative authoritative information sources (e.g., teachers, assigned texts) as hypertext: There is a worry (sometimes justifiable) that nonhierarchical commentary, let alone change or critique, can be taken as a judgment or even attack. Users can also go in the other direction, commenting on and/or changing information for their own needs or purposes (without thought to cooperation). The commentary/change may be primarily to create tension, to get a reaction out of the author, straining individual and community relationships, and making collaboration and/or cooperation that much more difficult (in online communities these individuals are recognized as trolls), or to achieve predetermined ideological or personal aims.

Two complementary goals of Open Source educative processes are (1) to make sure that students are ready to add to the work of others in a responsible way and (2) to enhance students' abilities and perceptions of efficacy in putting their own generated work out into the online community, readily accepting that the moment they do it becomes a continuously developing product of shared ownership. One of the best ways to develop responsible Open Source community participants is to make sure students engage in hypertext-based activities and understand their role, along with the role of others in their local development community, always moving dynamic knowledge building toward making information better suited to immediate and if possible long-term needs of the group as a whole, at the very least creating a minimum of trust among members of the shared community that they will do no harm either to the authors who have gone before or the shared problem-solving community as a whole (this is the other side of the differentiation coin).

Education needs to deal with, and perhaps embrace, Open Source in all its guises and the new types of human-information and human-human relationships they engender – relationships that can be critically different from those of (pre-Internet) place-based information/knowledge-centered activities. It is not only about developing skills but road maps to a hypertext ethics where it becomes easier and more natural for students to recognize and take part in well-functioning Open Source communities, understanding both the possibilities and the prerequisites for developing and sustaining working groups respectful of information/knowledge as a shared enterprise – communities where the work of the self and others is naturally open to change, to collaboration, to critique, and students who are willing to go out and explore the cyberspace range, open to new and unexpected feedback loops.

Developing open source educative processes through blogs (but wikis not so much)

The following is one example of developing Open Source Educative Processes through a series of courses that evolved over time using both Open Source Educative Processes and an action research approach (see Glassman et al. 2013 for a detailed discussion of the methodology). The original intent of the curriculum was to integrate wikis and blogs into graduate (Glassman et al. 2011) and then large undergraduate courses. Open Source ideas were always in the background of course development, but the initial purposes of the courses/research was to find a way to meaningfully mix applications into courses with the goal of developing a Deweyan democratic atmosphere (1916) in classes that moved easily between traditional place-based classroom practices and an online community. It was assumed that Internet technology could offer a second chance for bringing Dewey's ideas back into the mainstream of education (Glassman and Kang 2011).

The wiki and blog applications were chosen for two different reasons – the wikis because of possibilities for group collaboration as Dewey envisioned, the blogs because the teaching team had observed and at times participated in successful blogging communities (mostly political and entertainment oriented). Initially the idea of distributed thinking played a central role in the development of the curriculum – while collaboration between students was assumed. All students needed was a chance to connect with each other and the collaborative relationships similar to what Raymond (1999) described for the Linux community and in his own Fetchmail experiment would soon emerge. In the first experiment a graduate class was divided into small groups of students (the groups remained constant through the semester) and distributed across a small city, communicating with each other through the blogs (and wikis) during and between assigned class times. There was a syllabus of assigned readings and a common project (a topic-driven, course-related academic paper) established on a wiki platform (Glassman et al. 2011).

The wiki part of the experiment was a complete failure for many of the reasons described in Chapter 8. The graduate students were reluctant to comment on, let alone to change, each other's writing. In interviews students remarked on how wiki collaboration was not a process they were comfortable with. The blogging was more successful but still did not work in the way(s) the instructor envisioned. There was little community building and almost no merging of perspectives. The posts were for the most part standalone short papers based on predetermined reading assignments. The students showed almost no commitment to the community blog outside of traditional time boundaries (most posts occurred during class time because that is what students thought they were expected to do). At the end of the class the experiment fell prey to the same difficulties the activity theorists Hakkarainen and Paavola (2009) and Hung and his colleagues (2006) found in the Finnish and the Singapore schools systems: The students had taken the new technologies and simply adopted them to their (pre-Internet) institutionally driven needs and expectations. Integration of the Internet into coursework seemed to change little.

The one difference found in student interviews between wikis and the community blog was that students found little value in the wikis but did see potential in blogs – they enjoyed blogging even if they only did it to fulfill class requirements. Two of the students from the graduate class approached the instructor about applying the same technologies to a large undergraduate class but attempting to integrate ideas from the Open Source communities we had been discussing informally in a more direct way. The students would overtly be given more freedom on the blog to take the conversation in any direction they wanted (free as in free speech), more emphasis would be placed on hypertext (especially through open commentary), and more emphasis would be placed on multidirectional development of ideas (by having students add their own links to the discussion). An open community blog became the centerpiece of the course. Students were encouraged to bring their laptops to class and make posts whenever they felt the need (the blog was projected on a screen at the front of the class and continuously updated). Students were required to create a post, comment on another post, and provide an interesting link at least once a week outside of class time. To increase motivation for postings students were told there would be a competition for the best blog posts and comments, where students could earn extra credit (on a weekly basis) and the possibility of an automatic A in the class (on a unit basis) if their posts were identified as the strongest on a particular syllabus topic by the instructor and teaching assistants. Loathe to give up the possibilities of the wiki in spite of the warnings from the graduate students – the grapes just out of reach – a collaborative writing platform was established. Again hoping to increase motivation, instructors told students they could use the wiki to collaboratively write their own test questions.

The undergraduate class was if anything a bigger disaster than the graduate class. One student added to the wiki on quiz/test questions over the course of the semester. The blogging was perfunctory (students blogged because that was what they were required to do) and commentary was minimal. If anything there was the opposite of community development on the blog. One group of students started attacking another group of students for spending so much time on their blog posts – which the attacking group assumed were public attempts to get better grades, but also made the less active posters look bad. The teaching assistants had to make multiple interventions to calm the online waters; there was even an in-class discussion of blog etiquette. There were, however, some unantici-pated successes. The instructor – at some of the students' requests – posted examples of what he thought were quality blog posts during class. This sometimes led to extended in-class discussions on the topic of the posts, which a number of students then followed up on when doing their own weekly writings for the blog. For short periods students were overtly communicating with each other on the blog and there were some early vestiges of community – which quickly disappeared.

The instructor and the teaching assistants met to consider moving forward with what they began calling a blogcentric classroom. Several decisions were made based on the previous (painful) class experience. The first was to move away from wiki technology. Integrating the wiki into the course had not been successful in any meaningful way (those grapes were probably sour anyway). The second decision was to attempt to even more directly integrate key principles from Raymond's "The Cathedral and the Bazaar" into the curriculum. The development of Open Source communities had been an influence on the curriculum develop-ment from the beginning, but the instructors had been holding on to a number of traditional education processes involving adherence to the syllabus, grading, and individual ownership of information. These pro-cesses seemed to be working against the development of the type of online (learning) community we were trying to establish. In particular there was an overt attempt to apply at least some of Raymond's ten lessons for an Open Source approach to the curriculum.

1. Good software starts by scratching a developer's itch
This is true of education even more than software design. Students learn best about what they are immediately interested in (this also mirrors Dewey's ideas in *Interest and Effort in Education*, 1913). It is so obvious as to be almost tautological: Students (and for that matter humans) learn best about what they want to learn about – and yet we rarely seem to apply this idea to education. The syllabus would be a starting point, but if a topic of interest developed, class discussion would move in that direction, even if it took time away from planned lessons.

2. Good programmers know what to write, while great ones rewrite
Some of our best work is done building on the work of others (this is an idea that goes back to Vannevar Bush and before). The course, and

especially the blog, would emphasize that nothing was to be gained from individual ownership of ideas. Students could build on each other's posts in any way they liked. This idea was partially implemented by the decision that there would be no grading of content (a very dangerous concept for traditional education) – all emphasis would be on participation so there was no need to claim ownership (the opposite of what happened based on rewarding the best individual posts with extra credit).

3. Treat your users as codevelopers

The instructor had to be willing to hand ownership of the course trajectory over to the students, and the students needed to be willing to take it. One of the few successful parts of the previous course (which emerged more or less by accident) was after discussing blog posts as a class that students would expand on the ideas in their own way in their subsequent posts. It was decided to make this a regular part of each meeting, taking the first part of the class to discuss student posts. It was a conscious decision that this would not be based on how close the post adhered to the syllabus and assigned topics/readings but how much interest it generated on the blog. Both instructor(s) and students had to believe and demonstrate that the blog belongs to all participants equally (more important and difficult for the instructor than the students – at least in the beginning).

4. Release early and release often

Raymond takes this from the original Linux program development that "The Cathedral and the Bazaar" is based on. Linus Torvalds, the originator of the Linux community, would release new versions of the operating system as soon as he thought there was a qualitative change to the program through additions and/or patches. This was interpreted from an educational perspective as building up traffic on the blog as early as possible and working to maintain as high a level of ongoing blogging participation as possible. It was decided that posts had to be done every week, even the first week when students may think they have little to add to the conversation. The students were told to post or comment as soon as they had a semiformed idea that they thought might be of some value to the community. They were also told they should not wait until the end of the semester to fulfill their blogging requirements – which is often a natural inclination of college students. The blogging assignments are front-loaded, not based on assessment of knowledge gained but valued based on (potential) knowledge added. If they thought their idea was important, they should post it without worry of how it might be received (another reason it was important not to grade content).

5. If you treat your beta testers as if they're your most valuable resource, they will respond by becoming your most valuable resource

A close watch was kept on the blog. Open Source Educative Processes are dynamic, and the most important resource in continuous development of the curriculum is the students who are using the curriculum. The teaching team met weekly not only to discuss what was and wasn't working but to change the curriculum and the blog, and the relationship between the two, on the fly. Members of the teaching team would develop dialogues with students, specifically to discuss what they were thinking at the moment about the blog and the class. The students were at first required and in later iterations of the course asked voluntarily to do a summing up of what they thought of the course as a learning/teaching model.

The second version of the course, and subsequent courses using the developing Open Source–influenced curriculum that followed, were more successful in level and quality of participation on the blog and the degree to which students felt comfortable taking an ownership role (Glassman et al. 2013). What became apparent as different instructors used the curriculum is that it was the general approach and not any specific activities that are important. An Open Source curriculum needs to be constantly readjusting to the subject matter (how do you use an Open Source approach with positivist-oriented material?), the students' levels of Internet self-efficacy (what types of positive experiences have they had for using Internet applications for knowledge building?), students' levels of autonomy coming into the class (is Open Source fair to students who are more comfortable in highly structured education environments?), opportunities for strong voices to emerge on the blog (which can often be tied to specific subject matter – see the discussion of an Open Source blog and space place relationships in Chapter 6), the teaching style and educational belief systems of the instructor(s) (how much is the instructor willing to give up or even share ownership with the class as a whole? What role does assessment play? How important is teacher immediacy to how the instructors see their roles in the classroom community?).

Questions remain that we have not yet dealt with in an Open Source Educative Processes approach. It is critical that students understand Open Source–type licensing such as offered by the Creative Commons. But share and share alike licensing means free use of material, including for the students. Is it possible to align share and share alike use of information with traditional warnings against anything even resembling plagiarism? Fear of plagiarism within a fluid information ecology has led to the emergence of mechanical programs that use bots to crawl through documents to find similarities. At what point does free use become defined as plagiarism? If a student uses a phrase or a sentence or even a passage from another source but links the reader back to that source, is that plagiarism or good scholarship in an Open information world? To what degree is the student encouraged or even allowed to move away from accepted knowledge in their own explorations? There are more variables and complex questions, but these are some of the educational issues we will need to struggle with in the twenty-first century.

Open Source Educative Processes are a work in progress, and if done right they always will be. The fluidity of information leads to fluidity of education.

References

Best, R. A., Jr., and Cumming, A. (2007). *Open Source Intelligence (osint): Issues for Congress* (Vol. 5). December 5. Washington DC: Prepared for Members of Congress.

Dewey, J. (1913). *Interest and Effort in Education*. New York: Houghton Mifflin. (1916). *Democracy and Education*. New York: MacMillan Publishing.

Glassman, M. (2013). Open Source Theory. 01. *Theory & Psychology*, 25, 675–692.

Glassman, M., Bartholomew, M., and Hur, E. (2013). The Importance of the Second Loop in Educational Technology: An Action Science Study of Introducing Blogging in a Course Curriculum. *Action Research*, 11, 337–353.

Glassman, M., Bartholomew, M., and Jones, T. (2011). Migrations of the Mind: The Emergence of Open Source Education. *Educational Technology*, 51(4), 26–31.

Glassman, M., and Kang, M. J. (2010). Pragmatism, Connectionism and the Internet: A Mind's Perfect Storm. *Computers in Human Behavior*, 26(6), 1412–1418. (2011). The Logic of Wikis: The Possibilities of the Web 2.0 Classroom. *International Journal of Computer-Supported Collaborative Learning*, 6(1), 93–112.

Hakkarainen, K., and Paavola, S. (2009). Toward a Trialogical Approach to Learning. In B. Schwarz, T. Dreyfus, and R. Hershkowitz (eds.) *Transformation of Knowledge through Classroom Interaction* (65–80). London: Routledge.

Hung, D., Tan, S. C., and Koh, T. S. (2006). From Traditional to Constructivist Epistemologies: A Proposed Theoretical Framework Based on Activity Theory for Learning Communities. *Journal of Interactive Learning Research*, 17(1), 37–55g

Kon, F., and Souza, B. (2012). The Open Source Ecosystem. http://flosscc.org/spread-the-word.

Nelson, T. H. (1974). *Dream Machine*. Chicago: Hugo's Book Service.

Raymond, E. (1999). The Cathedral and the Bazaar. *Knowledge, Technology & Policy*, 12(3), 23–49.

Sharma, A. (2008). Learn about Open Source Software. https://dl.dropboxusercontent .com/u/2814392/asharma-osi-what-is-opensource-presentation.pdf.

Stallman, R. M. (2010). *Free Software, Free Society: Selected Essays of Richard M. Stallman* (2nd ed.). Boston: GNU Press.

Tuomi, I. (2001). Internet, Innovation, and Open Source: Actors in the Network. *First Monday*, 6(1).

Index

Brilliant, Larry, 171–172
browsers. *See* Mosaic browser
Burns, Ken, 251
Bush, Vannevar, 15, 40–41, 45, 131, 265, 298
  associationism and, 44–45
  on cognitive load, 71
  as contextualist, 45
  cybernetics and, 177
  on human thinking, 44–46
  hypermedia and, development of, 25–26
  hypertext and, development of, 25–26
  on innovation, 41
  Memex machine, 15–18
  as visionary of pre-Internet technology, 13–19
  web of trails for, 16

Calilou, Robert, 29
Carnegie Mellon Open Learning Initiative, 221–222
Carr, David, 86
Castells, Manuel, 175, 185
The Cathedral and the Bazaar (Raymond), 293, 312–313
Cerf, Vinton, 13, 26–27, 29
CERN. *See* European Center for Nuclear Research
chaos/complexity theory, 99–100
  emergent knowledge and, 127
  Hole in the Wall experiment and, 100
chunk hypertext, 49
  cognitive load and, 74–75
  Internet self-efficacy and, 78
  scaffolding and, 91–92
CISLE. *See* Computer Supporter Intentional Learning Environments
Clark, Andy, 40, 184
classroom communities, online, 159–162.
  See also massive open online courses
  cMOOCs, 267–271
  group facilitation in, 160–161
  learning styles in, alignment of, 161
  Math Forum, 164–165, 215
  participatory multi-layered education in, 284–288
  scripting for, 162–164
  size of communities, 162
  social equality in, 161–162

  space and place in, 187–191
  teaching styles in, alignment of, 161
  transactional distance for, 160
classrooms. *See* blended classrooms; flipped classrooms; traditional classrooms
Clynes, Manfred, 182
cognitive group awareness, 150–151
cognitive load
  Bush on, 71
  chunk hypertext and, 74–75
  controlling information processing, 71–75
cognitive load theory
  educational research and, 75
  short-term memory in, 71–72
  working memory in, 71–72
cognitive presence, in Community of Inquiry model, 115–117
cohesiveness, social, 141–142
collaboration
  in Community of Inquiry model, 110–111
  with CSCL, 114–115
  in CSLE, 110–111
  Dewey on, 110–111
  openness to, 300
  user agency and, 109–111, 131–132
collaborative intelligence, 50–53
  ARC and, 51
  CISLE and, 51–52
  complexity of, 65–66
  defined, 39
  discrete hypertext in, 52–53
  hypermedia in, 53
  Internet-derived, 40
  through Memex machine, 53
  new connectionism and, 51–52
  POLOS and, 51
collateral hypertext, 49
collective agency intelligence, 44–46, 59–62
  collective efficacy as part of, 60
  complexity of, 65–66
  Internet-derived, 40
  Linux operating system and, 60–62
  in virtual communities, 60–62
collective wisdom, 55
common carrier, 191
communication frame, of ARPANET, 20–27
communities. *See* classroom communities, online; online communities; virtual communities